Feasting and Foraging in Costa Rica

A Comprehensive Food and Restaurant Guide

By Lenny Karpman MD

Published in Costa Rica,

Café Britt, S.A.
2008

Acknowledgements

If all books were this much fun to research and write, I might never stop playing the restaurant-kitchen-cookbook-farmers' market-word processor game. My playmates deserve much of the credit. First and foremost is Joan Hall, a.k.a. Juanita, Noni, Honey or wife - companion, critic, supporter, first line editor and lover. When we entertain, she sets a glorious table appropriate for the occasion and cuisine, I cook, she arranges flowers from the garden, I cook, she plays hostess and pours the drinks, I cook, she serves coffee, cordials and desserts and yes, I cook, eat and enjoy our friends' company.

A host of outstanding cooks who have lived in Costa Rica for many years or their entire lives add to my knowledge and understanding of local fare every time we break bread or visit farmers' markets together. Many thanks and heartfelt hugs to Bob, Cecilia, Flory, Gail, Graciela, Harry (Oswaldo), Joann, Kay, Laura, Linda, Lisette, Lucrecia, Myrna, Olga, Paula, Pirkko, Susanna and Winnie.

Thanks to fellow ex-pat writers in Costa Rica for support, constructive critiques and information – Carol, Greg, Jo, Roberta, Sandy and Walden. Thanks to Marcos for sharing his knowledge of fruits and vegetables and to Maria Jesus and Graciela for tasting everything and restoring pristine order to my kitchen and cupboards.

Thanks too to Linda Xiques former editor of the Pacific Sun and Jay Brodell editor of AM Costa Rica for printing so many of my food articles and restaurant reviews, to the interactive readers of my former columns and to Angela Hoy of Writers' Weekly and Booklocker for printing two previous books, *Chana's Legacy* and *Noni, Baloney, Puddin' & Pie.* Finally, much appreciation to the editors and publishers of this book, *Feasting and Foraging in Costa Rica,*

Lenny Karpman
La Guácima, Costa Rica, 2007

Table of Contents

Chapter 1
OVERVIEW

Feasting and Foraging in Costa Rica is a nonfiction love story. To those of us who adore well prepared ethnic food, we see museums in markets and history and culture reflected in kitchens and pantries. Few travel experiences are more rewarding than breaking bread with local people, on their turf, sharing their comfort food. Immersing ourselves in a new land and unfamiliar cuisine is like gaining a new intimate friend for life.

After half a dozen trips to Costa Rica and a permanent move there in 2003, I became enamored of such a new intimate friend. The food culture and tropical splendor of Costa Rica became *mi novia*, my lover and metaphorical bridge. I continue to find incredibly diverse ingredients, ageless traditions and gentle people. They are generous to a fault, willing to share their feelings, aspirations, beliefs and recipes. For a year and a half, I wrote weekly food columns and restaurant reviews for an online Costa Rican English language website, AM Costa Rica that had over three million visits per month, mostly from the Americas. The enthusiastic readers of the columns expanded my horizons with insights and opinions.

Among the population in Costa Rica are émigrés from all of Europe and the Americas, parts of the Middle East, Australia, North Africa and most of Asia. Their contributions to Costa Rica's edible cornucopia include *anticuchos, antipasti, arepas, bacalao*, bagels, *carpaccio,* renowned cheeses, couscous, *crêpes,* curry, *dim sum*, dumplings, egg rolls, *falafel, focaccia,* fondues, herring, hot dogs, hot pots, *kimchi*, lasagna, lox, meatloaf and mashed potatoes, *paella*, pasta, *pâté*, Peking duck, pizza, *prosciutto, sashimi, schnitzel, shwarma, soufflés, sushi, tiramisu*, locally brewed German style beer and an assortment of imported wines.

The worn cliché that Ticos (Costa Ricans) eat only bland rice, corn and beans demands equal opportunity to expose the fabulous fusion of innumerable succulent tropical fruits, crispy vegetables, abundant meats and seafood, unique local flavors and savory immigrant accents. The cliché was born out of less affluent, more provincial and conservative culinary cultural times – all on the wane.

Costa Rica has oodles of everything that lives or grows – an artist's palate of innumerable colors for the Costa Rican family cook or grand chef to titillate and satisfy the most discerning diners. All you need to see and taste for yourself are time, modest means, adventurous spirit and this annotated road map.

Latin American food culture is fast becoming a trendy major player in the gourmet world. There is hardly a four star restaurant in the United States today that doesn't pair its meat or seafood centerpiece with an artistic *salsa (*sauce) or tongue-tingling citrus-based *mojo (*marinade or baste). Wine stewards may actually match the vintage to the *salsa* or *mojo*. When they are created with fresh ripe mangos, papayas, sour oranges, mandarin lemons, bananas, guavas and pineapples, they elevate dishes to another level. Welcome to *nuevo latino* cuisine, Costa Rican style.

When you taste fresh ripe pineapple, can you return to a can? Not likely. When you make a salad out of fresh Costa Rican hearts of palm, boiled lightly, still crispy like California-cuisine asparagus, you will never be satisfied with the softer, saltier canned variety again.

Can you imagine a salad of tender greens dressed in Seville (sour) orange juice-mango purée-virgin olive oil vinaigrette topped with tiny bits of warm *chicharrones (*pork *confit)?* Consider guava-honey or guava-molasses for a pork roast glaze or baby back rib barbeque sauce or a guava-tangerine salad dressing or banana-lime ice cream or meats tenderized with papaya-laden marinades.

How about a soup-sized bowl of fresh mahi-mahi *ceviche* for about a dollar in a market? Add avocado or mango to your homemade *ceviche*. *Tico* (Costa Rican) *ceviche* begins with seafood chemically cooked by citric acid from limes, lemons or sour oranges alone or in combination. Next come finely diced onions and sweet red peppers, with or without avocado or mango. The final touches are cilantro leaves and salt and pepper to taste. Are you phobic about hot chili peppers? *Ticos* rarely use them. Even when they pass you a jar of "fiery hot" peppers to satisfy your Mexican or Peruvian expectations, the peppers are fairly mild. On the rare occasions when chilies are liberally added to *ceviche* Peruvian style, cubed sweet potatoes are added as well to offset the heat.

The smell of freshly fried crispy potato chips pervades many markets. A "small" sixty cent bag feeds four. The primary addictive aroma, however, wafts out of myriad bakery doors and windows in nearly every town and neighborhood. A ritual in the "green" (euphemism for "rainy") season is to dart into a bakery and sip a latte or espresso and inhale a warm pastry until the shower passes. The tariff is pocket change.

Storefronts selling warm snack foods usually display corn flour chicken or meat *empanadas* (turnovers), Chinese egg rolls (*tacos chinos*) and fried chicken pieces in tandem under heating lamps.

Is fried fish really so bad when the basic corn meal batter contains ground pumpkin seeds, pulverized pistachios, cocoa powder, avocado purée, macadamia nut pieces or mashed plantains? There is no better grilled fish anywhere than the local fresh catch. Fillets baked in banana leaf wraps keep in all the juices and flavor.

Spit-roasted chicken is a staple near the equator around the world from Morocco to Tunisia to Syria to Indonesia to the Americas. None has a finer fragrance and flavor than the Tico version, never frozen and roasted over aromatic coffee tree roots.

Ticos have a sweet tooth. They love rich dessert cakes, puddings, tarts, paired fruit pastes and fresh cheese slices, caramel and coconut custards and ice creams. *Sandia* seems more flavorful than watermelon from any other location. Can you imagine a better simple conclusion to a complex meal than ice-cold watermelon or a sorbet of tropical fruit and hot rich coffee?

Do you crave international ethnic variety? In tiny Costa Rica you can sample Argentinean, Brazilian, Chinese (Sichuan and Cantonese), Indian, Italian, Jewish style, French, German, Japanese, Korean, Lebanese, Mexican, Nicaraguan, Panamanian, Peruvian, Philippine, Salvadorian, Spanish, Swiss, Thai, Turkish and international vegetarian cuisines. Yes, and there are fusions.

Restaurants change nearly daily when the chef quits, when the owners move back to Europe or Asia, when the supplier goes out of business, when a bad review destroys the business or when a rave draws more diners than the kitchen can handle. Restaurant reviews can be mercurial. What don't change are the well-crafted recipes from culinary artists in humble or grand kitchens. What they have confided to my friends and me, we will share with you. Let us add recipes to your collection and restaurants to your "must visit" list for Costa Rica.

Lenny Karpman MD
La Guacima, Costa Rica 2007

Chapter 2
Glossary of Ingredients

Abalone *(abulón)* The gastropod in a shell lined with mother of pearl appears on an occasional menu at a hefty price. Abalones come from the Pacific shallows from Oregon to Guatamala.

Acarajé These fritters, made from black eyed peas, probably came to Costa Rica's east coast from West Africa by way of Brazil and Caribbean islands.

Achiote, annatto The golden yellow color of rice, meats, chicken, stew, butter and cheese is often the result of a little added *achiote* powder or *annatto* seed oil. This "poor man's saffron" is from seeds of a tree. In markets, it comes as red orange powder, paste made with vegetable shortening, golden oil with red seeds (*aceite de achiote)* or packets of just the seeds. It imparts a very mild taste of musty nutmeg and pepper. When the seeds lose their bright color, they also lose their flavor. The seeds keep well in a tightly sealed jar in a dark place.

Aceite *Aceite* is the Spanish word for "oil."

Ackee See the fruit chapter, # 4, for details of this tropical Caribbean fruit that looks like scrambled eggs.

Adobo This very common stew from the Philippines is made with chicken or pork in coconut milk under a layer of red-tinted oil. In Mexico, *adobo* is a red sauce or marinade of a purée of *chipotle* peppers and vinegar. In Costa Rica, it is used very sparingly in stews. In Spanish, *adobo* simply means "seasoning" and the term refers to either dry rubs or marinades. Chipotle peppers are often packed in *adobo* sauce.

Agave This family of succulents grow well in Central America, Mexico and the American southwest. *Tequila, mescal* and *pulque* are potent alcoholic drinks distilled from plants in this family. Aloe is a family member. The leaves and stems can be baked and eaten.

Agua dulce This drink, served hot or cold, is brown cane sugar dissolved in water.

Ahi *Ahi* is the Hawaiian name for yellowfin tuna, a common inhabitant of Costa Rica's Pacific coast. It is usually filetted, grilled in garlic butter, breaded and fried or served with a white sauce.

Ahumado *Ahumado* is the Spanish word for " smoked." Although some bacon is not smoked and smoked fish is rare, Costa Rican meat and cheese processors do smoke pigs' feet, pork chops, necks, most bacon and a variety of cheeses. Smoked chickens and turkeys appear rarely around holiday time, but they are usually imports.

Al ajillo *Ajo* is the Spanish word for "garlic." *Al ajillo* describes any dish cooked with garlic or dressed with a garlic butter sauce.

A la parilla Typically Argentinean, meats are roasted over glowing coals in a fire pit on a grill. *La parilla* is the name of the grill itself. *A la parilla,* on the grill, describes both the style of cooking and the type of restaurant.

A la plancha *A la plancha* literally means "on the plank." In modern parlance, it refers to searing and cooking on a solid metal griddle or hot plate.

Albóndigas *Albóndigas* are meatballs. Whereas most cuisines add breadcrumbs or milk soaked bread to chopped meat along with the usual egg binder, herbs and spices, Ticos usually use corn meal instead. The meatballs are often served in soup or with a tomato-vegetable sauce.

Al horno See "baked."

Allspice *(Jamaica, pimiento gordo)* Brown berries from this evergreen tree taste like a combination of clove, cinnamon and nutmeg, hence the name "allspice." They have the size and shape of peppercorns. Native to Central America, the center for production moved from the land of the Aztecs, who flavored their chocolate drinks with allspice, to Jamaica, the leading supplier of allspice in the world. My neighbor has a *jamaica* tree growing in his front yard.

Almidón See "yuca starch" in chapter 6.

Americano Bitter Campari, sweet vermouth and club soda over ice are the ingredients of this mixed drink, usually served before dinner.

Ancho The smoky flavored dry poblano chili pepper, the *ancho*, is one of the very few chilies that finds its way into Costa Rican cuisine because it is relatively mild.

Anchovies *(anchoas, boquerones)* Silvery anchovies in olive oil are staples in Spanish *tapas* restaurants. Canned and salted dark brown ones are included in only a few menus, usually with pizza, pasta or in Cesar salad dressing. Native recipes only rarely include anchovies.

Anis seed (*anis*) These licorice flavored straw colored seeds can be found in local markets. The plants grow well from seed in my herb garden and look like paler green dill. You are most likely to encounter the flavor in potato-cheese dishes in local Peruvian restaurants, of which there are many. Anis flavored liqueurs are numerous worldwide, but none seems to be popular here.

Apio This is the word for "celery", in Costa Rica, but, in other Latin American countries, it is also the word for a knobby root vegetable called "*arracacha*" in Costa Rica.

Appetizers *(antojitos, bocas)* Whimsical little things or bites accompany drinks and may be complementary during Happy Hour.

Apples (*manzanas*) See the fruit chapter, # 4 for details.

Arepas A common first course or snack in Colombia and Venezuela, these cornmeal cakes or buns topped with cheese can be found in a few *sodas* and restaurants in the Central Valley of Costa Rica. The runny white cheese on top or inside the opened bun is similar to French-style *crème fraîche.*

***Arepas* flour** *(masarepa)* The classic corn used to make this flour has very large bland starchy kernels. Among all the varieties of flour in Latin America, it is the only one that is precooked.

Armadillo (*carachupa)* Armadillo used to be a food source in the American Southwest, Northern Mexico, Western China and Central America. During the Great depression, armadillo "Hoover stew" was common in Texas, where the old joke about the chicken crossing the road, went like this: *Why did the chicken cross the road? To show the armadillo it could be done*. It was the main ingredient in more apocryphal than real "road kill stew." Ultimately, microbiologists showed that armadillos carry Hansen's bacillus, the bacterium that causes leprosy. Human transmission is not proven, but consumption fell dramatically. There is one restaurant in Fort Worth, Texas and an occasional soda in Guanacaste, Costa Rica that serve it. They are sold in the Masaya Market in Nicaragua. No, I haven't tasted them, but one came scampering through our open front door one evening with dog in hot pursuit. We removed it outside our fence, away from our pets. In Yunan, China, where it once was common, it seems to have disappeared according to locals. In rural Costa Rica, when a farmer catches one, the family relishes eating it.

Arracacha, arracacia For details about this knobby root vegetable with parsnip similarities, see the vegetable chapter, # 5.

Arrabiata This Spanish spelling of the Italian word "*arrabbiata*" *(* angry), is the name of the spaghetti sauce with more heat than any other in Costa Rica. It is made with tomatoes, bacon and chile peppers.

Arroz con Leche See Rice Pudding

Asado criollo The importance of the *asado criollo* (traditional barbecue) in Argentina can be measured by examining the standard device for cooking meat. Unlike Americans with our Webber grills, Argentines like to char flesh in something that resembles real estate: an outsize brick and mortar affair called a *parrilla*. Squatting in the backyard like a guesthouse, it's used for every cut of meat imaginable (including the occasional whole lamb, piglet, or kid). In addition to steaks and ribs, an *asado* may feature kidneys, sweetbreads, *chinchulines* (tripe), and morcilla (blood sausage). After this carnivorous odyssey, the only dessert required is a toothpick.

Asadero This cow's milk cheese melts easily in the oven. In Mexico, it is also called Oaxaca or Chihuahua cheese. It has the mild flavor of a jack cheese and is less salty than white fresh cheeses.

Asapado A soupier version of *paella*, it is called *asapao* in Puerto Rico. It is colored with ancho and usually contains sweet red peppers, onions and garlic.

Atemoya This fruit is a cross between cherimoya and sweetsop. See the fruit chapter, # 4 for details

Atole This ancient Meso-American drink is like a fruit smoothie thickened with corn meal and sweetened with honey.

Avocado (*aguacate)* Avocado is a staple in Costa rica. See the fruit chapter, # 4 for details.

Ayote For details about this common squash, see the vegetable chapter, # 5.

Babaco This South American fruit is a rarity in Costa Rica. See the fruit chapter, #4 for details.

Bacalao See salt cod in this section.

Bacon *(tocinetta, tocino*) Bacon is common in Costa Rica. It is usually salt cured and smoked.

Baked (*al horno*) Baking is less common than in temperate climates because of the unwanted extra heat in a kitchen, be it from a modern oven or old fashion clay or brick beehive. The latter is usually under a roof without walls outside the home and takes center stage for fiestas.

Bananas (*bananos)* See the fruit chapter, # 4, for details.

Barbados Cherries *(acerola)* See the fruit chapter, # 4, for details.

Basil (*albahaca*) It grows like crazy in Costa Rica, but is not a local favorite. Costa Ricans consider it a medicinal herb. Its use is widespread in ethnic restaurants.

Batido Called "*merengada*" in some other parts of Latin America, it is similar to a smoothie, see the drink chapter, # 15, for specifics.

Bay leaf (*laurel en hoja*) Rounded California type bay leaves are sold all over. They are used in soups and stews as in North American cooking and are removed before eating the food they have flavored.

Bean mash fritter (*acarajé)* These Brazilian fritters are made from purée of black-eyed peas, a bean that originated in Western Africa and occasionally visits Tico markets. Caribbean restaurants serve them on occasion.

Beef heart (*anticuchos)* Kabobs of spicy marinated chunks of grilled beef heart are a common appetizer on the menu of nearly every Peruvian restaurant. They are a little chewy with the consistency of chicken gizzards. Argentinean grill/steak houses in Costa Rica also serve charred pieces of rubbery beef heart along with kidney, tripe, blood sausage and sweetbreads.

Beer *(cerveza)* German style beer comes from local breweries Bavaria, Pilsen and Imperial. It may not be up to snuff with Belgian, Dutch or Czech beer, but it is superior to many North American brands. Here, refrigerated beer comes with a glass of ice cubes.

Bell Peppers *(chiles dulces)* Green and riper red sweet peppers are available and inexpensive all year. See the vegetable chapter, #5, for more information.

Black Bean Purée *(muñeta)* As a topping for chips, side dish or filling for *pupusas* or *empanadas*, black beans, mashed, seasoned with garlic, oregano, cumin, salt and pepper in any combination and thinned with oil, are a Tico staple.

Blackberry *(mora)* Very common in Costa Rica, blackberries flavor gelatin, ice cream, jelly, syrup, candy, juices and smoothies.

Black pepper (*pimenta negra*) Standard black pepper comes from Asia. When you see "Jamaican pepper" for sale, it is allspice, not pepper.

Blaff Haitian émigrés to the Caribbean coast of Costa Rica poach red snapper that they have marinated in a spicy sauce of chile peppers, lime juice, garlic and allspice. They call it *"blaff."*

Boniato This Caribbean sweet potato has dark red-brown skin and off-white flesh.

Bread (*pan*) See chapter 6 for descriptions of bread and bread products.

Breadfruit *(fruta de pan)* See the fruit chapter, # 4, for details on this large starchy fruit and magnificent tree with huge leaves.

Bread pudding (*budín)* Tico bread pudding contains the usual ingredients: milk, bread, eggs, cinnamon and vanilla. Some cooks substitute condensed or sweetened evaporated milk for added richness.

Breakfast (*desayuno)* Fresh fruit, rice and beans, egg or cheese on top, bread and hot coffee are the norm in the rural areas where workers leave the house a little after dawn and don't return before dusk.

Broth (*caldo)* See the soup section of chapter #3 for more details.

Buñuelo This sugar and cinnamon topped fried pastry is more common in Mexico than in Costa Rica.

Burrito This *tortilla* wrapped package contains shredded pork or beef, cheese, rice, beans, sour cream or chicken in any combination.

Butter (*mantequilla) Dos Pinos,* two pine trees, is a largest cooperative dairy for all dairy products in Costa Rica. Their butter is creamy, rich, tasty and not oversalted. Monteverde is smaller but every bit as good. Numar is the brand of local butter alternatives. The company acknowledges that its product is high in saturated fats, but has gone to great lengths to omit all trans fats for health reasons, despite the opportunity for greater profits.

Cacao This tropical evergreen is the source of chocolate. Although it grows in Costa Rica, it is not a major cash crop.

Cajetas These cellophane-wrapped sweets are made from sweetened condensed milk cooked to a fudge consistency, cut into squares and displayed at check out counters virtually everywhere. They can be chocolate, caramel and/or coconut flavored.

Cake *(queque)* Since most Ticos are fonder of sweets than most North Americans, it is not surprising that cake is quite popular. *Tres leches,* three milks, is the names of the most coveted variety, a white cake drenched in sweet evaporated, condensed and whole milk and topped with whipped cream or a sugar and egg-white frosting. Bakeries with cake displays and cakeries abound. Cheese cake is surprisingly common. Other options include pound cake, angel food, chocolate and sponge cake, together with cakes frosted and adorned for all occasions.

Calabazas See pumpkin in the vegetable chapter, # 5.

Caldo *Caldo* is broth or soup. *Caldo de res* is beef broth with chunks of meat, squash, carrot, potato, yucca and corn, often served with a side dish of avocado, onion an cilantro, all diced and piled to be added to the *caldo* at the diner's discretion. *Caldo verde* is Portugese green cabbage or kale soup that occasionally turns up on Brazilian menus.

Callaloo A number of similar Caribbean leafy greens and a soup made from any of them are called *"callaloo."* The most common green is from the taro leaf. It is prepared like mustard or collard greens. Look for the soup in Limon or south along the same coast where it is made with greens, coconut milk, fish and lime juice.

Candies *(confites)* The most common kinds are cane sugar, coconut and caramel fudge.

Cane sugar loaf (*tapa de dulce)* Sugar cane is pressed and boiled into a rich brown sap, poured into a mold, hardened into a loaf and sold to homemakers who shave off as much brown sugar as they need for a recipe or to dilute in water for a hot or cold Tico drink called *"agua dulce."*

Capers *(alcaparras)* Not native to the tropics, capers are surprisingly common in Costa Rica, usually imported from Spain. They are often added to Mediterranean salads, Italian antipastos and tomato sauces or sprinkled atop smoked salmon or *carpaccio.*

Caramel cream (*dulce de leche) Dulce de leche* is a made from whole milk and sugar cooked slowly with frequent stirring until it turns to peanut butter colored syrup. It can be used like peanut butter on bread, toast or crackers, but is more often used to fill spaces in sweets. When made with goat's milk, rarely in Costa Rica but commonly in Mexico, it is called *cajeta,* the same name as caramel-like candy in Costa Rica. Don't ask for or about *cajeta* in Argentina, where you might be misunderstood. It is the local slang word for "vagina."

Cardamom The plant originally grew only in India and Ceylon. Now it grows in Central America. In the markets, it comes in three forms, the grayish pod, the dark brown kernels or fine powder. Guatemala is an exporter. Costa Rica is a lesser grower. It is used to flavor Arabic coffee, Indian tea and curries.

Caribbean style cuisine (*comida Caribeña)* The Caribbean coast of Costa Rica is inhabited mostly by English speaking dark and light skinned people originally from the islands throughout the Caribbean, where many are descended from West African slaves. Their cooking reflects a mixture of African cuisine, Caribbean island flavors, seafood aplenty, lots of coconut milk and more spice than the food of the rest of Costa Rica.

Carne seca Similar to jerky, this is the Latin American version of salted beef dried in the sun.

Carnitas Similar in appearance and use to shredded meat but very different in taste and texture, pork is braised until all that is left of the liquid is the rendered fat from the meat. All the flavor has been absorbed and the final bit of fat frying makes the meat crispy.

Carob This tropical tree has long pods that look like leather. The pulp inside is an edible sweet facsimile of chocolate.

Carpaccio Because of the large number of Italians and Italian restaurants in Costa Rica, *carpaccio* has become a standard appetizer on many restaurant menus, not only paper thin slices of beef, but also tuna, salmon, sea bass, octopus and a variety of others. They are most often served with a little extra-virgin olive oil on top with a twist or two of the pepper grinder. Other versions include mustard sauce, aioli, lime juice, capers and onions or plain mayonnaise.

Carrot (*zanahoria)* Tico carrots are enormous, cheap, tasty and plentiful year round. Half carrot and half orange juice is a popular Tico drink. See chapter #5.

Cascabel This is the Spanish name for a child's rattle. It is also the name of a dried red chile pepper whose seeds rattle when it is shaken. Because it is hotter than Ticos like, it is not common here.

Cashew The cashew tree is common in Costa Rica. Locals eat the red fruit, the cashew apple, from which the kidney-shaped seed, which we call the nut, is suspended. See chapter #4 for more details.

Cassareep The juice of the bitter cassava is sweetened with cane sugar and reduced to make syrup that is an occasional component of food along the Caribbean coast. It is similar to the sweet and tart flavor of tamarind.

Cassava This tropical tree is common in Costa Rica. The root is sold in many markets. Toxic unless boiled, the bitter variety is the source of cassareep (above) and the non-toxic sweet variety is the source of tapioca pearls.

Cauliflower *(coliflor)* Cauliflower is grown readily throughout the Americas and seems to be in Costa Rican markets year round. The heads can achieve enormous size here. See chapter #5 for more details.

Celery *(apio)* See the vegetable chapter, #5, for more details.

Ceriman, *monstera (piña anona)* See chapter #4 for details of this strange looking tropical fruit.

Chalupa *Chalupa* means "boat" in Spanish. This first course or light main course is an underlying fried corn *tortilla* "boat" upon which are layered chicken, beef or pork, an optional cheese layer and a topping of fresh green salad or cooked vegetables dressed with lime juice and/or mayonnaise.

Chamomile (*manzanilla)* Bunches of stems with leaves and small flowers are used for brewing tea. It is a local favorite.

Chancleta Stuffed and baked *chayotes,* made with cheese and cream, *chancletas* actually translate as "old slippers."

Chayote *(chuchu* in Brazil) This green thin-skinned member of the squash family has a u-shaped invagination that looks like the smile of an elder who forgot to put in his false teeth. The taste is mild, like cucumber and Asian pear. The texture is crunchy. It does well cubed in a salad, boiled lightly like squash, baked or in soups or stews. Like potato and orange, it is a good source of potassium.

Cheese (*queso*) Many different types of cheese are made in Costa Rica. Go to chapter #10 for specifics.

Cheese turnovers (*quesadillas)* The simple form, grilled *tortillas* sandwiching melted cheese, is made with corn *tortillas* in Costa Rica, unlike the Mexican style made with wheat flour *tortillas*. Both kinds usually combine crumbly white fresh cheese with a yellow cheese that melts better.

Cherimoya See chapter #4 for details of this tropical fruit.

Chicasquil The large glove shaped leaf, *chicasquil,* is chopped and cooked much like spinach as a side dish or in a hash (*picadillo)* with other chopped ingredients.

Chicha Fermented corn is the basis of this punch drink which can be golden, slightly alcoholic and beer-like. The Peruvian version uses purple corn and the drink, *Chicha moreada,* looks like a deep burgundy wine cooler with bits of diced fruit floating on top, like *sangria*. *Chicha de maiz* is a punch using local pale yellow cracked corn as a base.

Chicharrónes There are two types, skin and meat. Both are pork, deep fried in rendered pork fat and salted. The meat variety is cubed cut into pieces about two or three inches in any dimension. The pieces of crispy skin are flatter. Both are very popular. Every weekend, *chicharrón* sellers line the roadsides in every small town, boiling pork chunks and skin in large metal hemispheres over wood fires. Even if you usually avoid fats, sample a small piece of the meat for a taste treat.

Chicken *(pollo)* There are probably as many fried or roast chicken eateries per capita in Costa Rica as there are pizzerias in Italy. A two-piece order of fried chicken usually costs $1.25 to $1.50 with green plantain *ceviche* and a few warm *tortillas.* Add a fruit drink and your have lunch for $2 or less.

Chick peas (*garbanzos*) These legumes are sold dry or canned throughout the world. In Latin America, they find their way into soups, stews, salads and as side dishes.

Chilaquiles This cheap menu item in *sodas* is a mixture of sautéed strips of leftover corn *tortillas,* mixed with bits of pork, chicken, beef, cheese, onions, sweet red peppers or any combination thereof. In fancier venues, the ingredients are layered, topped with shredded cheese and run under the broiler.

Chiles Of the two hundred or so types of chilies or chili peppers, only two are part of the Costa Rican parlance, sweet red and green – *chilies dulces,* and spicy – *chilies picantes.* The former are bell peppers that turn red as they mature. The latter are all the dozens that produce heat around the world.

Chile con Queso Mexican restaurants in Costa Rica often serve this yellow cheese and green Chile pepper dip with fried *tortilla* chips.

Chiles Rellenos These cheese stuffed baked or breaded and fried peppers differ from the common Mexican type. Ticos substitute sweet for mildly spicy peppers in the recipe.

Chili con Carne Not part of the typical local cuisine, a decent bowl of *chili* is common fare in sports bars and Tex-Mex restaurants.

Chimichurri This green pesto of cilantro, garlic, olive oil, parsley, vinegar, salt and pepper is one of the mandatory side dish additives for steaks and chops in Argentinean steak houses. It can also be slathered on roasted chicken or grilled fish.

Chimichanga Basically a fried *burrito* wrapped in a corn flour *tortilla,* it is rare to see a *chimichanga* outside a local Mexican restaurant.

Chinese Mustard Greens Savoy cabbage is called "*mostaza china,* Chinese mustard," in Costa Rica. It is used is soups, stews, salads and as a cooked side dish in a vegetable hash (*picadillo).* It is more popular locally than any other leafy green, including spinach.

Chipotle Jalapeño smoked peppers are called "*chipotles.*"

Chiverre The flesh of this white spaghetti squash gourd is baked, separated from shell and seeds, stripped of a dark bitter internal stripe, mashed, sweetened and used to fill *empanadas* year round, Easter and Christmas pastries and is sold as jam. It is very tasty and mahogany colored.

Chocolate *(chocolate)* Refer back to *Cacao* above.

Chop Suey This western dish of Chinese-style diced meats or seafood and vegetables served over white rice, is a noodle dish in Costa Rica, similar to chow mein. Unless you order it dry (*chop suey seco*), it will come in a bowl in soupy brown gravy. To add insult to injury, it is often served with sliced white bread.

Chorizo *Chorizo* in Costa Rica is only a little redder and a little spicier than ordinary bland native sausage. If it were not called *chorizo* on the label, you would never guess. Imported Mexican *chorizo* is orange from lots of paprika, fiery hot from chili peppers and savory from garlic and spices. Soft *chorizo* from Spain has the color but not the kick of the Mexican. Cured Spanish *chorizo* is firm, dry and almost like ham.

Chow mein Tico chow mein is more like American chop suey, but is served with crispy fried thick noodles.

Churro This fried long thin donut has longitudinal grooves or twists. The dough is sweet and the outside is covered with cinnamon-sugar. *Churros* are common at street fairs, carnivals and snack stands.

Cilantro *(culantro)* *Culantro* would be the national herb, if one were so designated. Look for it in every sauce, dip, soup, stew or *ceviche*. It is used as parsley would be in North America both for taste and as a decoration.

Cinnamon *(canela)* Bark and powder are used in a variety of pastries, sweets, drinks and even savory dishes. Most of it seems to be of the Mexican type, sweeter and spicier than its East Indies cousin.

Citron This lumpy tart lemon is prized in Israel as a gift for a particular holiday. Its fingered form, “hand of Buddha (chapter # 4),” appears from time to time in Costa Rican farmers’ markets.

Clove *(clavo)* Cloves are easy to find in supermarkets. The distinctive flavor emerges in rice pudding, cakes, a fermented corn drink called *pitarrilla* and a sweet dessert made from a zucchini cousin, *pipián*. Allspice, a fairly common flavor in Caribbean food, can be a source of confusion. Clove does grow throughout the West Indies and Brazil. The famous fish sauce from Vera Cruz, Mexico is clove flavored.

Coconut candy *(cocadas)* Shredded coconut and egg yolk are added to sugar-water syrup and baked until they turn a pale golden color. You can find them alongside the milk fudge squares (cajetas) next to the cash register in nearly every small market. Similar sweet spheres covered with shredded coconut are called *bolitas de coco*.

Coconuts *(cocos)* Coconut drinks, ice cream, candies, cookies, milk, cream and Caribbean sauces, soups and rice are well worth a try.

Coffee (café) The Colombian government sued Costa Rica in International Court in The Hague because of bumper stickers that read "Juan Valdéz drinks Costa Rican coffee." Ticos are rightfully proud of their rich mountain grown coffee. Local brands of good quality sell for about $2 per pound. Volio is my personal favorite.

Comál There are two types of *comáles, tortilla* pans. One type is a thin tin hemisphere that looks like an inverted shallow wok. The other is flat unglazed ceramic.

Coriander Cilantro *(cilantro)* Costa Rica's number one herb is *culantro*. Its seeds were named *"koris,"* bedbugs, by the Greeks and are now called coriander. Powder from grinding the seeds is a component of many spice mixes and curry recipes, but Ticos harvest the plant green before it goes to seed and use seeds mainly for propagation.

Corn (*maiz)* Corn rivals rice and beans as the number one national staple. Corn flour, cornmeal, corn kernels, corn tortillas, corn pudding, corn pancakes, corn on the cob and popcorn are not even the whole picture.

Corn boiled (*elote cocinado)* This Spanish term refers to boiled kernels or ears.

Corn dough (m*asa harina*) The similarity of Spanish terms for ground corn products may be confusing, and, at times, appears to interchange. *Masa* harina is moistened dough sold in tubs or packages. A lump of *masa harina* made from finely ground corn flour mixed with water, flattened in a round press and toasted on a grill becomes a *tortilla*. Coarser dough filled with a host of savories and steamed inside a plantain leaf emerges as a *tamal* (tamale*)*. The same dough with different additions fry into croquettes.

Corn flour (*harina de maiz)* Corn flour or meal is more prevalent than wheat flour in Costa Rica. The finest grind is used for breads, rolls, dumplings, turnovers and pastries in similar fashion to wheat flour in North America. Coarser grinds coat foods for frying, are the basis of fritters, cook up into hot porridges and become fillers in hamburgers and stuffing mixtures.

Corn Pancakes (*chorreadas*, *cachapas)* *Chorreadas* are slightly sweet corn pancakes made without flour. Corn kernels are puréed in a blender with a little milk and sugar to taste. Because local corn has little water content, the purée requires some milk to thin it to the consistency of batter. It also is less sweet than North American corn, so sugar is added to taste. Pancakes are then browned on both sides in a buttered skillet or on a griddle and served hot. The corn kernels in Venezuela are plump and juicy like those in the US. They don't need added milk. Instead they need a little corn flour to keep the batter from being too runny. Their corn pancakes are called *cachapas*. Either can be topped with cheese, sour cream, fruit compote, eggplant caviar, apple butter, marmalade or maple syrup.

Corn pudding *(masamorra)* When you spy something in local markets and roadside stands that looks like more yellow than usual cheesecake, it is probably dense, sweet, tasty *masamorra*. If you visit the extremely popular La Paz Waterfall Garden Park, the restored old rancho serves free samples.

Corn roasted (*elote asado)* Elote asado is corn-on-the-cob roasted on a grill, common fair at open air festivals.

Corn starch *(maicena)* The dried central embryo of a corn kernel contains starch that, when mixed with liquid, is a potent thickener once the mixture boils. Its uses are the same in the tropics as they are in temperate climes.

Crêpes *(arepas, prestiños)* *Arepas* are unsweetened Columbian-style crêpes, common in Costa Rica. *Prestiños* are sweet dessert crêpes. Recently, crêperies have begun to appear in upscale malls. Their menus usually include savory lunchtime crêpes, sweet dessert ones, waffles, pastries and ice cream.

Croissants These flaky, crescent-shaped yeast rolls, originally from France, have begun to appear in breakfast venues, usually as part of morning egg and cheese sandwiches, and in a few bakeries.

Croquettes or fritters (*croquetas, buñuelas*) With such a plethora of starchy tubers in Latin America, it is understandable that so many are boiled, mashed, stuffed, shaped into a patty and fried as one of dozens of different kinds. Be they Brazilian *acarajés*, Tico *patacones* or *yuca croquetas,* Colombian *fritangas,* Ecuadorian *pristiños,* Peruvian *picarones,* Caribbean codfish cakes or Cuban *boniato croquetas con cerdo* they are all croquettes.

Cumin *(comino)* I associate cumin with cuisines of the Middle East, North Africa and the Asian sub-continent. All of these cuisines are underrepresented in Costa Rica. Nevertheless, cumin is used commonly, albeit in small amounts.

Custard (*flan*) Baked or steamed egg custard is a favorite dessert throughout Latin America, China, France and Spain. The only local variation on standard *crème caramel* is the frequent addition of coconut.

Custard apple See chapter #4 for details of this tropical fruit.

Dessert (*postre*) In small Tico restaurants throughout the country, dessert menus tend to be short and repetitious. They usually include ice cream, *tres leches* cake, *tiramisu,* cheesecake, rice pudding, gelatin and *flan.*

Desayuno *"Desayuno" is t*he Spanish word for breakfast.

Dinner (*cena)* The evening meal is not necessarily the main meal of the day, nor does it begin at 9 or 9:30 as in Spain. Mealtime usually begins between 6 and 7:30, a little later on Friday or Saturday nights in restaurants. Multigenerational family meals on Sundays are usually afternoon affairs at home or in restaurants. Many restaurants close at 5PM on Sunday. When the midday meal is the main offering, the evening meal may resemble a North American light lunch of soup, salad, sandwich, leftovers or rice and beans. When dinner is primary, expect appetizers, main course of meat, starch and vegetables, and dessert and coffee.

Dragon fruit, strawberry pear (*pitaya, pitahaya)* See chapter #4 for details of this unusual tasty tropical fruit.

Dressing *(aderezo)* Salads tend to be underdressed. Cold cooked vegetables with a little mayonnaise or lime juice is unfortunately common. Options may include oil and vinegar, pseudo-Russian mayo and ketchup, vinaigrette, ranch or the same cilantro pesto, *chimichurri,* that goes on steaks or chicken breasts. Blue cheese, Roquefort, authentic Cesar and *miso* dressings are uncommon.

Duck *(pato)* A few Chinese markets in San Jose carry authentic lacquered and Peking duck that hang from hooks in the window. Upscale Chinese and French restaurants serve duck. Otherwise, duck is uncommon to rare. The only visible wild duck species in the skies is merganser, and even they are not common.

Durian The slow-growing durian tree produces large green melon-sized ovals covered with fleshy spines. The foul smelling fruit is prized throughout Southeast Asia. Durian trees do grow in Costa Rica, but few have endured the fifteen to twenty year span required to bear fruit.

Eggnog *(rompope)* Similar to North American, the Central American version appears on market shelves in glass bottles, usually in liquor sections.

Eggplant *(berenjena)* The large oval dark purple variety of eggplant is common. See the vegetable chapter, # 5, for details.

Egg Roll *(taco chino)* Egg rolls are common, not only in Chinese restaurants, but also in snack stands throughout the country. The fillings are more likely to be chopped cabbage rather than bean sprouts, and ham rather than roast pork.

Eggs *(huevos)* Eggs are cheap and ubiquitous. In local breakfast *sodas,* they are generally prepared fried or scrambled, often atop *gallo pinto,* rice and beans. Poached eggs, deviled eggs and egg salad are relatively uncommon. Omelettes are usually limited to cheese, ham or both. Quiches and frittatas appear only in delis, upscale markets and ethnic restaurants. Unfortunately, Tico custom is to cook eggs in a hot frying pan in oil. They are nearly always overcooked - dry scrambled or bottom browned sunnyside up.

Empanada Literally, it means baked in a pastry crust. *Empanadas* are typically hemispheres that range in size from quail eggs to loaves of bread. The most common size would just cover your hand. They can be savory or sweet and vary significantly coast-to-coast and country-to-country. Standard Costa Rican turnovers are made with corn dough, baked or fried and filled with savories – meat, cheese, puréed beans, chicken or potatoes; or sweets – sweetened cheese, *chiverre,* coconut cream or pineapple. For variety, try Caribbean *pati* or Argentinean beef and gravy-filled pastries.

Enchilada This crêpe made of a corn *tortilla* may be filled with chicken, pork, shredded beef or cheese; dressed in tomato sauce; topped with crumbled white cheese and browned under a broiler. The Tico version is chili-pepper free.

En gelatina *En gelatina* means encased in jelly, as in aspic. Aspics and molds are popular neither in Costa Rican homes nor in restaurants. They are uncommon offerings in upper end deli counters where foreigners shop.

En papillote *En papillote* implies that the dish is cooked in a wrapping of foil or parchment paper. Foil wraps are more frequent than parchment, but neither are common here.

Enyucados Eggs and salt added to boiled and mashed yuca make the dough for these *empanada*-cousins called "*enyucados.*" Savory fillings of pork, cheese, beans or chicken, mixed with garlic, onions and/or sweet peppers top small circles of rolled out dough, that are then folded over, pinched closed and fried golden brown.

Escabeche Copied from a popular Spanish dish, *escabeche* is a pickling sauce spooned over lightly fried small fish or tossed with vegetables. It typically contains allspice, bay leaves, chili peppers, diced sweet red peppers and carrots, olive oil, onion rings, salt, sugar or honey, pepper and vinegar. The same marinade can be turned into a dressing for salads, shrimp, cubes of pork and chicken fingers.

Fajitas *Fajitas* are originally a staple of Tex-Mex cuisine. They are the southern border equivalent of Philly steak sandwiches. Tough cuts of beef, e.g. skirt steak, are marinated for many hours in lime juice, oil, garlic, oregano and cumin. Some people add beer or tequila to tenderize the meat. The meat is removed, cut into thin strips that look like small belts, called "*fajitas*" in Spanish. The strips are grilled and added to separately grilled onions and sweet red peppers. The mixture is wrapped in soft warm *tortillas* and eaten like sandwiches.

Fiambres See cold cuts in the meat chapter, # 7.

Fish (*pescado)* Chapter #9 contains descriptions of all locally available fish.

Flauta Shredded meat wrapped in a corn *tortilla* is deep fried until crisp and brown and served hot, topped with *guacamole* and sour cream in most Mexican restaurants. The tubular shape is similar to a flute, hence the name.

Focaccia *Focaccia*, Italian flat bread, is quite common and usually very well made in the dozens of Italian restaurants in Costa Rica. The top is most often drizzled in olive oil and sprinkled with salt and rosemary on its way into the oven.

Fricassee (*fricasé)* Another name for "stew," the French term appears on menus and in cookbooks on rare occasions.

Fried *(Frito)* Generalizations are always dangerous, but it is fair to say that locals eat lots of fried foods. The big three taste preferences are probably fried, sweet and without heat (no chili peppers). A dish called *"frito"* is not fried. Go on to the next heading for a description.

Frito This holiday stew of pig parts, head and organs is unlikely to grace menu pages. Look to stands with big pots and soup bowls at carnivals and town festivals. It is most popular with older folks, for whom it conjures up fond memories of community events from bygone days.

Garlic *(ajo)* Garlic makes its way into a huge number of dishes including beans, soups, stews, sauces, marinades and dips. Nearly all Tico restaurants offer as a choice for preparation of steak, fish or chicken, a garlic butter sauce.

Gazpacho This cold tomato and vegetable soup is uncommon in native cuisine but enjoys much more favor in Spanish and international restaurants.

Gelatin Flavored gelatin is a Tico favorite. Moms feed it to kids for dessert. Cubes of red gelatin are often added to fruit salad or ice cream. The top of cheesecake may have a thin layer of red gelatin as a cover, and the cake itself is often lightened by the addition of unflavored gelatin to the batter.

Ginger *(jengibre)* Ginger grows in amazing profusion in Costa Rica. It is more popular as an ornamental flower than as an herb, but it is easy to find in most farmers' markets.

Goose *(ganso)* Geese are not common in Costa Rica. On occasion, they are used as watch animals. Intruders beware. They are loud and aggressive. Restaurants rarely feature them and in my only home experience with one, it was stewed. *Foie gras* is not made locally.

Goosefoot *(epazote)* This dried-leaf potent herb is quite common in Mexico but also appears in very small cellophane packets from California to Panama. The flat sharp pointed leaves are sometimes added to bean dishes to decrease gas. They are a little bitter.

Grapefruit *(toronja)* Yellow, red and thick skinned pommelo are all common in Costa Rica.

Green sauce *(salsa verde)* The green color comes from parsley, cilantro or basil puréed in oil with ground nuts like pesto. The Tico version doesn't often contain basil, which is thought of as a medicinal rather than a flavoring agent. It usually has cilantro, garlic, capers, sieved egg yolks and is poured over fish fillets.

Griddled (*a la plancha*) I have heard that the origin of this term derives from cooking on a wooden plank over coals. Now it means seared on a solid metal grill, or griddle.

Grilled (*a la parilla)* Enormous Argentine style fire pits with rotisseries or parallel bars down to Weber Kettles and small hibachis all coexist under this rubric. When a restaurant sign out front advertises "*a la parilla,*" it usually signifies Argentinean steak house. Less often, it refers to barbequed chicken.

Guacamole *Guacamole* is mashed avocado seasoned with lime juice, cilantro, salt and pepper. In Costa Rica, diced sweet red pepper, onion or tomato may be added. It is used as an appetizer with chips, sauce, condiment or side dish.

Guaro *Guaro* is a colorless, cheap, potent, white alcoholic drink consumed mostly by local weekend revelers, in exotic combinations by imaginative bartenders and from hip bottles by impoverished alcoholics.

Guava *(guayaba)* See chapter #4 for details of this tropical fruit.

Guinea fowl (*guineas)* These beautiful birds live wild in the mountains of Costa Rica. Domesticated, they mix easily with chickens and rid the yard and henhouse of ticks. Their eggshells are lighter colored and more asymmetrical than chicken eggs. Unlike chickens, the female is the noisy one, honking like a goose with a kazoo. They are larger than chickens, smaller than geese and are much tougher than either when cooked. They are often stewed or simmered for about an hour in a pressure cooker.

Guinea pig (*cuy)* In the highlands of Ecuador and Peru or in South American restaurants in Costa Rica, gutted guinea pigs, divested of their fur, are deep fried to a crispy golden brown and served intact, teeth and all, on a platter. Don't let the kids see their pets' siblings on your plate. They taste much better than they sound. If you visit Odavalo Market in the mountains above Cusco, locals will direct you to neighboring villages where *cuy* are raised and eaten.

Guineo *Guineos* are green plantains used in festive stews like *frito (*see above).

Habanera *Habanera* means "prepared Havana style," as in *picadillo habanero,* a hash of potato, ground beef, onions, garlic and chili peppers. The incendiary Scotch bonnet chili of the Caribbean is called "*habanero"* in Spanish.

Hamburger *(hamburguesa) Ticos* alter hamburgers by adding a slice of ham and a swath of mayonnaise to the burger, along with lettuce and tomato. Grilled or raw onions and ketchup are optional. The buns are the standard soft type, some with white sesame seeds.

Hearts of palm (*palmitos)* Tender inner stems of a number of different palm trees are lightly boiled and salted. As a side dish or in a salad, they have a delicate flavor and mild crunch. The most common source in Costa Rica seems to be the thorny *pejibaye* palm. In Florida, they come from the state tree, the cabbage palm. Their flavor has been likened to artichoke and appearance to white asparagus shafts.

Honey *(miel)* Fresh local honey and an assortment of standard commercial brands are common. Farmers' markets are the best places to find the former. Among the unusual sweets called honey in Costa Rica are white spaghetti squash honey *(miel de chiverre)* and cane sugar honey *(miel de tapa de dulce)*. Either may actually be devoid of honey but bear the name because of similar consistency.

Horchata *Horchata* is a cold drink that looks like a milkshake, but is usually dairy free and low fat. The most common variety is made from rice and flavored with cinnamon. Others are made from nuts, usually almonds, grains or starchy root vegetables that are ground, soaked, strained, flavored and chilled.

Huachinango a la Veracruzana Perhaps Mexico's most famous fish dish, Caribbean red snapper is dressed with a sauce named after the coastal city of Vera Cruz. It contains a fine dice of green and yellow peppers, onions and tomatoes seasoned with clove and cinnamon.

Huevos rancheros, ranch style eggs This classic Mexican breakfast dish is now common all over the Americas. It begins with *tortillas,* hot off the grill or skillet. Next come a pair of fried eggs, usually sunny side up. The final component is red sauce – diced tomatoes, chili peppers, onion and garlic. In Costa Rica, the chili peppers are omitted unless you order *huevos rancheros* in a Mexican restaurant and the sauce may be a little soupy.

Ice Cream *(helado)* Vanilla, rum raisin, strawberry, blackberry, tutti frutti, chocolate, peanut and coconut seem to be the common local flavors. Generally good quality and low prices make ice cream a favorite.

Jerk In Jamaica, and subsequently along the Caribbean coast of Costa Rica, a paste called “jerk” is used as a marinade, to coat meat, poultry or seafood before cooking or as a baste to be applied during cooking. The usual component parts are these: allspice, chili pepper, cinnamon, garlic, green onion, hot sauce, nutmeg, paprika, pepper, salt, thyme and vinegar. Pork and chicken are the most common meats. As you might guess, chili peppers and hot sauce are used more sparingly, if at all, in the Costa Rican version.

Jerky (*charqui, carne seca)* Sticks of dried meat seasoned with spices similar to the antecedent Jamaican mixture are called jerky in the United States. Sun dried salted slices are *carne seco* in Costa Rica.

Jerusalem artichoke, sun choke (*topinambur)* An uncommon visitor to Costa Rican markets, this tuber is much more prevalent in South and North America, farther away from the equator. It grows better in Canada than in Costa Rica.

Jicima Similar in taste and texture to Asian water chestnuts, these pale brown skinned roots with white flesh are members of the morning glory family. See chapter 5 for details.

Kiwi See chapter #4 for details of the fruit of this tropical vine.

Langosta, Langostino These are the Spanish words for lobster and prawn, respectively.

Lard (*manteca)* These days, you have to read labels. Also sold as *manteca* is all vegetable shortening. The leading Costa Rican brand is Numar.

Lasagna Surprisingly popular even outside of Italian restaurants, Tico lasagna may be made with canned tuna, white sauce, sweet red peppers, green peas and mushrooms.

Leek Leeks are seasonal visitors to farmers' markets, but are not a common ingredient in traditional recipes.

Lemon *(limón)* *Limón* is used interchangeably to denote lemon or lime. Limes are much more prevalent. See chapter # 4 for details on both.

Lemongrass Native to Southeast Asia, lemongrass is available at times in La Garita nurseries and grows well in my herb garden. Its mild lemon flavor is a standard in Thai soups and sauces.

Lima bean A large pale kidney shaped bean, it is most frequently sold dry. Known to the Incas and Algonquins long before Columbus, it is ubiquitous in the Western hemisphere.

Liver *(higado)* Beef and pork liver are more popular in Costa Rica than in the US. Preparations are similar, the most common being pan fried with onions.

Long cilantro, *(recao, culantro largo)* Larger than cilantro leaves, arising singly from a long stem, this herb is much less common and a little more peppery than ubiquitous cilantro. The leaves have sawtooth edges. The stems and leaves are used in salads, soups and stews.

Loquat, Japanese medlar *(nispero)* See chapter #4 for details of this tropical fruit.

Lunch (*almuerzo*) Lunch can be anything from a burger to the main meal of the day. Daily specials usually cost between $3.50 and $4 for a large plate of meat (beef in sauce, chicken, pork cutlet or fish fillet), salad, cooked plantain or banana, yuca, rice and beans and a fruit drink or bottled soda.

Macadamia nuts Many people have tried and a few have successfully raised orchards of macadamia trees in Costa Rica for a cash crop. Unfortunately, it takes about ten years for the trees to produce. Although they can grow virtually anywhere that coffee grows, most seem to be along the Caribbean slope, north of Turialba.

Mahi mahi *(dorado)* This Pacific dolphinfish is great to catch and better to eat broiled, grilled, in lime juice as *ceviche*, raw as *sahimi* or sliced paper thin into *carpaccio*.

Manchego Imported *manchego* Spanish sheep cheese is very popular in Costa Rica (and throughout the world). Local facsimiles are not bad, but don't compare to the Spanish imports.

Mandarin orange *(mandarina)* The Mardarin orange or tangerine is quite popular and easy to grow here. It is sweet and juicy when the skin becomes loose, even if the color is partially green.

Mangos *(mangos)* See chapter #4 for details of this queen of tropical fruit.

Marjoram *(mejorana)* Marjoram is a fascinating herb. It belongs to the greater mint family and is a cousin of oregano, but is much milder and sweeter, particularly when grown in warmer climates. It is a great herb in tomato, lamb and vegetable dishes. Marjoram is an ingredient in many premixed poultry and Italian seasoning packets. It is commonly used in head cheese, bologna and liverwurst. In Germany it is called *wurstkraut,* sausage cabbage, because it is part of so many different sausage recipes. Because it is not very strong, its flavor is best preserved if it is added to any dish in the last minutes of cooking. Sweet marjoram tastes like fruity, aromatic thyme. The same herb, grown in colder climates, becomes an annual rather than a perennial, loses its fragrance and becomes bitter.

The sweet dried leaves are available in most Tico supermarkets, but it seldom appears in local recipes.

Maté This tea, made from the leaves of a type of holly, is a caffeine rich beverage most popular in Andean countries, but available in most Central American cities. You are most likely to find it in Costa Rica in Argentinean restaurants. It may appeal to you when a friendly waiter offers you tea in an ornate silver or gold trimmed gourd or cup and a silver straw. Beware. The tea is bitter and the caffeine content may be enough to cause cardiac rhythm problems e.g. rapid heart rate or extra beats.

Melon pear (*pepino dulce)* See chapter #4 for details of this tropical fruit.

Melons *(melones)* See chapter #4 for details of these tropical fruits.

Merengue (*suspiro)* This egg white meringue, seasoned with sugar and the zest of an orange or lime, is probably the primary dessert in Peruvian restaurants. Upscale Costa Rican restaurants often serve it as well. Some places call it by its Australian pseudonym, "Pavlova."

Milk fudge (*cajeta)* On the counters of every little grocery, you will see pale beige squares wrapped in cellophane. They are fudge made from milk and sugar, flavored with citrus peel and cinnamon. Most of the steak houses and many other restaurants in Costa Rica are owned or run by Argentineans. Be careful not to ask for *cajeta* in such places. It is slang for "vagina" in Argentina.

Mineral water (*agua mineral*) Tap water is safe to drink but many French and Italian mineral water brands are available.

Mint *(menta)* Mint is a common Tico herb. It grows rapidly and aggressively in herb gardens and existed in many varieties in pre-Columbian Inca and Mayan cuisine. *Menta* is peppermint. *Yerba buena* is spearmint.

Mojo *Mojos* are sauces and marinades that vary from country to country. Most are citrus vinaigrettes with imaginative spice combinations, garlic and tropical fruit purées. They are major players in *Nuevo Latino* cuisine, particularly in the hands of Cuban chefs. *Tico mojos* are usually lime juice, garlic, cumin, cilantro, salt and pepper with or without tropical fruit purée such as papaya, pineapple, mango or guava. For marinades in other Latin American countries, to the same ingredients, chefs add Scotch bonnet, *jalapeño* or *habanera* chili peppers.

Mole In Mexico there are entire families of *mole* sauces containing spices, nuts and seeds. Perhaps the most famous also contains unsweetened chocolate – *Mole Poblano,* a dark rich sauce served on and with chicken and turkey. There are also red and green *moles.* Perhaps Mexico's most famous sauce, this labor intensive multi-ingredient sauce of many herbs and spices, ground seed and nuts and unsweetened chocolate, exists only in Mexican restaurants in Costa Rica.

Mombin (*caimito*) This sweet and delicious plum-like fruit is described in chapter #4.

Morcilla *Morcilla,* a sausage, is uncommon but not unknown in Costa Rica. It is thicker, darker and much more aromatic than other local sausages. Basically it is a pork blood sausage filled with about forty percent rice. The aroma comes from clove, cinnamon and either anis or nutmeg.

Muñeta, frijoles negros molidos *Muñeta* is a mash or purée of black beans. A very common dip with corn chips, see the section on *bocas* in the next chapter.

Mushrooms (*hongos*) The vast majority of mushrooms in supermarkets and farmers' markets are the mundane cultivated white ones. Boletus, chanterelle, oyster and russa mushrooms do grow in Central America, but seldom appear in Tico markets. Keep an eye out for *hongos de maiz,* corn mushrooms. They are actually a paste or purée made from the fungus and the corn kernels it grows on. In Mexico, the paste is called *cuitlacoche,* and is used to fill turnovers or season cream sauces.

Mussels (*mejillones*) A seafood mainstay from Lima to coastal Chile, mussels are a minor player in seafood markets, behind octopus, squid, shrimp and tiny clams.

Napa Cabbage (*mostaza China*) Called Chinese cabbage in Costa Rica, Napa cabbage is used as a fresh salad green, as a cooked green in soups and stews, as a stir fry ingredient with ginger and garlic or as white matchsticks in Sichuan dishes.

Naranjillas*, lulos* These 'little oranges" are the fruit of spreading shrub, that indeed are orange and round when ripe and taste like tart strawberries. See chapter #4 for more details.

Nopal These fleshy pads of cactus are boiled and sliced. The strips become salad ingredients, more in Mexico, but occasionally in Costa Rica. These are the same cacti that bear prickly pears.

Nougat (*turrón*) Nougat is a sweet made from roasted nuts, honey and sugar. It is a fairly common addition to flan and frozen mousse and is often crumbled over frozen desserts.

***Nuevo Latino* cuisine** Roughly fifteen years ago, Chef Douglas Rodriguez began a culinary revolution. Born in New York of Cuban parents and trained at Johnson and Whales Culinary Institute, he introduced bold fusions of Caribbean, Central American, South American and Mexican tropical fruits, marinades, sauces and spices in Miami. His trainees, later dubbed the "mango gang," dispersed the new style throughout North America. You need only consider the successes of his and their restaurants Chicana, Pipa, Calle Ocho and Sol in New York; Alma de Cuba and Pasión in Philadelphia; Mas, Cuatro and National 27 in Chicago; Ceiba in Washington, D.C. and Limon and Destino in San Francisco to appreciate their expanding appeal to gourmands.

Octopus *(pulpo) Pulpo* is a common ingredient in all mixed seafood dishes in Costa Rica. It is also mixed with rice, sautéed in garlic butter and shaved into carpaccio.

Okra Uncommon except on the Caribbean coast, this pod is used primarily for its mucilaginous properties in stews, soups or tomato sauces. It may also be battered and deep fried.

Old clothes (*ropa vieja) Ropa vieja* literally means "old clothes." This stew of shredded meat from calf, kid or lamb, green olives, onions, garlic and peppers can be found in Costa Rica on the menus of Cuban restaurants or in the homes of Cuban, Puerto Rican or Venezuelan expats. In some South American countries, *ropa viejo* is a salad of shredded leftover meat and cabbage. There is a Tico version which is an in-the-home meatless soup made with stale shredded pieces of corn tortillas. Tomato, onion, pepper, garlic, cilantro and salt are sautéed in oil and mixed with the tortilla strips which have soaked up enough water to moisten throughout. Milk is added and heated to the simmer. Eggs are cracked open and gently added to the hot chowder so that every bowl gets an egg with firm white and soft yolk.

Onions *(cebollas)* See chapter #5.

Orange *(naranja)* See chapter #4.

Orange pudding *(atol de naranja)* Made from orange juice and pulp, milk, corn starch and sugar, it is sometimes served in the scooped out skin of the orange halves that sourced the juice and pulp.

Oregano *(oregano)* A common herb in Costa Rican cooking, fresh oregano leaves are often used, even in Tico-Italian restaurants here. In Italy fresh oregano is never used, only the dried crumbled leaves.

Oven *(horno)* Pizza ovens, bakery ovens and outdoor old fashion beehive clay or ceramic ovens are used more frequently, it seems, than modern kitchen ovens, probably because of the tropical climate. Some people even have a separate small out-building for home baking.

Paella There are many versions of *paella*. The dish is Spanish in origin, named after the shallow wide pan with two handles in which its ingredients are cooked. Classic *paella* begins with medium grain rice, saffron, sausage, chicken parts and seafood, usually decorated with strips of red pimento and green peas. In Costa Rica, you can find *paella* in nearly all the Spanish and Peruvian restaurants, although no two are the same.

Palillo In Central America, this yellow coloring agent and mild spice is similar to turmeric, but less costly.

Pancakes *(panqueques)* Go for the local corn pancakes, *chorreados*. They are a little sweet, but delicious. North American pancakes are generally made with simple add-water-mixes and are underwhelming. Maple flavored syrup is quite the bargain here. Another dish worth trying is *panqueques dulce de leche*. These are hot crêpes, spread with slowly cooked sweetened milk until it has a peanut butter consistency. The crêpe is then rolled up like a cigar. You are most likely to find them in fancy B&B's or upscale breakfast buffets.

Pan Bon *Pan bon* is sweet bread, Caribbean style. The recipe includes flour, sugar, cinnamon, vanilla, nutmeg, raisins, baking powder, shortening and crystallized fruit.

Pan de maíz This sweet dense corn bread is honey colored and has the consistency of firm pudding or heavy cheesecake. It is often sold by the slice or kilo in weekend markets.

Papas secas Peruvian dried potatoes have a history that antedates the arrival of the *Conquistadores*. *Chuños,* whole potatoes from the Andes, were frozen outdoors and squeezed free of liquid repeatedly, until they were rock hard and had a shelf life similar to dried beans. Modern freeze dried cooked potato cubes, *papas secas,* can be browned in a skillet and re-hydrated in water before being added to soups, stews and hashes.

Papaya (*papaya*) See chapter #4 for details of this tropical fruit.

Passion fruit (*maracuya, granadilla*) See chapter #4 for details of this tropical fruit.

Patacones, tostones Twice fried coin shaped pieces of plantain come out like thick potato chips. Often served with *ceviche,* seafood, fried foods or dips, they must be salted while very hot or they will be bland.

Pati *Pati* is a spicy Caribbean meat turnover similar to a juicy empanada.

Peach *(melacatón)* See chapter 4 for details of this tropical fruit.

Peanuts (*mani*) Roadside vendors sell large bags of roasted peanuts in the shell. They are also plentiful in markets.

The shelled variety is common as well, with a variety of seasonings.

Pear *(pera)* See chapter 4 for details of this tropical fruit.

Peruvian potato salad *(causa)* In Quechua, the language of Peruvian Andes natives, *causa* means an entire meal. It begins with boiled, peeled cubed potatoes tossed or layered with yellow corn kernels, green and red sweet pepper matchsticks, chopped celery, sliced olives, avocado cubes, cilantro leaves and seafood (shrimp, crabmeat, octopus pieces, sea bass, lobster, etc.) in any combination, dressed with citrus, olive oil, mustard, hot sauce and herbs blended. It is typically served at room temperature or slightly chilled. With contrasting colors, textures and tastes, it truly is an entire meal. You would be hard pressed to find any of the fifteen or so Peruvian restaurants in Costa Rica without *causa* on the menu.

Picadillo, hash The Costa Rican version of hash is predominantly cubed pieces of potato, cooked in a little liquid with ground or diced meat. It is frequently part of *plato del dia,* the daily mixed plate. It looks more like ground turkey chili in Cuba. There are dozens of other *picadillos* of chopped or cubed plantain, papaya, squash, beet leaves, radish, pumpkin, *pejibaye*, *yuca, chicasquil* and a host of other starches or vegetables.

Pie (*Pastel*) Savory pies are more popular in Latin America than sweet North American style dessert pies. Turnovers, *empanadas,* are first on any *Tico* hit parade.

Piña Colada Mix coconut cream, pineapple juice and rum. Pour it over ice and garnish it with a piece of tropical fruit.

Pinchos These very small bite-sized *tapas* cost only about thirty cents apiece and consist of no more than a mouthful serving of potato frittata, tiny *empanada,* cube of Manchego cheese, etc.

Pineapple *(piña)* See chapter # 4 for details of this tropical fruit.

Plantains (*plátanós*) See chapter # 4 for details.

Pinilillo This not very common drink is made from corn and cocoa.

Pinto beans These medium sized speckled beans are more widely used in Mexico than in Central America.

Pisco sour This cocktail is probably the national alcoholic mixed drink in both Peru and Chile. It is often on menus of upscale Costa Rican watering holes and occasionally in few restaurant bar lists. The liqueur, *pisco,* is an ancient brandy made from Muscat grapes. The brandy is mixed with lime juice, fine sugar and egg white, chilled and served as is or with additional nutmeg or cinnamon

Plum *(ciruelas)* See chapter #4 for details of this tropical fruit.

Poblano *Poblano* chilis are milder than most and, therefore, occasionally make their way into local food.

Posole, pozole More common in Mexico and Guatemala than in Costa Rica, this rich soup of hominy, pork or chicken, onions and garlic is a weekend or holiday treat. It is usually served with small mounds of diced green chili peppers, cilantro leaves, radishes, lettuce, sliced avocado, crumbled white cheese and/or crispy fried corn chips to be added to the soup at the discretion of the diner.

Pork *(cerdo, lechon, puerco)* My guess is that pork sales outdo beef in Costa Rica. Pork sausage, cold cuts, ham, *chicharrones,* chops, ribs, loins and bacon are in every market. Necks, liver, skin, tripe, kidneys and feet can be found in central market butcher shops.

Potato *(papa)* Potatoes are thin skinned, usually yellow inside and firm, similar in texture and taste to Yukon gold. These properties make them perfect for soups, stews, potato salad and hashes (*picadillos)*, but not for baking whole. As a side dish, potato is probably fourth fiddle for starch after rice, beans and yuca. Because of unusually high water content, these potatoes can be a challenge for mashing. I suggest that after you boil, drain and skin them, you return them to the heat in a dry pot to remove more moisture, before you add butter and mash them. If you want to add a dairy product, use cream instead of milk, and only sparingly or you will end up with potato paste.

Prestiños Deep fried thin squares of sweetened dough are topped with syrup and eaten as a sweet snack or dessert.

Pudding *(pudin)* Pudding is a common dessert or snack. Rice pudding loaded with sugar and cinnamon is number one. Corn, bread and chocolate puddings follow in popularity.

Pumpkin, green pumpkin, (*calabaza*) Not like Halloween orange pumpkins, Latin American and Caribbean pumpkins are really varieties of winter squash, many of which have the size and shape of a pumpkin, if not the color. They can be green, yellow, beige, multicolored and striped.

Quesadilla *A quesadilla* is a toasted *tortilla* thin sandwich. First, the *tortilla* is covered with cheese, meat, chicken, beans or a combination. Next, it is topped by another *tortilla* or the original is folded in half and pressed down. Then it is crisped on both sides in a skillet or under a broiler. If two large *tortillas* form the top and bottom, the thin pie is sliced into wedges like a pizza.

Queso *Queso* is the word for cheese of any kind. Locally made fresh white cheese is the hands down country favorite, although American, cheddar, *feta, gorgonzola, gouda, mozzarella, palmito* and Swiss are among a host of cheeses made in the Central Valley by *Dos Pinos,* around Monteverde, near Barva or in Turrialba.

Queso blanco This ubiquitous white salty farmers' cheese is sold in blocks. It is fresh white cheese that is a little crumbly and salty. The standard local homemade or mass produced farmers' cheese, it is used in slices with cold cuts or fruits, crumbled on salads soups, inside turnovers or stuffed vegetables or layered in sandwiches and lasagna. Women in their first trimester should avoid it along with feta, camembert, blue and a host of soft white cheeses because of the possibility of getting a type of listeria infection that can cause abortions.

Rabbit (*conejo)* Rabbit can be bought in butcher shops, particularly in larger central markets. It is an uncommon feature on Tico restaurant menus, but not in the homes of Colombian expats, who sauté herb coated pieces in onion and tomato sauce, then add coconut milk to offset the inherent dryness of the tasty meat.

Raisins *(Pasas)* Raisins are common in pastries, stuffing and puddings. Local and imported varieties grace market shelves. There do not seem to be any golden raisins other than California imports.

Recaito This thick green sauce gets its name from one of its ingredients, *recao (see below).* It is a purée of onion, garlic, black pepper, sweet pepper and cilantro. *Recaito* is used as a marinade, base for stews and in soup.

Recao *Recao* is a large leaf green herb, more akin in flavor to parsley than cilantro.

Refrescoes *Refrescos* are fruit drinks made with juice alone or juice mixed with water, served chilled and/or served over ice.

Relleno It means "stuffed," as in *chile relleno,* sweet pepper stuffed with cheese, battered and fried or baked.

Ribs (*Costillas)* Small pork ribs are the norm. Large beef ribs can be had in American steak franchises and Argentinean restaurants.

Rice Local rice is long grain and not very starchy. It is a staple mixed with meat, chicken, pork, seafood, fried Chinese style, mixed with beans, in soups and stews, and as sweet creamy pudding.

Ring (*corona)* *Corona* means "crown." The noun, *corona,* is the name for a ring shaped coffee cake, usually laced with cinnamon and pieces of jellied fruit. As an adjective, it describes anything prepared in the shape of a ring.

Roast *(asado)* Rotisserie roasted chicken over glowing roots from old coffee tree roots, hams and pork loins are the major roasted meats. Of course, there are roast turkeys in ex-pat kitchens on Thanksgiving or Christmas.

Rondon *Rendon* or "rundown" is the Caribbean equivalent of *olla de carne,* a stew of meat and starchy root vegetables more strongly spiced and containing breadfruit.

Rosemary (*romero)* Rosemary grows well in my herb garden and is common in herb markets. Its leaves look like pine needles and the strong flavor is slightly resinous. Since lamb doesn't appeal to native palates and roasted chicken utilizes other more typical herbs, I don't notice the distinctive flavor very often in native dishes. Despite its potency, it is used in white sauces for seafood and inside whole fish before baking, roasting or frying. In a few Lebanese restaurants in San Jose it makes its mark with lamb. *Foccacia* is frequently sprinkled with rosemary in Italian restaurants.

Roti An émigré from India to Trinidad and Tobago, this flat bread is stuffed like a Mexican burrito.

Russian Salad *(ensalada rusa)* Diced cooked beets tossed with mayonnaise are the basic parts of this common side dish in Tico *sodas,* often as part of the daily special.

Salmon *(salmón)* Imported whole fish, fillets, smoked or canned salmon cost more than local fish, but are easy to find. The bulk of salmon in Costa Rica comes from Chilean waters.

Salmuera More than just salt water, *salmuera* is sea salt which becomes mildly acidic when dissolved in water. In Argentina style steak houses, it is brushed over roasting meats to lessen the fatty taste.

Salpicón This dish is a cold mixed green salad topped with seafood or meat.

Salsa crudo *Salsa crudo* is a sauce made from uncooked ingredients, usually tomato based.

Salsa frita *Salsa frita* is a sauce wherein the components are cooked in hot oil

Salsa oscura *Salsa oscuro* is a dark opaque sauce as opposed to a clear sauce – *salsa claro,* or a white sauce – *salsa blanco.*

Salsa picante Be it a red hot liquid like Tabasco or local equivalent brands (Alfarro, Lizano) or diced red chili peppers and onions in vinegar, *salsa picante* is hot sauce.

Salsa verde See green sauce above.

Salt cod *(bacalao)* You need only read Mark Kurlansky's treatise on the history of cod to realize how important and ubiquitous salt cod has been in the history of the western world. Basque cod fishing forays in North America were probably the first commercial endeavors in the Western Hemisphere. They salted their catch and sun dried the fish on the northern American rocky shores. Cod fish fritters are common in the cuisine along the Caribbean coast. Salt fish, often cod, is partnered with *akee* to make Jamaica's national dish

Sangria Derived from the Spanish word for blood, this drink gets its color from red wine. Add some club soda, diced fresh fruit and ice to the wine, and you have a mildly alcoholic bubbly fruit punch. When you order it in a Mexican restaurant, speak clearly or you may get *sangrita,* a spicy chaser for tequila consisting of lime, tomato and orange juice plus enough Tabasco sauce to tingle your tongue and lips.

Sardines (*sardinas)* Fresh sardines are a treat, but they deteriorate by the end of the day they are caught. If you find them in a morning market as part of the day's fresh catch, have them for lunch pan grilled or pickle them in vinegar for 24 hours as soon as you get them home. To grill them, spray coat or very lightly oil a skillet, crisp them on both sides and enjoy. Flavor them with salt and a little dried thyme before cooking. To pickle them, wash them well and cover with white wine vinegar or Japanese wine vinegar. The following day, pat them dry and dress with cilantro and a little olive oil. Canned sardines are common locally.

Sausage *(salchicha, salchichon)* Local sausages are as bland and mild as British bangers. Even when local varieties are labeled "Italian," "chorizo" or "Polish," they have only a little more flavor.

Scotch bonnet This potent *habanero* chili pepper is the most common type used throughout the Caribbean.

Sesame seeds *(ajonjoli)* White and black sesame seeds are available in upscale markets.

Seville orange (*naranja agria*) See chapter #4 for details of this tropical fruit.

Short ribs (*costillas a la brasa)* From the tail end of the chest wall come these beef ribs with a flat bone, large layer of lean meat and a surface of pure fat. For fat haters, the outer surface can be easily removed, but for flavor and succulence a little should be left behind.

Shredded meat (*carne mechada)* *Mechada* is braised for hours until tender, mixed with its flavored cooking juices, and used to make *burritos, empanadas, picadillos, ropa vieja (*old clothes) and *tacos.*

Shrimp *(camarones)* Shrimp of all sizes are caught, sold and eaten in Costa Rica. Most of the jumbos get exported for profit. The smallest, called "pinkies," show up in rice dishes and local Chinese food.

Sirloin (*lomo)* Tasty and a little tough, sirloin is a popular local choice, grilled with onions or garlic butter. Tico grass fed beef has an earthier flavor than North American corn fed beef. Because local beef has less fat, it is less "juicy" and, therefore tougher.

Smelts (*pejerreyes)* Smelts are a favorite along the Peruvian and Chilean coast. You can find them on occasion in Costa Rican markets. They average about eight inches long. To prepare them, break the backbone with your thumbnail just above the tail. Give the body a little squeeze between your palms to loosen the innards. Then grab the head between your fore-finger and thumb and pull off the head downwards along the ventral (belly side) surface to the tail, removing the guts along with the head. Snip the fins with scissors. Dredge in three parts wheat flour to one part fine or medium ground corn meal, salt and fry crispy golden brown to make delicious *pejerreyes arrebosados.* You can prepare sardines, fresh anchovies or any other small fish this way. When they are half the length of smelts (about 4 inches) or less, you may leave the head and insides intact.

Another option is to remove the head and innards as above, layer the smelts in Pyrex dish, salt them lightly, cover them with any white vinegar (my home preference is Japanese rice vinegar) and let them pickle in the fridge for 48 to 72 hours. To serve *pejerreyes en vinagre*, pat them dry, top them with chopped cilantro leaves, splash with a little lime juice and drizzle with a little good quality olive oil.

Sofrito Step one in making a stew throughout the world is to sweat herbs and spices in oil, lard or butter – to make a *sofrito.* In Latin America, garlic, peppers and onions constitute the *sofrito* of choice with or without tomatoes.

Sopa seca Literally, "dry soup," but how can that be? You probably won't see it on menus. It refers to leftovers at home, such as rice, beans, pasta or strips of *tortilla,* added to a soupy sauce and boiled until the liquid is absorbed.

Soup *(sopa, caldo)* Soups are described in detail in the next chapter. *Caldo* has two meanings. Generally it refers to clear broth, often prepared from bouillon cubes or powder, but when the name is combined with an ingredient e.g. *caldo de res* or *caldo de pollo,* it is soup with chunks of potato, vegetables and corn on the cob in the soup, in addition to the main ingredient.

Soursop (*guanabana*) See chapter # 4, for details of this tropical fruit.

Stamp and go Caribbean codfish cakes carry this moniker.

Star anis (*anis estrello*) This dark brown star-shaped herb is a mainstay of Chinese cuisine. Its licorice flavor identifies it as one of the spices in Chinese five spice mix. You can find it imported on most spice shelves in Costa Rican markets

Starchy tubers *(arracache, camote, name, ñampi, tiquisque, yuca*) All of these tubers are boiled or baked, used in soups or stews and often found in *olla de carne,* a traditional meat and tuber weekend stew. Many are dried, ground into flour and used for baking or as a thickening agent.

Star Apple *(caimito)* See chapter #4 for details of this tropical fruit.

Star fruit *(carambola)* See chapter # 4 for details of this tropical fruit.

Steamed (*al vapor, sudado)* Rice, *tamales,* seafood, chicken breast and vegetables are frequently steamed.

Stew, ragu *(guiso, cocido, guisado, ajiaco)* Stews seem to be more popular in other parts of Latin America than in Costa Rica. *Olla de carne,* beef and root vegetable stew, is a common weekend dish, but other signature stews are more common in other countries, e.g. *feijoada* (black bean and pork parts) or *vatapa (*coconut meat, yuca flour and palm oil stew) in Brazil, *ajiaca de pollo Bogotano* (Bogotá chicken stew) in Colombia, *ropa vieja* (old clothes shredded beef stew) in Cuba and Puerto Rico, *carbonada de criolla (*beef stew with fruit in it) in Argentina, *carbonada en zapallo* (veal stew with fruit, baked and served in a pumpkin shell) also Argentinean, *birria (goat stew)* in Mexico and *cocido de Brasiliera,* a hearty one pot stew from Brazil's mountains. Central American corn stew is *guiso de maiz.*

Sticky Rice *(arroz guacho)* Because short grain rice has so much starch, the individual grains stick together. Used to mop up sauces in Thailand, sticky rice is occasionally employed to make risotto or pudding in Costa Rica.

Strawberries *(fresas)* Smaller, firmer, paler but tastier than North American strawberries, they grow at higher altitudes in Costa Rica.

String beans *(vainicas)* Green string beans that resemble French *haricot* grace the market stalls most months. From September to December, you may find yellow wax beans.

Stuffed or filled *(relleno)* Chili peppers, sweet peppers, cucumbers, squash, pumpkin, beets, zucchini, chicken breast, meatloaf, pork loin and various other butterflied cuts of meat are stuffed and baked *relleno* style.

Stuffed breast of veal or flank steak pocket (*matahambre) Hambre* means "hunger" and *mata* is a form of the verb "to kill." The stuffing is usually well seasoned ground pork or veal mixed with spinach, chopped nuts and diced carrot, onion, celery and sweet pepper. The well sealed meat is usually boiled then roasted. When it is eaten, it kills hunger.

Stuffed sirloin (*lomo relleno)* Similarly stuffed as the entry above *(matahambre), lomo relleno* replaces flank steak or veal with sirloin, cuts it thin, pounds it thinner and rolls it up around the stuffing. It is often served cold, sliced, as a party buffet dish.

Sweet potatoes (*camotes* in Costa Rica, *batata* in Colombia, *boniatos* in the Caribbean) Sweet potatoes are a staple throughout Central and South America and the Caribbean. In Central America, the most common variety has purple skin and pale yellow flesh. More common in South America is the kind with rusty red skin and orange flesh.

Sweet potato chips (*camote frito)* Banana chips, yuca chips and sweet potato chips look like thicker white potato chips and are usually more flavorful.

Swiss chard (*acelgas)* Attractive bunches of silvery green Swiss chard appear in the markets periodically. The leaves can be used in salads, cooked like spinach, substituted for *callaloo* in Caribbean cooking or cut up with the stems in *picadillo,* hash. Diced or cross sliced stems go well in soups and stews. A favorite Central American pairing is Swiss chard and garbanzo beans flavored with cumin.

Tacos *Tortilla* sandwiches in North America are often fried and crisp. In Central America, they are usually soft. Fillings include shredded pork, sausage, minced beef, *cabeza (*tongue, cheek and neck meat), beans, cheese, lettuce and tomato, onion, avocado, fish and chicken.

Tamales asados These are baked sweet cornmeal cakes.

Tamales *Tamale* making is a seasonal family affair and art form. Labor intensive, multiple generations of family cooks assemble pork, vegetables and herb fillings in rectangular packets of freshly made corn meal, wrap them in folded plantain leaves and tie them decoratively with reeds or twine. They are traditionally given to neighbors at Christmas, and steamed or simmered before eating. In Colombia and Venezuela, they are called *hallacas* and may contain raisins or olive pieces. In Mexico, they are wrapped in dry corn husks.

Tamarind *(tamarindo)* The pod of this tree has seeds and soft flesh that is both bitter and sweet. The flesh is used to season stews, soups, curries and Worcester sauce. It is sold in markets as dark brown bricks in plastic wrap. . See chapter # 4, the fruit chapter, for more details.

Tangerine (*mandarina)* See chapter # 4, the fruit chapter, for details of this common tropical fruit.

Tapas Originally, small dishes served in bars in Spain quenched the appetites of people whose evening meal often began around 10pm. In time, *tapas* graduated from olives, cheese, ham, omolette slices, small sandwiches, squid, mushrooms, stuffed pimentos and anchovies to become international fusion food on small plates artistically presented and carefully paired with boutique wines.

Tap water (*agua coriente)* Specify *agua coriente* when you want a glass of water in a restaurant or you might get a pricey bottle of imported mineral water. *Con hielo,* with ice, is worth adding to the order, because not all restaurants chill tap water. Costa Rican tap water is safe to drink and ice is fine to use in drinks.

Tarragon *(estragon)* This mildly anis-flavored herb with pretty little yellow flowers grows very well in Costa Rican herb gardens.

Tea *(té)* Black, jasmine and chamomile are the most commonly used teas but hot tea is unusual and ice tea is nearly always sweetened.

Tenderloin *(lomito)* Perhaps the most tender cut of steak available in ordinary markets and restaurants, tenderloin is less tasty than sirloin or marinated cheaper cuts (*churasco).*

Tequila Tequila is the alcoholic drink made from fermented agave juice.

Thyme (*tomillo)* Thyme grows in my herb garden year round and can be found fresh in all the upscale supermarkets. The dried herb is common as well.

Tilapia Originally from Africa, this farm fish is now grown worldwide. In Costa Rica, tilapia appears in *ceviche* and seafood stews, breaded, fried and grilled.

Tiquisque This pink skinned starchy root has no English name that I have found, nor have I ever seen it in North America. It is a frequent ingredient in *picadillo,* a vegetable hash, and in *olla de carne,* a soupy stew of meat and an assortment of root vegetables.

Tiramisu *Tiramisu* is a classic Italian dessert flavored with coffee and almonds. Its base is mascarpone cheese. In even the smallest Tico eateries, if desserts are available, *tiramisu* is usually available along with *tres leches* and *flan.*

Tomatillo Mexico's marvelous green sauces begin with this small green tomato in a husk. Technically a fruit, it appears on occasion in Tico markets. In our cuisine it is seldom used raw.

Tomato Roadside tomatoes are sold in boxes of thirteen for about 80 or 90 cents. They are firmer and tastier than their North American cousins, more like plum tomatoes in taste and texture, less uniform in size, shape and color.

Tongue (*lengua*) Beef tongue is relatively expensive in the meat markets, but is very popular in Tico restaurants and homes. It is typically boiled, sliced and served in a tomato – onion sauce or brown gravy (*lengua en salsa).*

Tortillas *Tortillas* are flat circles of *masa harina,* dough made from cornmeal soaked or cooked in lime water. They are the daily bread of Central America. In Mexico, similar unleavened thin pancakes are more often made from wheat flour than corn, though both types exist in both cultures. They are lightly browned on a dry griddle called a *comal.*

Tostada *Tostadas* are crisp fried *tortillas*, large or small, covered with meat, crumbled cheese, sour cream, mashed beans, *guacamole* or salad in Mexican restaurants. In Tico restaurants, they are the same and are often called *chalupas,* but *pan tostada* is toast, and a dip *con tostadas* is a dip that comes with corn chips.

***Tortilla* soup** (*sopa vieja, sopa tortilla)* Very popular in its native Mexico, *Tortilla* soup appears on a number of Tico menus, including the large popular *Rosti Pollo, El Fogoncito* and *Huaraches* chains.

Tree tomato *(Tamarillo)* See the fruit chapter, # 4, for details of this tropical fruit.

Tres leches The national cake of Costa Rica, *tres leches,* is a moist white cake made with three kinds of "milk" – whole milk, sweetened condensed milk and evaporated milk frosted with sweetened egg whites. Even if your preference is for low fat and few calories, try at least a bite of someone else's.

Tripe *(mondongo, menudo* in Mexico, *chinchulines* in Argentina*)* Costa Rican style tripe is a thick soup, not quite a stew. The tripe is simmered for hours in salted water flavored with carrots, onions, garlic, garbanzos, cilantro, oregano and lime juice until everything is tender. *Chinchulines* are tripe pieces charred on an Argentinean grill.

Trout *(trucha)* Wild (planted years ago) and farm grown trout are fairly common in the mountains.

Tuco When a large piece of beef tenderloin, eye of the round, flank steak, etc. is braised in a hearty tomato sauce, the resultant incredibly rich liquid is called *tuco* and goes great with pasta. If it gets too thick, the addition of a little red wine before re-simmering does the trick.

Tuli machi From neighboring Panama comes this seafood stew made with coconut milk, mashed cooked ripe plantains, collard greens, shrimp, sea bass, crab meat, corn kernels, and garlic.

Tuna *(atún)* Tuna caught on both coasts are processed and canned in Costa Rica and make for components in multiple home recipes including tuna lasagna, tuna empanadas, salads and sandwiches.

Turmeric The yellow powder with a delicate flavor is sold in packets everywhere to add color, but *achiote* seems to be a little more popular as a coloring spice in Latin America.

Turkey (*pavo, guajalote)* Wild turkeys once lived all over North and Central America. Turkey is still a Guatemalan specialty, but it has become uncommon in Costa Rica. Supermarkets carry frozen North American birds for Thanksgiving and Christmas.

Turnovers *(empanadas)* *Empanadas* are baked or fried turnovers filled with beans, cheese, potatoes, pork, beef, pumpkin seeds, chicken, in any combination. There are as many variations as there are countries in Latin America. Costa Rican *empanadas* are made from corn flour and usually fried. Argentinean *empanadas* are probably the most juicy and tasty. They are usually made from wheat flour and baked. In Colombia and Venezuela, they are made from precooked corn flour, *masarepa*. When stuffed with brightly colored chopped peppers, onions and tomatoes, they are called "little parrot turnovers" or *empanadas de perico*. Turnovers are *empadas* in Brazil, *patis* in the Caribbean.

Vanilla *(vanilla)* Alone or combined with cinnamon, vanilla flavor is frequent in pastries and puddings. Whole beans come to market on occasion. Supermarkets and small town markets carry real and imitation vanilla liquids.

Vatapa Brazil sends us this thick stew, originally from Africa, made from ground peanuts, yuca flour, coconut meat and palm oil.

Venison (*venado)* Wild and farmed deer exist in small numbers in Costa Rica. Venison is as expensive than lobster or giant prawns in the very few restaurants that carry it.

Water (*agua)* Water is safe, good tasting and healthy all over the country except in a few remote locations, where there tend to be warning signs. New comers and visitors need to remember to actively drink enough to re-hydrate their bodies in any tropical climate.

Watercress (*Berro)* Outdoor markets normally have shade cover. Perhaps it's the tropical heat, but unless watercress is fresh picked, it wilts in a day, even when stored in a glass of water in the refrigerator. When you find it fresh and use it soon, it is great in salads, cold cream soups and on sandwiches.

Watermelon *(sandia)* See the fruit chapter, # 4, for details.

Yuca, manioc, cassava This starchy tuber can be baked, boiled, or fried like potatoes and potato chips or made into flour for making bread, buns or pastries.

***Yuca* starch** (*almidón)* It can thicken gravies, soup or stews in the kitchen like corn starch and works equally well in the laundry room to starch clothes.

Yucca Oh the confusion over the one "C" yuca and the two "C" yucca! In so many books they are used interchangeably, but they are very different. *Yucca* is related to all the other southwestern desert euphorbias including century plants, aloe and the agaves - source of tequila, mescal and pulque, Mexican alcoholic brews. Although seeds, flowers and fruit may be edible, they have nothing in common with the potato–like starchy root with one "C".

Zapallito See the vegetable chapter, # 5, for information about this ridged tubular squash.

Zapote See the fruit chapter, # 4, for details of this tropical fruit.

Zucchini (*calabacín*) I suppose that zucchini grows in gay profusion everywhere in the world except the polar ice caps. The vegetable and a half dozen of its cousins are cheap and plentiful here as well. In the summer squash plethora, it ranks second to *chayote*. See chapter # 5.

Chapter 3
Common Costa Rican Dishes

Bocas

Literally, *bocas* are "mouths" in Spanish. Figuratively, they are bites or small plates like *tapas* from Spain or *dim sum* from China. The diminutives, *boquitas* and *pinchos,* are little bites or nibbles, usually served with drinks, often free in bars.

Chips and dips are common *bocas*. The "chips" are one of four kinds. Fried corn tortilla pieces (corn chips) are the most common. Also popular are *patacones,* twice fried chunks of plantain. They are half inch thick diagonal slices, fried until tender. They are then smashed flat and deep fried a second time to form a crunchy golden wafer with the long circumference of an egg and half the thickness of a slice of bread. Less common, but tasty, are thin slices of deep fried yuca and banana that look like oblong thick potato chips. Potato chips work as well, particularly the homemade fresh kind sold in Alajuela's Central Market.

Number one on the dip parade is purée of black beans, smooth and savory. Black beans boil up in only 90 minutes without soaking. Blended to a paste with garlic and onion and softened in a little oil, the dip requires only salt and pepper to taste. The Mexican version adds jalapeño peppers, cayenne, oregano and cumin. The North American version adds mayo, sour cream or orange juice to thin it, and often layers the paste with grated cheese, diced tomato and onion, olives and cilantro leaves. Other variations utilize pinto beans, kidney beans or garbanzos, separately or in combination.

Second is tomato *salsa,* diced fresh tomato flavored with raw onion, cilantro and lime juice. Careful, a request for *salsa de tomate* can get you either this diced tomato sauce or a bottle of ketchup.

Third is avocado dip - buttery yellow local avocados mashed with any combination of sour cream, cream cheese or mayonnaise until smooth; to which diced tomato and onion are added, salted and peppered to taste and topped with a squeeze of lime juice and a few cilantro leaves. The addition of Tabasco is more Mexican than Tico, but a bottle is always at hand on the table. Frequently, a jar of carrot, cauliflower, onion and cucumber in vinegar with chili peppers graces the table or lunch counter. A little of the juice or a small serving of the veggies usually adds enough heat for bolder local palates.

A fourth combo may be used as a dip, alone, or added to other ingredients. *Pico gallo***,** literally the beak of a rooster, is a juicy mixture of chopped tomato, onion, cilantro, oil and lemon juice. Similar to tomato salsa (above), the oil distinguishes it. It is quite nice on chips. Mixed with crumbled cheese, half white and half yellow, softened with cream cheese or sour cream, *pico gallo* becomes a tasty cheese dip**.** Yet another dip adds tuna to the cheese concoction.

Pejibaye, rich palm fruit, boiled, puréed and mixed with finely diced sweet red pepper and green onion, and enough lemon or lime flavored mayonnaise to soften, is an elegant dip on crisp thin crackers or toasts.

Nachos are chips covered with melted yellow cheese and beans - plus or minus green chili pepper slices. Plain mayo may occasionally be served with chips. In Peruvian, Argentinean, Brazilian, Mexican and Indian style restaurants, hot sauce is served in a dish and may become a dip for those with asbestos tongues and lips.

Another large *boca* group are ***gallos***. Three meanings for *gallos* are 1) sandwiches made with fresh corn *tortillas* instead of bread, 2) any small plate or bite and 3) anything served atop a *tortilla*. Toasted bread sandwiches, a possible fourth meaning, may also be called *gallos* in some places. In humble breakfast and lunch eateries called *sodas*, the usual *gallos* are pork, ham, beef, chicken, fried fish, bean or cheese. In homes, peanut butter or cream cheese with strawberry marmalade or guava jelly and canned tuna with oodles of mayo are common *tortilla* fillers. The beef is often shredded leftovers from making soup. Tough cheap cuts boiled until soft can be pulled apart into thin strands.

Tico tacos are baked or fried stuffed tortillas. Tea sandwiches of sliced white bread *sans* crust, filled with cream cheese and sliced cucumber, often appear on potluck Tico buffet tables.

Yet another very common snack, ***ceviche,*** is cubed fresh fish, chemically cooked in lime juice, flecked with finely diced sweet red pepper, white onion and cilantro leaves. It is served chilled in dessert bowls accompanied by chips or soda crackers. Ketchup, mayo and Tabasco are provided for the minority who require a different taste. Larger meal size bowls are always available. Sea bass, marlin, snapper, mahi mahi and tilapia are the usual fish choices. They are all fine, but mahi mahi and marlin are my choices because of a slightly preferable flavor of the former and a firmer texture for the latter.

Crispy fried **chicken wings** are another common *boca*. Two to four of them come with chips and a small cup of green banana *ceviche* to which strips of mild green chili pepper have been added. Yes, *ceviche* is the same word, but it refers to the lime juice pickling, not the fish or banana main ingredient.

Tamales are cornmeal patties, stuffed with pork or chicken and bits of decorative veggies, wrapped in plantain leaves and boiled or steamed. The Mexican version uses corn husks for wrappers.

Empanadas are another class of snack food. They are baked or fried half-moon shaped turnovers filled with chicken, meat, beans or cheese.

Enyucados are *empanadas* made from boiled yuca dough, rather than cornmeal, stuffed with savory chopped or shredded meat and deep fried.

Maduras, ripe plantains, browned in butter and topped with *natilla,* local sour cream, is a delicious and common snack.

Chorreadas are corn pancakes that are light and flavorful despite the fact that they contain neither flour nor eggs. The only seasoning is a little sugar to taste and an optional pinch of salt. Local white corn is scraped from the cob into a bowl, mashed to a paste, diluted with a little milk and poured onto a griddle or into a lightly greased frying pan to brown on both sides. Only a little thicker than a crepe, they may be paired with butter, syrup, jam, sour cream, eggplant caviar, egg salad, chutney, etc.

Fried squid, breaded and fried to crispy crunch, tentacles and body rings grace the menus of restaurants, *tapas* bars and watering holes during "happy hour." They usually come with mayonnaise, catsup or tarter sauce.

Picadillos, nicely seasoned chopped vegetable hash of potato, leafy greens, other roots like *arracacha, pejibaye,* plantain and many more can be spooned on tortillas warm or at room temperature as snacks or appetizers. They are more commonly served as side dishes with meat, fish or poultry, particularly in the regional cuisine of the northwestern state of Guanacaste.

It would be easy to fill an entire book with an endless variety of *boca* descriptions, but this is the basic group.

Soups and Stews

Soups are surprisingly common in this country only eight to eleven degrees north of the equator. Common traditional ones are usually served hot. Nearly all *Nuevo Latino* varieties are cold.

Perhaps the most common hot traditional kind, ***sopa negra***, black soup, begins with the nearly black, dark brown water in which black beans are cooked, flavored with garlic, cilantro, oregano, a drizzle of lime juice and salt. Drop in a few hard-boiled eggs and heat - that's it, rich tasty, filling and very inexpensive to make. Each bowl has an egg, usually quartered. A staple in Tico homes, it seldom reaches restaurant menus. The key to its richness is to limit the volume of water in which the beans are cooked to a depth of only a few inches above the beans and to mash in a few of them if it is too thin. A small dollop of sour cream on top is a nice touch

Fish and seafood soups are very common. They exude the flavor of fresh ingredients from the sea. Unlike New

England chowders, they are mostly flour, potato and milk free. Neither do they contain the pastes or purées of Mediterranean fish or seafood soups. They are usually light and clear. Step #1 is to simmer fish heads in water with bay leaves, carrot and celery with a little salt and pepper. After an hour or more, strain the broth. Step #2, heat a little oil, garlic and onion in a skillet. Barely cook bite-size pieces of fish fillet in the oil. Step #3, add fish, garlic and onions to broth, heat thoroughly for a few minutes, top with cilantro leaves and serve with *patacones,* boiled rice and lime wedges on the side. Substance derives from fish and/or shellfish, not thickened broth. Costa Rican cooks use sea bass, tilapia, marlin, tuna and snapper for the fish and tiny clams, crabs, octopus, squid, shrimp and mussels for the seafood. In most homes and restaurants, only the broth is made ahead. Steps #2 and #3 occur after the order is taken.

Pejibaye (pronounced peh-hee-**bah**–yay) is calorie-rich palm fruit. You can spot it in markets or on roadside fruit stands as the handsome cluster of multicolored golf ball size spheres – yellow, orange, red, green or striped; or they may appear floating in a caldron of water in which they have been boiled. **Cream of *pejibaye* soup** has the flavor of chestnut purée and Japanese pumpkin. The ingredients are cooked and puréed *pejibaye,* reduced cream, salt and pepper. It is so rich that a little too much reduction of the cream renders it nearly inedible. Absolutely a "no-no" for dieters. Prepared properly, it is among the best of the world's cream soups.

Among the other hot soups are **chicken soup, vegetable soup, minestrone, lentil soup, tripe soup, noodle soup, meatball soup, beef soup, cream of mushroom, cream of asparagus, cream of chicken and corn and cream of potato and leek.**

The template for **cold soups** is four or five parts chicken broth to three parts puréed fruit or vegetable to one part heavy cream, blended smooth, chilled and decorated with cilantro or mint leaves, a dollop of yogurt or sour cream or a few drops of flavored oil. This scheme works for asparagus, banana, beet root, cantaloupe, *calabaza* (Latin American pumpkin), *chayote* (squash), cucumber, mango, papaya, passion fruit, *pejibaye*, potato, red pepper, sweet potato, watercress and watermelon. The blander cucumber, chayote and potato need more seasoning (dill, garlic, basil, oregano) and extra salt and pepper. Sweet potato does well with the addition of allspice, nutmeg and a little apple sauce. When cantaloupe is seasonally sweet (March to June), blending two parts melon with one part plain yogurt is sensational. Counter too much natural sweetness with lime juice or too tart a flavor with a little guava jelly, honey or maple syrup. To make it fancy enough for formal entertaining, top with a small dollop of sour cream and a mint sprig and perfume with a few drops of rose water or orange flower water.

Olla de carne is one of three typical weekend specials. It is a delicious root vegetable and bone-in beef chunk stew. The starches and veggies are potatoes, carrots, *camote (*sweet potato*), chayote (*pear shaped squash*)*, plantain, *tiquisque (root)* and *yuca*. Another weekender is hearty ***Sopa de mondongo*,** made from tripe and vegetables**.** The third and final end of the week special, ***chicharrones****,* are neither soup nor stew, and will be discussed in the meat section**.**

Salads

Repollo, **cabbage slaw**, is the most common salad in Costa Rica. It cohabits the plate with roast chicken, ribs, daily special combos and many snacks. A little shredded carrot, diced sweet red pepper and/or tomato slices may supplement the otherwise Spartan slaw. The salad is usually very lightly dressed or served with a wedge of lime.

A noteworthy local salad is made with crispy ***palmito***, **hearts of palm**. Accompaniments often are *avocado* slices, quartered hard-boiled eggs or strips of roasted sweet red pepper.

Mixed green salads, chef salads and **Caesar salads** grace the menus of most upscale restaurants. They are pretty conventional except for the Caesar which seldom has romaine lettuce leaves or authentic dressing.

In addition to the cabbage slaw, inexpensive eateries, particularly in rural areas, often offer **macaroni salad**, **green bean salad** and **Russian salad** made with diced beets. Tuna, chicken and, less commonly than in the U.S., egg salad take center plate for a light meal or as a sandwich stuffer.

Casados

Casado is the Spanish adjective that means "married." It also stands for mixed platter, blue plate special or dish of the day in common eateries. On the single large plate are a centerpiece of pork cutlet, beef steak, roasted or fried chicken, fish fillet, grilled calves liver with onions or tongue slices in tomato sauce; white rice; red or black beans flavored with garlic; a cabbage and tomato salad, dressed simply with lime juice or salsa and a sweet browned ripe plantain.

Gallo pinto

If any one dish were to typify Costa Rican cuisine, it would be *gallo pinto* (pronounced **gah**-yoe- -**peen**-toe). The literal translation is "painted or spotted rooster," referring to the color, black and white with red and green flecks. The dish combines precooked black or brown beans with precooked rice. In a little oil, dices of onion and sweet red pepper cook for a couple of minutes. The rice is added and heated. Local English sauce, Salsa Lizano, cilantro and the beans are mixed in and heated. The beans are usually mildly garlic flavored from their original preparation. If not, you may wish to add a little garlic to the onion and red pepper dice.

A mound of *gallo pinto* is the basis for most Tico breakfasts. It comes with eggs, fried or scrambled, tortillas or toast and, frequently, meat, cheese or cooked plantain and sour cream. Less often, but commonly, *gallo pinto* is the starch at lunch as well. If not, separate small scoops of rice and beans replace it, providing the leftovers for the next batch of *gallo pinto.* On occasion, *gallo pinto* is a side dish at the evening meal as well.

Main courses

Main courses include beef, pork, chicken, fish, seafood, rice and pasta dishes described in subsequent chapters. Notably absent most of the time are lamb, mutton, goat, rabbit, turkey, Caribbean conch and dishes made with spicy curry or hot chili peppers. Despite their popularity in other parts of Latin America, they seldom appear on Tico tables. To find them, you need to go to restaurants serving foreign cuisines.

Desserts

There is a certain sameness to the dessert portion of most typical Costa Rican restaurants. The cast of limited characters include the national cake - *tres leches,* white cake, soaked in sauce made from whole milk, condensed milk and evaporated milk (hence the name which means "three milks") while the cake is still warm, frosted with an egg-white and sugar topping. Caramel topped (after it is inverted) custard, *flan,* is as ubiquitous as *tres leches*. For reasons I don't know, Italian style *tiramisu* and fairly light cheesecake made with gelatin run a close third and fourth, followed by fruit, ice cream and gelatin alone or in combination and rice pudding, which is laden with cinnamon.

Suspiros, a frosted meringue is similar to Australian Pavlova. Chocolate cake, sponge cake and pound cake line bakery shelves along with elephants' ears, sweet turnovers, palm leaves, coffee cakes and cookies, Napoleons and turnovers.

Chapter 4
Fruit

Acerola See Surinam cherry.

Ackee Originally from Africa, ackee is a Caribbean fruit that has the consistency and flavor of spongy scrambled eggs. You are likely to encounter it on menus along the Caribbean coast paired with rice and fish dishes. It is actually toxic under-ripe or overripe.

Ambarella *(yuplón)* *Yuplón* is not really the Spanish name of this fruit. It is the Costa Rican version in "Spanglish." Among a dozen or so other names, ambarella is called Jew plum in Jamaica. It came to Limon from Jamaica. When the "J" becomes a "Y" and "M" and "N" are interchangeable, the English name becomes Latinized into *yuplón*. Other names include golden apple, hog plum, Tahitian quince, *Otaheite* apple and *caja-mango (*in Brazil). A cousin of the mango, it suffers by comparison. It ripens months before the mango. The trick is eating it at the right time. Unripe it is sour and overripe it becomes fibrous. In between, the three inch fruit yields a tart apple resemblance around a spiny central pit. Cluster of yellowgreen fruit hang down like a Berber necklace. The tree drops its leaves for a few weeks, once a year. Ticos salt fresh slices. I have never tried the combination, but I hear its tartness combines perfectly with the sweetness of guava to make jellies or pork glazes.

Apple *(manzana)* Good crisp tart apples require cold winters. Costa Rica has neither cold winters nor good apples. The local red variety is small, on the soft and mealy side of perfection and lacking tartness. The horses in the adjoining pasture prefer carrots. Doesn't that say it all? Imports from the United States and Chile fill the void, albeit at a higher price. A newer small green apple seems to be better.

Atemoya This self propagating hybrid of *cherimoya* and water apple is green, heart shaped and covered all over with pendulous firm tear drops. It looks like a mango with dreadlocks. Its taste has been compared by some to a *pińa colada*. The many black seeds are inedible. It grows well here, but seldom shows up in markets. In Florida and Israel it has become a commercial crop.

Avocado (*aguacate)* Of the three major types of avocado - Guatemalan, Mexican and West Indian – all but the West Indian antedate Columbus. The name itself is Aztec. It means *tree with testicles*. The lone member of the laurel family that produces commercially significant fruit, the avocado, now grows in Asia, North America, Africa, Southern Europe, Polynesia, the Philippines, Israel, New Zealand and Australia. The pearshaped fruit is creamy and mild. The Mexican has black wrinkled skin and pale green flesh, the Guatemalan bright green smooth skin and yellow flesh. In Costa Rica, the yellow, buttery flesh has given the fruit the name *aguacate mantequilla.* Locally, avocado slices lightly salted compete with a milder than Mexican version of *guacamole,* omitting the hot sauce. Slices of avocado often complement *ceviche,* soups and salads. A small wild variety of avocado is the favorite food of one of the world's most beautiful birds, the resplendent quetzal. The best way to spot this rare beauty is to find the tree loaded with fruit during the mating season and look for a vivid green fern frond sticking out of the trunk. It is likely to be the tail of the male quetzal which covers the entrance to the nest and eggs or babies by filling the hole from inside with his long green feathers.

Babaco This South American fruit is a rarity in Costa Rica. It is about the size of a sweet potato, has yellow-green edible skin, is pentagonal in cross section and tastes like a sweet, slightly acid banana-flavored melon.

Banana (*banano)* Bananas grow everywhere from the steepest hillsides to the humid coastal lowlands. They come in several sizes, shapes and colors, including bright red. Commercially, workers wrap bunches loosely in blue bags to keep insects and birds off the fruit. They look like dry cleaning hanging from the trees. When barely yellow, bunches are cut, stems hooked onto pulleys and they get pushed to packing areas along overhead wires, often a few hundred yards away. Ticos prefer to cut them as they turn yellow and store them in tool sheds or other places away from bugs and birds until the skins begin to blacken. They like them softer and riper than North Americans and Europeans do. When a bunch of fifty ripens, the rush is on to share, to make banana bread, banana pudding and banana cream pies. The leftovers go to the chickens, guinea fowl and pet parrots, all of whom love them.

Blackberries (*moras)* Blackberries are plentiful in Costa Rica. They account for the ubiquitous purple smoothies (*batidos)* made with fruit, milk and ice that accompany many meals in local *sodas*. Blackberries and sweetened sour cream, jams, and ice cream toppings complete the purple panoply.

Breadfruit (*pan fruta)* About eighteen months ago, I planted a twelveinch breadfruit tree on a rocky hillside. It now stands about fifteen feet and seems to produce new large serrated leathery leaves daily. It is almost like time-lapse photography. What a beauty. No fruit yet, but when it fruits, I plan to use it the same way I use yuca and potatoes – boiled, mashed, fried as chips and in soups and stews. Originally from Southeast Asia, the breadfruit traveled to Tahiti, was brought to the Caribbean as a source of starch for slaves by direction of King George 111, made its way to Limon with refugees from Jamaica and now shows up in a number of Costa Rican Caribbean recipes. The thin skin is patterned with small pentagons and hexagons, each bearing a central barb. The outer color transforms from green to yellow as it ripens. There are a hundred or so types of breadfruit but only one kind each of the seedless and the seed-containing grow here. The seedless type predominates. The smaller, less common seeded fruit is loaded with pseudo chestnuts.

Calabaza (*calabasa, calabaza,* West Indian pumpkin) The orange Halloween pumpkin, given to the Pilgrims by the Indians of New England, is a rarity in the tropics. Pumpkin-like squash are very common. *Calabaza* is the usual variety in the Caribbean and Latin America. Its typical size and shape are like a rounder watermelon. Colors range from tan to green to orange to pink. The flesh is similar to butternut squash, sweet and firm.

Canary melon (*melón Amarillo)* In March, April and May these bright yellow oblong beauties sell along the roadsides, particularly in and around Orotina on the Pacific slope of the Central Valley, near sea level. The sweet juicy flesh is similar to ripe honey dew.

Cantaloupe (*melón)* Coincident with the canary melon season, cantaloupe explodes on the scene in bags of five or six for a dollar. Pick the ones without soft spots, with a fairly tight pattern of lacey webbing on the outside and with yellow, rather than green under the webbing. They are so good, I make smoothies (*batidos)* out of them daily and serve dinner guests a first course of cold soup made from equal parts puréed melon and plain yogurt, sweetened with a little honey if the yogurt is tart, accentuated with a dash of rose water and adorned with a sprig of fresh mint. Refrigerated melon chunks are a family snack favorite.

Cashew apple *(mariñon)* Not only is the cashew apple not an apple, it is not even a fruit. It is the thickened stalk or peduncle that supports the true fruit, the cashew nut. In an eclectic restaurant in San Rafael, California, Bogey's, the sign over the kitchen door reads "Life may be short, but it's wide." So too, the cashew tree is at least as wide as it is tall. Nuts form first from blossoms. Then the peduncles thicken and transform into waxy vivid lipstick red, pear shaped, pseudo-fruit. The nut hangs off the bottom. When both are ripe, they fall to the ground attached. Ticos twist off the nut, throw it away and eat the succulent, though tannic acid flavored fruit. On enormous cashew plantations in India, the nuts are twisted off and the fruit is left to rot on the ground. The nuts are inedible unless roasted and the double shell contains toxic phenols – a lot of labor for a single kernel. The apple also has its problems. If bruises easily, is fibrous in its center and has too short a shelf life for commerce except in farmers' markets. Whatever cashew apples we miss from our trees, the local wild parrots consume with gusto. We have to scurry to save a few treats for our aviary of rescued parrots.

Ceriman, monstera *(piña anona)* This ornamental rapid growing vine has leaves that look like split leaf philodendrons or the even larger *mano de tigre,* hands of the tiger, but they have holes instead of splits in the leaves and bear flowers and fruit at the same time. The flowers are large off-white wrapped cylinders with pointed tops that unfold to expose encased fruit. The fruit look like tall thin pinecones, nearly a foot long. The hexagonal scaly segments, which taste like pineapple and banana custard, can be eaten when they separate from the inedible core.

Cherimoya The sweet and fragrant creamy flesh of the *cherimoya* has been described as tasting of vanilla, banana, mango and pineapple. The custard is laden with inedible large black seeds and covered with a tough green skin that looks like a heart-shaped hand grenade. *Champus* is the name given to Peruvian hot *cherimoya soup.* If you order *champus* in Colombia or Venezuela, you get a *cherimoya batido* or icy smoothie. The hairy tree branches arise close to the ground giving it a bushy appearance. Native to Central America and/or South American highlands, *cherimoya* is now cultivated all over the tropical and semi-tropical world. I tasted it first on a ferry boat in Viet Nam, then in a Mexican market in San Francisco and, for the third time in rapid succession, in Harrod's food court in London – all in the space of a month many decades ago. Now it grows on my small farm in Costa Rica. At times, the terms *cherimoya* and custard apple are used interchangeably. Although the two species are related, they are quite different. To add further confusion, a hybrid of *cherimoya* and sugar apple, the *atemoya* is also mistakenly called custard apple or *cherimoya* at times.

Cherry (*cereza*) The leaves of this cherry tree are larger and darker green than those from Japan and North America and the bark doesn't have horizontal striations. The fruit is smaller, less sweet and more astringent than, for example, a Bing cherry. The fruit is much more common in Guatemala, El Salvador and Mexico than in Costa Rica. As is often the case, names may be confusing. *Capulin* is another name for this fruit in some Latin American countries, but *capulin* is the name of a totally different non-fruiting tree grown for its wood in Costa Rica.

Coconut *(coco)* As in many a tropical clime, coconut appears in candy, cookies, cakes and pies with regularity. Coconut caramel flan is the number one custard. Cold coconut juice (*pipa fria)* is a roadside staple in the lowlands. Coconut milk and cream are basic to the cuisine on the Caribbean coast where even rice is boiled with coconut milk.

Custard apple, bullock's heart *(anona*) Compared to the other members of the genus annona, the custard apple is the least special. It is creamy and sweet but not as distinctive as the others (the hybrid *atemoya, cherimoya* and sugar apple). Neither is the tree attractive. The brownish skin has reticulated markings like the *cherimoya*, but they are flatter. The fruit tends to be a little smaller as well. The seeds are very hard. Despite the fact that toxic kernels reside within the seeds, the impregnable shell renders them harmless if swallowed. The fruit is usually cut along the long axis and eaten with a spoon.

Dragon fruit, strawberry pear (*pitaya, pitahaya)* There are several types of climbing cactus in Costa Rica, some epiphytes with air roots and some growing out of soil. This particular climber has striking very large perfumed yellow flowers that open at night. The fruit comes in two colors, lipstick red and canary yellow. The red ones are bigger with fruit as large as two pounds each. They are most often chilled, halved and scooped out with a spoon, tasting like a kiwi/pear combo, but related to neither. Peeled and sliced, the red or white flesh dotted with tiny edible black seeds, often compliments fancy salads. On our farm, the cactus grows with air roots in a dead tree and has red flesh. Every arm bears three or four fruit that go from small, oblong and green to large, round and bright red. The same red dragon fruit appear in farmers' markets in May, June and July.

Durazno In Costa Rica, *durazno* is a firm, tart peach that is picked green. Before it can ripen into softer yellow flesh, birds and insects devour it. The trunk divides early into a mass of smaller branches that grow upward rapidly. Small white blossoms in April give way to fruit in May and June. Although they are chopped, canned and dried in other parts of Latin America, I have only seen them eaten out of hand here. The central pit is small and red and can easily be removed. Freestone yellow peaches, *melanzanes,* are imported from less tropical climes.

Durian The town of La Garita, Alajuela, only a few miles from home, has about a dozen nurseries. One of them now sells durian trees. The resident gardener insists that there is now a growing demand. Twenty-five years ago I encountered this fruit for the first time. My expat Thai friend insisted I bring some to her mother's house when we went to dinner. "My mother will be so pleased. She asked me to look for some extra special durian during your visit. It is a tradition in our country to honor revered guests with this wonderful delicacy. She was a little hesitant that you might not like it, but I assured her that you eat all kinds of Thai foods in markets here and in restaurants back in San Francisco. You are not squeamish like some Americans. You'll see. It is delicious, even if it does smell spoiled." Reckoning came at dessert. Under the durian's yellow-green skin was a thick white rind. Inside it were sections containing large black seeds surrounded by golf balls of the acrid yellow flesh. It was served as if it were custard. The entire family riveted their beaming eyes on me, proud to honor my presence with an overly large portion of the best ripe durian in the land. There was no escape. I clenched my left fist in my lap until my fingernails burrowed into the flesh of my palm, and locked my facial muscles in a rigid smile to overcome any other response. On a large spoon that trembled imperceptibly, I hastened the silky custard past my lips and down my throat, shortening the duration of contact with my tongue as much as possible. It worked, but barely. I was nauseated for only a moment. To my relief, the durian had a flavor different from its stench. It tasted like mushroom pâté and Juicy Fruit gum, eaten in a dumpster, filled with rotting potatoes. My facial muscles ceased their throbbing and began to relax. The heat of my facial flush began to cool. I had survived this confrontation with a simple piece of fruit without humiliating my hosts or myself. No, I hadn't won. My near defeat had escaped detection. "*Kaup koon mak kap*", thank you very much, I blurted aloud. My hosts mumbled pleased you-are-welcomes, not knowing that my thanks were actually intended for the deity of intestinal fortitude. That they were audible was purely an accident of the moment. Durian is grown in several locations in Costa Rica, but not commercially as yet. I planted one down wind from my house, but (luckily), it died. Undoubtedly, it is an acquired taste.

Egg fruit, yellow *sapote*, canistel (*zapotillo, huevo vegetal, siguapa* and a dozen more) *Zapotillo* is the common name in Costa Rica. The tree is slender at the base, not very tall, endowed with slender long leaves, and a furrowed bark redolent with sticky latex. The fruit has a heart or pointed oval shape. The skin begins green and ripens yellow. Not terribly popular, the yellow-orange innards are dry and a little mealy with the taste of a sweet potato. The center may be creamy like an egg yolk just barely hardened by boiling. When completely ripe, the fruit may be eaten fresh with a splash of lime juice, puréed into a smoothie or egg-fruit-nog, added to custard or used in confection recipes.

Fig (*higo)* Fig trees are among my favorites with lush foliage, large three fingered leaves, a canopy of shade, gnarled trunks with tuberous nodules and loads of delicious fruit. The fig loves tropical warmth and sun but is easily disease ridden in tropical wetness. Many other ficus cousins grow better in Costa Rica than anywhere else. Green and purple fruit find their way to market on occasion. Because the seeds are less commonly pollinated than in my former California home, they tend to be hollow and lack a little of the added nut-like flavor. They are otherwise every bit as sweet and juicy. A fresh ripe fig half wrapped in a paper-thin slice of *prosciutto* remains my favorite appetizer.

Grape (*uva)* Table grapes are mostly imported from northern or southern latitudes farther away from the equator. The scant wine industry uses sweet tropical fruits and is euphemistically less than memorable.

Grapefruit (*toronja)* I grow yellow and red grapefruit alongside thick skinned pummelos with remarkably little attention to fertilizer or pest control. Unfortunately, all three types and the pink ones contain a substance that interferes with our body's breakdown of the very commonly prescribed "statin" class of medicines that constitute the cornerstone of lipid (cholesterol, triglycerides, fatty acids) lowering for prevention of stroke and heart attack. A portion of grapefruit or a glass of its juice can magnify the effect of the drug by 40 times. Particularly for groups of baby boomers and seniors, you might want to avoid using grapefruit since it is likely that one or more of your dinner guests may be adversely affected. If you don't take those medicines and want to try a new sweet, candied grapefruit jelly making is a home industry in the lovely Costa Rican town of Atenas (Spanish for Athens) west of La Garita, on the road that runs from the Pan American Highway to the central Pacific coast (Jaco, Quepos, Manuel Antonio National Park, etc.). Look for the word *toronja* on hand painted signs in vendors' front yards. Atenas supposedly was chosen by National Geographic as having one of the world's best climates, although the specific reference eludes me.

Green coconut (*pipa*) Tico roadsides abound with piles of decapitated green coconuts outside of stands . The vender slices off the top with a machete, pops in a straw and serves refreshing chilled coconut juice to thirsty travelers. Look for signs that advertise *PIPA FRIA*. In the cities, venders sell plastic bags of the same thirst quencher out of street corner ice chests.

Guava (*guayaba*) Before coming to Costa Rica, my experience with guava had been limited to jars of jelly in Christmas baskets or on market shelves. In recent years, guava nectar appeared in cooler dispensers. Large cans of guava shells from South America came to Latino markets, joining blocks of dark red guava paste, *guayabate*. I tried them all.

The jellies, jams and marmalades were fine on toast with cream cheese. They were better as glazes for ham, pork roasts, ribs, roast chicken and turkey.

I added guava to barbecue sauces and to spicy Thai peanut sauces and used it to candy sweet potatoes and carrots. It went well in salad dressings, particularly vinaigrette, and softened the richness of balsamic vinegar. The nectar became a marinade, alone or in combination with olive or sesame oil, soy sauce, rice vinegar or sake. After a potent punch cup of guava and lime juices, coconut milk and rum, I fell asleep at the table.

The canned shells were only ok. They were guava halves, peeled, with the central seeds removed, packed in heavy sweet syrup. My best rendition was shell cavities filled with tart fresh fruit pieces and a sprig of mint to offset the syrup. A friend used the canned shells successfully as pie filling. The local pancake house offered guava syrup as one of six pancake toppings.

The dense guava paste that comes in blocks is fabulous, redolent with flavor and not too sweet. It pairs very well with slices of cheese from *queso fresco* to jack to *chevre* to *gorgonzola*. It works well mixed with ricotta, mascarpone, feta or cream cheese as a filling for tartlets, turnovers, puffs, profiteroles, blintzes or filo triangles.

On our little farm, we have *cas* and *guayaba* (guava) trees. Our problem with the fruit is that it ripens late in the rainy season at a time when little white worms invade it. Our undaunted and appreciative next-door neighbor, horses beyond our fence and birds in our aviary consume it worms and all. There are dozens of guava varieties. Let me help you differentiate and demystify the five you are most likely to encounter in Central America.

1) Guava, (*guayaba,* psidium guajava) The dimensions of the fruit vary from tangerine to orange size. It is pleasantly aromatic to some and cloyingly musky to others. The thin skin is green, yellow or purple. Flesh colors vary by species from white to yellow to pink to red. Next to the skin is a layer of pulp. The small gritty seeds fill the center and are a good source of dietary fiber. Some have softer seeds, some fewer and a variety from Indonesia is seedless. The fruit is very rich in Vitamin C and pectin. The bark can be used to tan animal hides. It is rich in tannin and peels easily like eucalyptus or sycamore bark.

2) Pineapple guava (*feijoa sellowiana*) When Joan and I lived in San Francisco, a flock of wild parrots lived nearby. They ate palm fruit, cherries, wild plums and a neighbor's pineapple guavas. With seasonal temperatures down to 50 F (10 C), the plants bore fruit in abundance. Here in Costa Rica, the plants produce glorious flowers but little fruit because of the absence of a cold season. The pear shaped fruit tastes to me of pineapple, pepper and spearmint. The flowers have a base of edible white petals and an inedible plume of white tipped long red stamens. Despite the similarity in the Portuguese names, *feijoa (*pineapple guava) and *feijoada (*Brazil's national dish of stewed black beans and pig parts), they are not related.

3) Strawberry guava (cattley guava, purple guava, *cas dulce*, psidium cattleianum) This variety is a gorgeous ornamental shrub, resistant to cold like its pineapple cousin, resplendent with sweetly fragrant all white flowers that are not edible and full of small red fruit. The fruit has none of the musky odor of larger guavas and tastes like a spicy strawberry. The flesh goes from pink near the skin to white in the center. A yellow variety (psidium lucidum) looks and tastes the same except for the color of the fruit.

4) *Cas* (Costa Rican guava, *cas acida*, psidium friedrichsthalianum) The tree is larger than strawberry guava and smaller than the common guava. Its leaves are a waxy deep green. Like its cousins, its bark peels easily and contains lots of tannin. The small round yellow colored fruit has no musky odor and is so acidic, a bite will pucker your lips and implode your cheeks. Sweetened, it makes wonderful drinks, good jelly and tasty pie and pastry filling. The parrots in our aviary (all rescue birds or abandoned pets unfit for survival in the wild) prefer *cas* to all other fruits except papaya, banana and cashew apples.

5) Brazilian guava (cas estranjero, guayaba agria, Castilian guava, psidium guinense) This small tree or large shrub has hairy leaves, a gray trunk, flowers with as many as two hundred stamens each and yellow fruit less than an inch wide. It is too tart to eat raw and I have not seen it sold in drinks. I include it only because it produces uniquely flavored jelly that aficionados seem to prefer to all others. I have not tasted it.

Guava flavors desserts everywhere; in and atop ice cream, rice pudding, flan and fruit salad. For the easiest introduction to home use, melt a little guava jam or jelly and spoon over one of these desserts or over bananas browned in butter. Google.com has pages of guava recipes including layer cakes, cheesecakes and pies. Try using guava jelly and nectar in place of apricot jelly and nectar in old recipes. Use melted jelly in place of honey for baking or stewing. Baked ham with imbedded cloves tastes great with a glaze of Dijon mustard, cinnamon and guava jelly for the last twenty minutes in the oven. Try the jelly alone or with your favorite barbecue sauce on any grilled, broiled or roasted meat or poultry. Jelly and lime juice together are great for grilled or broiled fish.

Hand of Buddha (*mano de Buddha)* Linda Watanabe McFerrin is a wonderful poet, novelist, travel writer, short story writer and friend. She titled a collection of spiritual stories *Hand of Buddha* after a tropical citrus fruit, the citron that appears in Costa Rican farmers' markets from time to time. Native to Southeast Asia, this bizarre fruit splits from its stem end into a number of tapering fingers several inches long. They hang down like yellow octopus tentacles. The skin and rind are very thick, the pulp and juice minimal. Marvelously aromatic, the whole fruit can be used as a natural source to perfume e.g. a bathroom with an essence similar to key lime. Candied rind is a popular Asian treat.

Inga *(guaba)* The fruit of the inga vera tree looks like a smaller, less curved boomerang, painted dull green. Inside the inedible skin and rind, sweet white flesh, as dry as cotton candy, surrounds green waxy seeds. The white flesh is eaten out of hand. The seeds are tossed out or added to *olla de carne,* a traditional weekend stew. The name of the dish, "pot of meat," is less than descriptive. The stew does contain beef chunks cooked with the bone in, but the rest of the mélange includes many unusual root vegetables and, at times, inga seeds.

Jackfruit The largest tree borne fruit in the world, the jackfruit looks like breadfruit on steroids, the size and shape of a large watermelon. Its skin is patterned five and six-sided little scale, with a short central spike. Ripe, it smells like a less rancid durian. About ten years ago, my wife and I went to a restaurant on Marlboro Road in Jogjakarta to try the chef's "world famous jackfruit." We arrived before the lunch hour so I could witness the preparation. After twenty minutes or so, the place got busy and I was exiled to the diningroom. Before retreating, I watched the chef do battle with a monster fruit, the size of his pot belly. He was covered in protective grease like an English Channel swimmer, as was his cleaver. Every cut liberated an ooze of sticky latex. Later I learned that the latex works well as a caulk for plumbing and tile or to glue broken pottery back together. He sliced and diced chunks, seeds and all in a cauldron of boiling salted water that grew a gum ring at the water line after only a few minutes. He cleaned the goo off his cleaver every few minutes with a greasy brush. Before the herbs and spices came on stage, I was asked to leave. The meal was underwhelming and the kitchen aroma hitched a ride back to our hotel on my clothing. Jackfruit can grow anywhere that is warm and moist. I have seen just a few in Costa Rica. They are rare in the Americas except in Surinam and Brazil. In India, they are grown in pastures to provide feed when the fruit fall from the trees for the cows and shade for their holy bodies.

If you want to try the fruit, I suggest you buy a can of cooked slices from Thailand in your Asian market. It is basically a bland starchy vegetable when not quite ripe, similar to breadfruit and plantain. The seeds are similar to chestnuts when boiled. In moist cultures, breadfruit is preferred because of more manageable size, the bothersome latex of jackfruit and the bad smell of the latter.

Jocote (purple mombin, red mombin, wild plum, *jobo, ciruela, prune rouge* and at least a dozen more names) The oval golf ball size fruit seems to attract construction workers, field hands and kids playing soccer on their R&R breaks from July to October, the end of the rainy season, when the trees are loaded with red or orange instant snacks. The flesh is yellow, juicy, sweet smelling and tastes like a plum. Squirrels love them. Like ripe bananas and mangos, fruit flies congregate around ripe *jocote* left in the open, even in a fruit bowl in the house. Some neighbors boil and dry them and store them in cupboards or bags where they last for several months as a snack food for kids of all ages. Others chill and serve them with a little honey for dessert. Although they are pleasant tasting, their popularity is disproportionate, probably because *jocote* feasting out of little hands was part of the pleasant childhood memory bank in rural Costa Rica. The branches of the lacey green tree accommodate youngsters by bending down to within a few feet of the ground.

Kiwi, Chinese gooseberry These russet brown egg-shaped fuzzy fruit grow on a vine. The green flesh is quite tart until it sweetens at peak maturity. It Costa Rica, it is peeled, sliced and eaten plain or as a salad component. Native to China, kiwis seem to adapt to diverse climates. Dogma dictates that they need a chilly season followed by a long period of warmth to bear fruit, but they appear commonly in Costa Rican markets and in people's yards.

Kumquat Growing kumquat trees requires care and patience. Their roots are poor, so they have to be grafted. They require nearly daily watering and frequent fertilizing. Even then, they grow very slowly. The small orange fruit have a poorer flesh to rind ratio than other citrus explaining why they are usually cooked in syrup and eaten whole. Mostly they are raised and sold as dwarfs in pots as ornamentals.

Lime (*limón*) There are no lemons to speak of in Costa Rica, so there is no confusion about the word *limón*. In other Spanish speaking countries where limes and lemons co-exist, limes may be called *limas*. Of the three major types of limes in the world, sour Mexican, Tahitian and sweet, Costa Rica has an abundance of two – Mexican (*limon agria)* and sweet *(limon dulce)*. Lime juice from the more common sour variety serves as dressing for shredded cabbage salad, as a marinade, as squeezable wedges with fish, cubes of pork, spare ribs, avocado, tomato slices and many other fruits and vegetables, in a host of cold drinks from club soda to beer and as the "cooking" liquid for *ceviches* of fish, seafood and bananas. The sweet variety is often eaten out of hand fresh off the tree. It is sweeter than any lime or lemon available in North American markets. It doesn't keep its marvelous flavor very long in storage, and fades fast after it is cut. Ticos, therefore, pick them or buy them fresh, slice them and drink the juice unsweetened as a breakfast drink or as lemonade. They make a lighter, less acid *ceviche*. Gingerale or Sprite is often added to lime juice when sour limes are used in *ceviche* making.

Loquat, Japanese medlar (*nispero)* The loquat is an ornamental evergreen that grows from subtropics to temperate climates. The amount and quality of fruit is dependant on the conditions. The sweet and juicy fruit is not a major seller in Tico markets, but it can be found. The skin is yellow to red, most often orange. The pale yellow flesh wraps around five inedible brown seeds.

Mango (*manga, mango)* The most common tropical fruits are clearly banana, papaya, pineapple and coconut. The best loved is probably the manga. It is perhaps the most diverse with some five hundred different varieties. The fruit may be small as a golf ball dangling on a long thin stand like a Christmas ornament or five pounds and close to a foot long hung on a short thick stem. Every color from pale yellow to dark purple tints the tough waxy skin. Small ones tend to be round. The larger ones tend to be lopsided or slightly kidney shaped oblongs with a tapered tip. Given proper soil, climate, altitude (up to about three thousand feet in Costa Rica) and decent drainage, the trees live a very long time and become giants. The town square of Alajuela is home to several of "the world's largest" well over a hundred feet tall. Wild parrots frequent their branches. About twenty years ago, I had the opportunity to snorkel the unspoiled endless coral reefs of the Andaman Islands off the West Coast of Southern Thailand. The only inhabitants were tan skinned boat dwellers called "Sea Gypsies" with Caucasian features and wavy to curly black hair. We spent an afternoon in the jungle together. I was looking to photograph wild orchids, but they were far more intent on showing me magnificent wild mango trees that they claimed were the first ones on earth. Some mangos are so fibrous, they can't be chewed. People usually roll them between their hands, cut a hole in the apex and suck out the juice. The less fibrous but small ones may be peeled with a sharp knife allowing the flesh to be eaten off the pit. Larger ones are most often sliced into two skin-coated fillets by running a sharp knife close along the flat pit. The severed cheeks can then be separated from the skin.

When the tree closest to our house is loaded with a few hundred fruit, we stash several ziplock bags with peeled chunks in the freezer for sauces for fish, smoothies, marinades for pork, glazes for poultry, pudding, mousse, crème brûlée or for baked desserts when mangos are out of season. Some authorities suggest a little added lime juice to prevent discoloration. Others suggest coating in sugar or syrup. It may be a result of the sugar and acid content of our fruit, but the chunks survive freezing and thawing unadorned. Our mangos ripen in May, early in the rainy season. Unfortunately, the strong winds that come to Costa Rica around Christmas and are supposed to leave by February, may linger into the weeks before the fruit ripens and cover the yard with dropped green fruit. There are dozens of recipes for green papaya, particularly in Thai and Indian cookbooks. Substituting green mango works just fine.For those of you who love mangos as much as I, satisfy your curiosity for more mango information and buy Allen Susser's lovely book *The Great Mango Book,* full of beautiful photos by Greg Schneider and recipes to salivate over. (Ten Speed Press, 2001)

Mangosteen A close second for mouthwatering flavor to the mango is the mangosteen. Unfortunately it is uncommon in Costa Rica. I have read that it is a commercial success in Guatemala and Coastal Peru. I include it only to dispel any confusion about its name; it is not even a distant cousin of the mango.

Marmalade plum *(mamey, mamey sapote)* The tree is beautiful. It looks a lot like a southern magnolia that has been sculpted to form a perfectly rounded top off a stout short trunk. Twice a year baseball size brown fruit hang down in perfusion. The skin is rough and leathery, but the smooth flesh is eye-catching salmon red. Seed remnants and skin are bitter and need be judiciously removed. The cleansed flesh is sweet smelling and tastes like a honeyed yam.

Melon pear (*pepino dulce)* *Pepino dulce* actually means sweet cucumber. The fruit of this hearty shrub or small tree tastes like melon and cucumber. The skin is yellow to green with vertical purple stripes. It grows at all elevations in Costa Rica, but is not a commercial crop.

Mombin (*caimito)* It looks like a plum and comes in all shades from yellow, to red to purple on a tree with silvery purple leaves. The fruit is delicious out of hand when it is ripe. Dark green flesh surrounds four or five small inedible pits. The flavor is a combination of ripe purple plum and kiwi to my taster. Less ripe, it can be acidic.

Nance (*nanzi, nanzi agria)* The tree often looks like a shrub in the wild, where it grows all along the Pacific coast. The fruit look like stemless Queen Anne yellow cherries. The pale flesh around a central pit is bland, a little sweet and astringent. Children eat them out of hand. Birds love them. When they come to farmers' markets or roadside stands, they are very inexpensive.

Naranjillas, lulos Even though the name translates as "little oranges," these shrubs of the deadly nightshade family are not citrus. Leaves and fruit can be covered with hairs. When the fruit ripens, it turns bright orange and the hairs lessen or disappear completely. They grow at higher elevations in Costa Rica, Colombia, Ecuador and Peru. Their skin is tough. Inside, pulp and juice are edible – seeds are not. The juice is light green and is often sweetened. The shells may be used for small baking receptacles for mashed pulp and bananas. *Naranjilla* fruit tastes like tart strawberries. To eat them raw, one should scrub the skin with a brush or sponge to remove the hairs before cutting the fruit in half and sucking out the innards, sans seeds. *Narajilla* is used to make drinks, pies, ices and mousse, particularly in Columbia.

Naseberry (*zapote, sapodilla, chicle, nispero)* Native to Central America, this hundred foot giant is called *zapote* rather than its other names. The canopy of shiny green leaves is dense and umbrella-like. At times it looks as though someone with a ten story ladder has shaped, trimmed and rounded the top. The fruit are small, about three inches along their egg shaped long axis, with rough brown skin. The flesh is sweet and crunchy like a crisp pear splashed with syrup and has a few black seeds that are not toxic if inadvertently swallowed. The flesh color varies from golden brown to rust. A cut into the bark releases milky latex that was an original ingredient in chewing gum.

Orange (*naranja)* No thick skinned seedless oranges grow here. The common variety is sweet and juicy, even before the thin skin changes completely from green to orange. Fresh squeezed juice is available nearly everywhere. A Tico favorite is mixed orange and carrot juice that comes in waxed cardboard containers in supermarkets.

Otaheite gooseberry (*grosella*) Nothing like Oregon gooseberries, these strange émigrés from Madagascar grow well and produce large clusters of fruit in wetter lowlands. The individual fruit is an inch across, half an inch from stem to tip, pale yellow, shaped like cookie cutter summer squash with eight rounded excrescences along its outer edge. Crisp and sour describe the little beauties. The flesh must be sliced from the pit and sweetened, and is then only used in jellies with other fruits, in drinks or in sauces. I have not seen them in the central markets and only rarely in roadside stands along the Caribbean.

Papaya (*papaya*) Papayas have single trunks like palms, two foot wide leaves like large ornamentals, fragrant white flowers and clusters of fruit, each of which can weigh up to twenty pounds. They are not really trees, but are hollow stemmed herbs. They require very little to no care and often appear as volunteers anywhere in Costa Rica where there is plenty of water, but good drainage. Their only nemesis is flooding for days, which can kill them. The fruit varies from oval to club shaped. It is ripe when the smooth, thin skin changes from green to at least three quarters yellow. The flesh is orange with varying shades of admixed red. Small black seeds in a gel fill the central cavity. These seeds are peppery and some people add a few of them to fruit slices to sharpen the flavor. More typically, Ticos peel, seed and slice them and squirt on a little lime juice before eating. They are frequent breakfast fruit but appear as street snacks and in virtually all tropical fruit salads. To my palate they taste like cantaloupe and apricot. A minority of people don't like the musky overtone. Green papayas are cut thin and served in Asian salads, but in Costa Rica, green papayas are always cooked like squash. Unripe fruit contain latex loaded with papain, a proteolytic (protein digesting) enzyme that is used as a commercial meat tenderizer and in brewing. Combining chunks of the green fruit and beef and cooking them together with onions, potatoes, tomatoes, garlic and carrots makes a fine stew with tender meat. Green papaya may be stuffed and baked. The white unripe seeds are not eaten.

Passion fruit (*granadilla, maracuyá*) It is hard to choose whether this hearty, rapid growing vine is better for its gorgeous flowers or delicious fruit. Different types of yellow fruited vines (there are also less succulent purple fruited types) produce either brilliant red or breathtaking complex purple blossoms. The fruit is an oval, tough skinned container of edible seeds and sweet tasty flesh. It is unique to my palate, though others think it is similar to guava.

Pear (*pera*) Several varieties of pear line upscale shelves of produce departments from yellow to red, but they are imported from temperate climates north or south. The firmer green skinned type survives well and even reach rural markets.

Pejibaye, *pejivalle* (Costa Rican spelling) A tall stately palm that grows abundantly in the wild on the Atlantic side of Costa Rica, it is covered all over with long stiff sharp spines. The caustic fruits are beautifully colored red, yellow, orange green or striped. Most often, they are boiled in salted water for about three hours, after which the skin comes off easily and the flesh separates from the central pit. At that point, the fruit may be eaten as is, mixed with a little mayonnaise as a snack or pureed as a dip. Cream of *pejibaye* soup is elegant and is described in detail in the section on soups in chapter 3. A cluster of fruit may contain 50 to 300 individual spheres a little larger than golf balls weighing a combined 20 to 50 pounds. They can also be roasted, fried, oven-dried, or baked. Oven-dried fruit can be rehydrated with a halfhour of boiling even up to six months later and the texture and chestnut flavor returns. Mashed or cubed cooked fruit mixed with corn flour, moistened with eggs and milk or broth, make a fine faux-chestnut turkey dressing. Love of the hearts of *pejibaye* palm by the invading Spaniards decimated entire forests. There still are many more in Costa Rica than anywhere else in Central America. Indigenous communities fermented the fruit and the sap into an alcoholic drink, ate the seeds, ground the dried fruit into flour and fashioned hard but flexible spears and arrows out of the wood. A single fruit contains more than a thousand calories according to folklore, but only 40 according to a local nutritionist, along with multiple vitamins, protein, calcium and fiber.

Pineapple (*piña*) Pineapple is actually a bromeliad. Unlike most of the other 2000 members of the Bromellaceae family which are epiphytes growing in trees, pineapple grows out of the ground as an herb, three feet wide and about four feet tall with sharp pointed long leaves. Hummingbirds are the principal pollinators of the flowers that form the fruit. The sweet yellow flesh from freshly picked ripe pineapple is so superior to what comes in cans, it is almost a different fruit. A second, less common variety with darker and greener skin and whiter, less yellow flesh is also grown for local consumption in Costa Rica. Although it may be referred to as "cooking pineapple" I prefer it to the yellow kind for its less acidic and less cloying fresh flavor. If you get the chance to try *piña blanca,* see what you think. Pineapple is available year round and is used widely as cut up fruit, in drinks, sauces, jams, sweets and pastries.

Plantain (*plátano)* The plantain or "cooking banana" comes in many sizes, shapes and colors, but usually looks like a longer, larger green banana. Unripe green ones have starchy firm insides that are usually fried, smashed and fried again (*patacones, tostones*). Still green or slightly brown, the insides begin to soften, to become creamier. These are most often boiled or sautéed in *picadillos,* soups and stews or as a vegetable. When they are so ripe that the skin turns black, they are roasted or grilled and served topped with melted cheese or sour cream (*maduras).* As easily as a ripe banana peels, a green plantain is difficult to undress. Most people oil their hands to protect them from the sticky resin in the cut skin, chop off the ends, make four long slits through the tough skin for the length of the fruit and soak in hot water for a few minutes to help loosen the skin. Once the skin and long fibrous strands are off, the flesh begins to oxidize (discolor) unless drizzled with lime juice or another acid.

Pomegranate *(granada)* The tree, *granado,* prefers a more temperate climate than Costa Rica, but some fruit come to market on occasion from higher elevations and single trees grow in yards.

Prickly pear *(tuna)* Prickly pears are the fruit of cactus of the same name. Like the fleshy edible pads, the fruit are also covered with long thin spines which must be removed. Flowers of the prickly pear cactus are brilliant yellow, red and purple on the same plant. The fruit is sweet, pink and has the flavor of fig and ripe pear. Because it is rich in fiber, the fruit supposedly can lower LDL cholesterol and blood sugar. When I was a college kid, we went to Bermuda to SCUBA and overdosed on prickly and its fiber and spent the night lined up at our outhouse. The pads, despined and sliced (*nopales)*, are a common element in Mexican salads. Usually vinegary and minimally mucilaginous, they add crunch, pleasant flavor and body. Because Costa Rica doesn't have comparable deserts to Mexico, *tunas* are not very common and *nopales* are rare.

Pummelo, *(pomelo)* The thickest skin and largest fruit in the citrus world belongs to this primitive grapefruit. Plant geneticists tell us that other kinds of grapefruit seem to be hybrids or mutations of pummelo. Favored in Southeast Asia, it is a secondary curiosity in the tropical Americas. It grows well here with very little care. Ticos seem to prefer traditional grapefruit.

Rambutan *(mamón chino)* Similar to its cousin the lychee, rambutan fruit is encapsulated, slightly translucent, soft, attached to a central pit, sweet and fragrant. The rambutan outer capsule looks like a sparse caput Medusa with a perm. The spines are soft, the color every shade from yellow to orange to red to pink to purple. The way to eat them is to split the capsule with a sharp fingernail or pocket knife, pop out the fruit, eat it off the pit and toss the potentially toxic pit away. Rambutan also comes in cans from Malaysia and goes well in fruit salads. The tall tree can be grown from dried seeds, flat side down, particularly in hot, humid lowlands like the Caribbean coastal plain.

Sour orange (*naranja agria, naranja ácida,* Seville) Similar to other oranges, the sour orange has sweet smelling flowers, evergreen leaves and round orange colored fruit. It is a little more erect and the ripe fruit have a reddish blush. The fruit and peel are very bitter. The peel may be candied and the fruit is the most common citrus ingredient worldwide for orange marmalade. Its other major use is in sauces and marinades.

Soursop *(guanábana)* The annona genus, famous for cherimoya, sugar apple and custard apple, has a larger, more acidic type of fruit that is the only one of the group that can be processed and preserved. The *guanabana* is oval, green, covered with soft, fleshy spikes and can weigh five or six pounds. As it ripens, it softens a little and the skin begins to yellow. At that point it should be picked, before it falls off the tree and smashes on the ground. Fruit and flowers may coexist. The flower begins as an odd looking Japanese lantern, yellow or orange, suspended by a very short stalk from the wood itself, away from the leaves. It is as often found on the main trunk or large inner limbs as on more distal branches and twigs. The skin is too bitter to be eaten and the black seeds too toxic. Pure white flesh, carefully seeded is also acid, but sweetened it makes lovely drinks puréed with milk and ice. Pops, the Tico Baskin Robbins equivalent, and Mighty Rivers farm make great *guanábana* yogurt. In other parts of Latin America, *guanabana* carbonated drinks, juices and concentrates appear in cans and bottles. When two large fruit approached picking ripeness fifteen feet from my front gate, a thief unlatched it and absconded with the pair despite my pack of six fierce looking dogs, which assuredly would have barked and growled and licked him or her had they seen the culprit.

Star apple *(caimito)* The tree is medium size with a short trunk and dense umbrella shaped canopy of dark green ellipsoid leaves that have a bronze patina. The small spherical fruit are about three inches tall and wide. Two distinct varieties bear either pale green or dark purple fruit. Both have white sweet flesh with jelly-like texture. The name derives from a starburst seed pattern in the center when the fruit is cut horizontally through its waist. The outer third, the skin and rind, contains bitter latex that renders the fruit inedible unless it is carefully halved and the core of flesh closest to the seeds is scooped out. Star apple pulp is a popular component of two unlikely named desserts in Jamaica, *matrimony* and *strawberries and* cream. Matrimony is a mixture of sour orange juice and sweet star apple pulp. Strawberries and cream mixes sweet orange juice, an ounce of sweet sherry or dry sherry and a little sugar, grated nutmeg and star apple pulp. You can find *matrimony* in Limon. I have yet to discover *strawberries and cream* there.

Star Fruit (*carambola)* Star apple and star fruit are unrelated. Their only commonality is that the star appears subsequent to a transverse cut. Whereas the apple has a central many pointed star produced by its seeds, the *carambola* or star fruit has five outer ribs that run from stem to stern. A slice from the middle looks a five pointed sheriff's badge. In the courtyard of a Hanoi monastery, a monk picked the fruit with the pinkest blush on its golden skin for us to eat out of hand. It smelled like star jasmine and tasted like a mild pear with a pucker. Its botanical family is called *Oxalidaceae* because of its oxalic acid content. The oxalic acid causes the pucker. There are two common varieties, a larger blander but sweeter one with less oxalic acid and a smaller sour type. Both are sour before they ripen fully. If you want to minimize the pucker, choose the larger type, very ripe with the rib edges beginning to turn brown and slice off the outer ribs where the majority of the oxalic acid resides. With the star shape intact, slices dress up salads, puddings and frozen desserts quite nicely. Younger fruit do well in *achar* and chutney in South Asia with or instead of tamarind. They grow well in Costa Rica. The fruit are common in farmers' markets.

Strawberries (*fresas)* Costa Rican strawberries are delicious. Don't be fooled by their appearance. Compared to North American berries, they are smaller, firmer, less juicy and more of a red- orange than a purple-red. A little yellow at the stem end is common. Nevertheless, they are more flavorful to my taste out of hand, in fruit salads or as jams and jellies. They grow up on the mountain slopes where roadside stands seem to have an endless supply.

Sugar apple (*anón)* When you spy a bumpy pink or red heart shaped fruit in the market, stop and eat one. They are a delicious treat. The sugar apple is a tropical native of the Americas that tastes like it should have come from India or North Africa. It has the flavor and aroma of rose water. Break one open and pop a segment into your mouth. Each segment is full of hard seeds. Separate them with your tongue and spit them out. Some people make a tea out of the leaves as a cure all for the digestive, genitor-urinary and upper respiratory systems. Green fruit may be used as an antidote for diarrhea. In India, dried leaves are sniffed to treat hysteria.

Surinam cherry (*pitanga, acreola,* Barbados cherry*)* The mirtacea or myrtle family includes all the guavas, *feijoa*, *jambo*, rum berries, water apples, rose apples and many other fruits, none of which resemble their kin, *pitanga* or Surinam cherry. The tree probably originated in the Yucatan or in Surinam, Guyana and British Guiana. It then moved to Brazil, but now grows from California, to Sri Lanka to China and the entire Caribbean from Florida to Costa Rica. A bushy small tree that barely reaches fifteen feet, it possesses white flowers followed in only three weeks by gorgeous plump little Chinese lantern or mini pumpkin shaped fruit that turns from yellow to bright red. A less common and reputedly sweeter variant goes from burgundy to nearly black purple. Each marble size fruit has ridges that go from stem atop to blossom below dividing the fruit into lobes.

After washing them, remove the stem and blossom and cut them vertically. Extract the seed and store for a few hours uncovered in the fridge to allow the volatile resins to escape. They are then ready to be eaten as is or in any recipe as a strawberry surrogate.

My friend, Winnie Orcutt, is renowned for her talents as one of Costa Rica's best birders and as an excellent cook. Her *pitanga* jam and bread and butter pickles are particularly popular. I gave her a bag of mustard seed for her pickles and she shared the following Surinam cherry jam recipe: Pick the ripest fruit, crimson red to dark purple, rinse well and put through a Foley food mill to separate out the seeds, stems and blossoms. Force the flesh through a strainer. Add granulated sugar, one and a half times the volume of the purée. Heat in a pot until the jam sheets. Sheeting is a term that implies that when a spoon is dipped into the bubbling mixture, the jam runs off the spoon, not as from a spout, but rather in a thin sheet, more like a waterfall. Pour into sterilized jars. Once opened, it should be refrigerated. The fruit are so rich in pectin, that none has to be added.

The flavor is unique. To me it tastes like strawberries and purple plums with a tart subtle resin addition. Although I dislike resin flavors in Greek wines and cough drops, a hint of it adds perfect complexity to *pitanga* jam. Other uses of the berry include syrup, wine, relish, pickles, vinegar, pie fillings and sherbet.

In rural Brazil, locals spread *pitanga* leaves on the floor so they release a citronella-like substance when walked upon, thus reducing the fly population indoors. In Surinam, a tea from the leaves is used as a cold remedy. Keep the seed away from kids. Ingested, they cause diarrhea. In Florida it is used as a hedge or ornamental bush. In Costa Rica's Central Valley they produce fruit non-stop in April and May. Unfortunately, they have a short shelf life raw.

The name *pitanga* is from the language of Brazil's Tupi Indians. Other names include *cereza de Cayena* in Spanish, with local variations – *nanga pire* in Argentina, *cereza quadrada* in Colombia, *guinda* in El Salvador and *pendanga* in *Venezuela; cerise de cayenne or cerises carrées* in French with local variations – *ceresa a cote* or *cerises côtes* in Martinique and Guadaloupe and cerises *du pays* or *cerises carees* in French Guiana; *Surinaamsche kersh*, or *zoete kers* in Dutch; and Surinam cherry or Florida cherry in English.

Tamarind (*tamarindo*) Tamarind trees are slow growing, but live long enough to become giants with circumferences of their trunks up to twenty-five feet and a height of ten stories. The combination of size, bright green feathery leaves and innumerable long grey-brown pods hanging down make the tamarind easily recognizable even at a great distance. They grow best and most prolific in areas that are less wet. With pods full of seeds, it is part of the leguminosae botanical family. The flesh around the seeds transforms from unripe green to a dark rust color when more mature. In Central American, tamarind pulp is sold in plastic bags, wrapped in corn husks, sugared and rolled in balls, as flat sweetened patties, in blocks, as canned jams and juices, as a syrup over shaved ice or in barbecue sauces. In Southern Asia (India, Pakistan, Kashmir, Nepal) tamarind is a major souring agent in chutneys and curries. Many brands of Worcester-type sauce contain tamarind.

Tangerine *(mandarina*) Unlike the fruit sold in North America, tangerines here are often sold while the loose peel is still partly or all green. The flesh is as moist and sweet. The hardy tree requires little care. It is eaten almost exclusively out of hand and doesn't seem to even have a place in fruit salads. It makes great juice and sauces.

Ugly fruit (*ugli)* The fruit looks like a small grapefruit with warts. But tastes like a sweet tangerine with banana overtones. The first member of this presumed hybrid was discovered growing wild in Jamaica in 1924. Growers call it a tangelo hybrid, but some botanists favor an origin of sour orange, mandarin and grapefruit. The flesh is pale yellow with a hint of orange. It has fewer seeds than a grapefruit. Saplings are sold in La Garita nurseries but there is no great commercial presence as yet. Judging by the popularity and high prices of the coveted fruit in the U.K., there must be a large industry evolving somewhere. In Jamaica, locals call the fruit "HOOglee", not "ugly" as it is called in the U.S. and the U.K.

Water apple (*manzana de agua)* Shaped like a large pear, the water apple is bright red skinned with white crunchy flesh that seems to be a favorite thirst quencher for kids from Southeast Asia, India and the Philippines to Central America. The attractive tree grows rapidly in wet areas that are frost free. The taste is a little bland, similar to jicima.

Watermelon (*sandia)* Costa Rican watermelon is sweet, tasty and inexpensive year round. During the peak periods, they sell at roadside stands for as little as twenty cents per melon. The two common varieties, pale green and striped, taste the same. Local lore suggests that those grown at or near sea level are the sweetest. Seedless varieties are becoming more common. Yellow watermelons are rare.

White sapote (*matasano, zapote blanco)* In Costa Rica, the wooly leafed white sapote grows well at the same altitude as coffee and is often planted to provide shade for coffee plants. The fruit is an unpopular afterthought, except as a powerhouse in folk medicine and mythology. At different times in history and in different cultures, white sapote fruit, seeds, bark and roots have been purported to alleviate the aches of arthritis, calm jangled nerves, cure insomnia, lower blood pressure and lessen the hyperglycemia of diabetes. The only commercially viable product to date has been a cockroach poison made from the seeds. Seeds may be fatal if eaten. The cream colored flesh is mild and sweet, somewhat similar to local butter avocados. It is decent eaten fresh in hand or in a salad and makes a nice smoothie (*batido*) with milk and crushed ice, but it doesn't preserve well in jellies or jams, frozen or canned. It is not a cash crop.

Zapote See naseberry

Chapter 5
Vegetables

Despite incredible variety in local farmers' markets and a host of imports in upscale chains, vegetables are minor role players in Tico diets. The exceptions are shredded cabbage salads, sweet red peppers, tomatoes, corn, carrots, cucumbers, *chayote, ayote,* beans and a mélange of root tubers in soups or stews. Bountiful broccoli, cauliflower, eggplant, okra, jicima, shallots, beets, Jerusalem artichokes, radishes, chives, asparagus, leafy greens and assorted lettuces are mostly ignored.

In mid to upper scale restaurants, the vegetable side dishes are most often broccoli, cauliflower, carrots, green beans, baby zucchini and squash alone or together, hot or cold, but usually at least a little overcooked.

Salad bars are beginning to emerge. The usual choices include beets, cabbage slaw, carrots, chayote cubes, cucumbers, onions, red peppers, sprouts, tomatoes and boiled yuca. The most common salad dressings are mayonnaise mixed with catsup, ranch, simple lime juice and vinaigrette.

***Arracache, arracacia,* Peruvian carrot** This knobby root vegetable looks like turnip with tumors. Because of its irregular shape, it is a challenge to peel. In soups and stews it resembles parsnip and celery root. *Apio* is the local word for celery. Unfortunately the same name is used for *arracacha* in some Spanish speaking Caribbean countries. According to my palate and preference, the best chicken soup needs celery, carrot, parsley and a generous amount of parsnip in the simmering water along with chicken to create the requisite sweetness and vegetable blend of flavors. Parsnips don't grow here. Neither are they imported. *Arrachaca* remains my substitute of choice.

Asparagus (espárragos) Occasionally, home grown asparagus appears in weekend outdoor markets. When it does, the spears are thin and crisp. More often, they are rather pricey imports. Since one can never be sure when asparagus will be in the supermarkets, I go to the hardhat warehouse in San Antonio de Belén, called Belca. For wholesale prices, they offer bags of frozen green asparagus or commercial size tins of soft white spears.

Ayote A hard round winter squash, *ayote* is similar in some ways to *calabaza,* although smaller, greener on the outside and paler inside. It is diced in *picadillos,* cooked in soup, boiled and salted as a side dish, made into bread and sweetened with milk caramel and served as a cold dessert or boiled and mashed to make popular Tico squash custard.

For every cup of *ayote*, dissolve a tablespoon of sugar, 2/3 tablespoon cornstarch, ½ teaspoon vanilla extract and ½ teaspoon cinnamon in two cups of warm milk. Heat carefully to avoid scorching, sticking or boiling over until it forms a sweet, slightly thick custard. Serve it cold.

Broccoli Standard green broccoli seems to be in season and inexpensive all year.

Cabbage (*repollo*) Green and red cabbage are always available and cheap. They grow well at middle to higher elevations. Napa cabbage, kale and collard greens are commonly grown in the lowlands.

Cauliflower *(coliflor)* Fresh cauliflower is always available and inexpensive. The pearly white heads can be twice the size of their North American brethren. They are usually boiled and dressed with salt and butter or vinaigrette. A Chilean variation is to serve cauliflower in a white sauce flavored with ground almonds.

Celery *(apio)* The local variety doesn't fare well in comparison with imports from more tempoate climes. It is hard, stringy and usually full of mud.

Chayote (*chuchu* in Brazil) This green thin skinned member of the squash family has a u-shaped invagination that looks like the smile of an elder who forgot to put in his false teeth. The taste is mild, like cucumber and Asian pear. The texture is crunchy. It does well cubed in a salad, boiled lightly like squash, baked or in soups or stews.

Cherry Tomatoes A specialty item in upscale markets, they are often grown in home gardens, staked. They do well in the Central Valley. Green, yellow, orange and red ones come pear-shaped or round. Most are sweet.

Chinese mustard *(mostaza de China)* A lettuce or Napa cabbage look-alike with a wide white central rib, this green has a delightful tart flavor, milder than arugula. It keeps well in the fridge.

Eggplant Only the plump dark purple variety is grown locally. It is abundant and inexpensive.

Green Beans *(vainicas)* Standard green beans are seasonal. They grow easily in sunny home gardens. Yellow wax beans are uncommon.

Hearts of Palm (*palmito*) Tender inner stems of a number of different palm trees are lightly boiled and salted. As a side dish or in a salad, they have a delicate flavor and mild crunch. The most common source in Costa Rica seems to be the thorny *pejibaye* palm. In Florida, they come from the state tree, the cabbage palm. Their flavor has been likened to artichoke and appearance to white asparagus shafts.

Jerusalem artichokes (*topinambur*) A few farmers grow them at higher elevations but mostly they are imported from Chile or North America.

Jicima Similar in taste and texture to Asian water chestnuts, these pale brown skinned roots with white flesh are members of the morning glory family. They provide crunch and moisture. In Mexico, they are eaten sprinkled with red chili powder or drizzled with lime juice. Older, less tender roots are added to stews.

Leek *(puerro)* Costa Rican markets sell leeks that look and taste the same as the North American and European standard. They appear in soups and stews.

Lettuce *(lechuga)* Open leafed heads of lettuce similar to Boston, red leaf and oak leaf grow well in Costa Rica. Closed or tighter heads like iceberg and romaine don't fare well in the tropics. They need protection from too much sun and too much rain with partial shade and good drainage.

Nopal Common in Central America, but much less so than in the deserts of Mexico, the nopal cactus grows to enormous size. My next door neighbor has one in his front yard trimmed like a tree for years. It is twice as tall as his house. Rows of this cactus are used as fences and as cattle barriers.

The fruit (actually a seed pod), prickly pear, is discussed in the previous chapter. The fleshy leaves or pads are also good to eat. Very common in salads throughout Mexico, *nopal* also appears on occasion in Tico markets. The pads look like green ping pong paddles with tufts of long spines. I use garden gloves and a vegetable peeler to scrape off the tufts of spines. Leaving the rest of the skin intact, I trim away the edges which can be hard and dice the flesh into pieces about three inches long and half an inch wide. Into boiling water they go until they are only a little bit crunchy. A byproduct of the cooking is an okra-like mucilaginous substance that can be prevented from appearing with the addition of a quarter teaspoon of baking soda to the boiling water. I like it tossed in lime juice, salt, black pepper and fresh cilantro leaves. In Mexico, radish and onion slices are often added.

Okra (*quiabo* Portuguese) I see okra in markets fairly often but never on menus or in Costa Rican cookbooks. Originally an African vegetable, it gained a foothold in Brazilian cuisine, parts of South America (Colombia, Ecuador, Peru) and in many Caribbean countries. Aside from the Caribbean style soups, stews and gumbos of Costa Rica's east coast, it doesn't seem to be very popular. I was served breaded and fried crunchy okra nuggets once in someone's home. They were not the least bit mucilaginous prepared that way.

Onion *(cebollo)* Ordinary looking yellow onions are surprisingly mild and sweet in Costa Rica, rivaling Vidalia (Georgia), Walla Walla (Washington) and Maui (Hawaii) cousins. Most shoppers in the country markets buy them by the braided bunch a dozen or so at a time and use them in nearly everything. Squat pure white Bermuda onions are more costly and, frankly, not as tasty. Their appeal is appearance only. So, too, purple Spanish onions are neither milder nor sweeter. Somewhat uncommon in North American are knob onions, (*cebollas de rabo*), scallion giants with a white onion bulb on the end, the size of a quail egg. Common in Central America, I have otherwise seen them only in the American southwest where they are called Texas scallions. Regular scallions or green onions are the same baby plants as in the north.

It seems that the pair, onion and cilantro, are in every Costa Rican sauce, dip, *ceviche*, soup, stew, ground meat dish, seafood combination and salad.

Pumpkin *(calabaza)* This pumpkin has the size and shape, but not the outer color of North American Halloween orange jack-o-lanterns. The flesh is little more squash-like and perhaps a little nuttier, but has a similar yellow – orange hue. It can be peeled, cubed and boiled like squash, added to soups or stews, mashed and seasoned like sweet potato, purèed and sweetened in a pudding or custard, mashed and fried into a fritter or croquette or used as a receptacle for baking or roasting savory stews.

Other names include Cuban squash, West Indian pumpkin, green pumpkin, Malabar gourd and winter squash. In Costa Rica it is in the markets all year long. The color can be solid, blotched or striped, tan, green or yellow.

Radish *(rabano)* In our garden, radishes virtually push up out of the soil, cruchy, sharp and huge. They can be so large that a first timer to a farmers' market may not recognize them.

Spinach (*espinaca*) Spinach appears infrequently in produce markets and only occasionally in frozen food sections of supermarkets. The canned version can be found, but why bother?

String Beans *(vainicas)* They grow well and stay bright green and crunchy if doused in ice water after brief cooking.

Tiquisque This pink skinned starchy root has no English name that I have found, nor have I ever seen it in North America. It is a frequent ingredient in *picadillo,* a vegetable hash, and in *olla de carne,* a soupy stew of meat and an assortment of root vegetables.

Tomatillo In Mexico, green husked *tomatillos* are everywhere. Despite similar appearance, they are not small unripe green tomatoes. Tomatillos require a few minutes of boiling or simmering. Their taste is delicate and a little acidic. They appear in a host of green gravies, sauces and dips. In Costa Rica, farmers sell them on occasion, but they play only a small role in the cuisine.

Tomato (tomate) Tomatoes are available all year and they are dirt cheap. Roadside stands sell them for about 98 cents for a box of thirteen. Where they differ from North American tomatoes, they come in all sizes and shapes and are often less red. Even when they retain a little green or orange color, they taste wonderful with, on average, much more flavor than North American supermarket tomatoes. In addition, the flesh is a little firmer, the skin a little thicker and they last a lot longer in the refrigerator like plum tomatoes.

Zapallito When this green summer squash is young and tender, the "ito" ending is used. When it matures and toughens, it is called *zapallo*. It tastes a lot like zucchini and has parallel ridges from stem-to-stern.

Zucchini (*calabacín*) Wherever zucchini and all its first cousins grow, at harvest time there is an overabundance and rock bottom prices. So too in Costa Rica do cooks resort to zucchini bread, fritters, fried slices, cheese casseroles, soups, stews, side dishes, salads and even flan.

Chapter 6
Starches, Roots and Tubers

Beans Legumes that have seed-containing pods, and are neither peas nor lentils, are beans. They are among the oldest known human foods, some dating back at least to 5000 BC. In drier parts of Latin America, they provided native people with their primary source of protein. To this day, the national dishes of Costa Rica, Brazil, Colombia and Venezuela are bean dishes, and beans may be part of all three daily meals.

Black beans (turtle beans, *frijoles negros, feijão* in Brazil, *caraotas negras* in Venezuela) They are sold dry and are about the only variety that doesn't require pre-soaking for several hours before boiling. Usually an hour- and-a-half to two hours will suffice. The higher the altitude, the longer the cooking time and the more likely home cooks are to pre-soak or use pressure cookers. The beans are never salted before they become tender, or they may remain hard.

When we first stayed in Costa Rica to study Spanish, my wife and I lived in the home of a great cook. I watched our Tica friend and hostess boil black beans in water flavored with a tablespoon each of diced onions and garlic that first sweated in a skillet. At 2500 feet above sea level, her beans became tender in a little under two hours. She added enough water to keep the beans covered by an inch or two. At the end, she salted to taste, ground a modest amount of black pepper on top and a pinch of oregano. She drained the cooked beans for use as a sidedish and a second recycle into the national dish, *gallo pinto*. The cooking liquid became black soup, *sopa negra,* loaded with flavor and reminiscent of garlicky Cuban black bean soup. To thicken it, she mashed a few tablespoons of the cooked beans and added them to the broth. Before serving the soup, she added a quartered hard-boiled egg to each, squeezed on the juice from a wedge of lime and topped with cilantro leaves. How extraordinary that a simple and economical dish could taste so great.

Were I at a formal soup-tasting, I could imagine overbearing tasters commenting on the undertones of mushrooms or truffles, the body of a rich demiglace and the aroma of earthiness. Simply, it was delicious.

Puréed black beans make a fine dip with corn chips. Side dishes of black beans accompany the very best steaks in the country and nearly everything else. Lightly fried leftover beans and white rice with a little Worcestershire sauce and a smattering of finely diced red sweet pepper and cilantro combine to make *gallo pinto,* a staple at the breakfast table.

The national dish of Brazil, *feijoada,* seems to be the Saturday midday meal for all large groups. It is a thick, savory stew of at least seven different pig parts, enough garlic to notice and black beans.

In Tex-Mex chili cook-offs, the hot stuff is usually paired with meat and black beans.

In Oaxaca, Mexico, *torta de plátano,* a layered casserole, has mashed bananas on the bottom, an omelette next, then a cheese layer and mashed black beans on top. In the Yucatan, cubed pork, hot chili peppers and black beans are the norm. Mexican refried beans, *refritos,* are not twice fried. They are boiled, mashed, seasoned with salt and a little hot sauce and then fried in lard. Different areas prefer pinto, kidney or black bean *refritos.*

Chinese fermented black beans and garlic bean paste are not related. These hot, salty beans are a variety of soy beans.

Cranberry beans They are uncommon in Central America, appearing fresh on rare occasions towards the end of the rainy season. I substitute canned Italian pinkish-white beans, *fagiola romanas, or* larger all white *canellis,* when the need arises for a special antipasto, or I soak dried packaged cranberry beans overnight and then boil them for four hours. Cranberry beans, Chilean *porotos,* are available fresh all year in that South American country.

Porotos garanados, a thick vegetable stew of pumpkin or squash, corn, onions, sweet peppers and cranberry beans is very popular in Chile. A Chilean friend says that fresh cranberry beans, cooked and mashed, taste like creamed chestnuts.

Lima beans Yes, they are named after Peru's capital. They seem to have been cultivated in the Andes several thousands of years ago. Red and black beans grow poorly in the Andes and require many hours of boiling at high altitude. Limas grew better and cooked quicker. In Spanish restaurants, white gazpacho is usually made from puréed limas. Whole limas occasionally appear in tapas with sausage, bacon, anchovies, julienned vegetables or black olives. They are not popular in Costa Rica.

Pinto beans "Pinto" is the Spanish word for painted. These beans begin as pink with brown streaks which disappear during cooking. They are the primary bean in Mexican cookery where, by tradition, they are cooked in crockery jars over low heat for many hours. Most Mexican refried beans and *chili con carne* dishes are made with pinto beans. In Costa Rica, they run way behind black and red beans.

Red beans Small red beans and kidney beans are both more a deep maroon than red. They have a small white dot near the inner bend. Their only appreciable difference is size – the small reds are indeed smaller. Like pintos, they are very popular in Mexico. My guess is that they garner a third of the Tico market, with black beans getting the lion's share. They are the Louisiana standard for making red beans and rice.

White beans Dried white northern and navy beans sit on market shelves in Costa Rica. One local dish combines white beans with pork ribs, cabbage, potato, garlic, onion, sweet red pepper and cilantro leaves. I saw white bean salads in Chile and read a recipe for Chilean sea bass baked with cooked white beans sewn into the cavity. Of course, white beans are more common in ethnic Mediterranean restaurants – Spanish, Italian, French or Greek.

Black-eyed peas Black eyed-peas are really beans. *Acarajé* fritters, made from black eyed peas, probably came to Costa Rica's east coast from West Africa by way of Brazil and Caribbean islands. They are deep fried ovals that look like hush puppies. They are cut nearly in half and filled with a traditional Brazilian sauce, *vatapà,* spicy shrimp, crab salad or a host of messy gravies. Hopin' John, another former slave dish from the American south, is supposed to bring a year of good luck if eaten on the newyear. Salt pork, black eyed-peas, a little hot sauce and white rice are the recipe.

Bread Often warm out of the oven, fresh baked loaves of bread are available all over the land. A 6 am parade of locals carrying large baguette-shaped breads home for breakfast and for brown bag lunches is common. The bread is crusty, airy and white inside. A meter-long loaf costs about 70 cents. Unfortunately, the bread dries out quickly, becomes stale and crumbles when cut. It makes pretty good French toast. Pull-apart loaves of torpedo-shaped rolls and smaller baguettes offer limited variety. Several brands of white and whole-wheat sliced bread, hamburger and hot dog buns and high fiber varieties line shelves in small town groceries. Up-scale super markets often have on-site bakeries that produce denser French, Italian, peasant, rye, challah, olive and herb breads of good quality, along with an assortment of buns, bagels and rolls. On their shelves are packaged dark rye, wheatberry, cinnamon-raisin and cheese breads. English muffins are a little less common. Bagelman and Boston Bagel produce multiple types of decent chewy rounds in their outlets. Fresh pita and imported lavash are available as well. *Croissants* are not nearly up to French standards. Because of their shape, they are called "*congrejos,*" crabs, in Spanish. Auto Mercado makes a decent sourdough on occasion.

Cassava (*yuca, manioc, tapioca*) The ubiquitous black bumpy root is a year long resident of virtually every market in Central America. It is about a foot long and a third as wide. This starchy tuber can be baked, boiled, or fried like potatoes, finely sliced like potato chips or made into flour for making bread, buns, yuca flour *empanadas (enyucadas)* or pastries. An English expat friend, who has lived in Costa Rica for decades, makes “Tico shepherds’ pie” substituting mashed yuca for mashed potatoes, local white cheese for cheddar, cilantro for parsley and seasoning for ground beef with Salsa Lizano, cumin, fresh tomato dice and oregano, rather than Worcestershire sauce and ketchup. There are two types of yuca, bitter and sweet. The bitter must be cooked to break down a toxin. The cooked juice from bitter yuca, becomes a Caribbean syrup when it is spiced and reduced with cane sugar. The product is called “*cassareep*.”

***Yuca* starch** (*almidón)*   It can thicken gravies, soup or stews in the kitchen like cornstarch and works equally well in the laundry room to starch clothes.

Cereal   Corn flakes are number one. Local brands sold in bulk cost a fraction of the American imports. All kinds from Muesli to All Bran to Fruit Loops vie for shelf space. Most selections are sweetened.

Corn *(maiz)*   Corn rivals rice and beans as the number one national staple. Corn tortillas, corn bread, corn flakes, corn flour, corn meal, corn kernels, corn pudding, corn pancakes, corn on the cob, corn dough and popcorn are all popular. Most of the corn is drier and less sweet than North American types. Fresh corn kernels are often scraped off the ears with a paring knife and mashed by hand or in a blender into a flour-free batter for puddings and pancakes. Corn-on-the-cob shows up at street fairs and carnivals more often roasted than boiled, in soups and stews and as a side dish. The growing seasons are very rapid in this land of a lot of sun and ample water. It is a matter of only a few weeks when seedlings reach heights of seven feet. Local rural custom is to leave the dry stalks in the ground as stakes for the subsequent bean crop, which returns nitrogen to the soil that the corn might otherwise deplete.

Arepas A common first course, snack or bread substitute in Columbia and Venezuela, these cornmeal cakes or buns, stuffed or topped with cheese, can be found in a few *sodas* and restaurants in the Central Valley of Costa Rica. The runny white cheese on top or inside the opened bun is similar to French *crème fraîche.* The centers of the buns are a little doughy. The buns are usually split open, a little of the center removed and the space replenished with butter, cheese or pork *chicharrones*. Another variation is to mix the simple batter of *arepa* flour, *masarepa,* and water with grated cheese and an egg yolk and fry like cheese hush puppies or bake them like French *gougere.*

***Arepas* flour** *(masarepa)* The classic corn used to make this flour has very large bland white starchy kernels. Among all the varieties of flour in Latin America, it is the only one that is precooked.

Cornbread Mashed corn kernels, wheat flour, sugar, a little salt, baking powder and eggs are the basic ingredients of Tico cornbread. Locals don't add molasses, bacon bits, cheese or green onions as they do in the American South and in Paraguay.

Corn dough (*masa harina*) This is the dough from which *tortillas, tomales* and most Tico *empanadas* are made. Cornmeal cooked in lyme water and a little salt yields the firm beige dough. *Masa* is the Spanish word for "dough." An instant dry form, *masa instantanea de maiz,* becomes dough when water is added.

Corn dumplings *(humitas)* Seasoned with basil and chili peppers, these mush balls from fresh blended kernels are mixed with diced onion and sweet peppers, lightly fried, packed into husks and boiled in Andean countries. They show up on Peruvian or Ecuadorian menus in Costa Rica.

Cornmeal, polenta, corn flour Dried ground corn is the basic flour or meal for dozens of Mesoamerican foods.

The color depends on the color of the original kernels. The coarseness of the grind dictates use. The finest powder-like type is best for making dumplings, polenta and baking bread and pastries. The coarse cut can morph into breakfast cooked cereal, coating for fried foods, *tamales* and croquettes.

Corn-on-the-cob (*elote*) Shucked ears are boiled, roasted or grilled over coals *(maiz tierno a la brasa).*

Corn Pancakes (*chorreadas*, *cachapas*) *Chorreadas* are slightly sweet corn pancakes made without flour. Corn kernels are puréed in a blender with a little milk and sugar to taste. Because local corn has little water content, the purée requires some milk to thin it to the consistency of batter. It also is less sweet than North American corn, so sugar is added to taste. Pancakes are then browned on both sides in a buttered skillet or on a griddle and served hot. The corn kernels in Venezuela are plump and juicy like those in the US. They don't need added milk. Instead they need a little corn flour to keep the batter from being too runny. Venezuelan corn pancakes are called *cachapas.* Either can be topped with cheese, sour cream, fruit compote, eggplant caviar, apple butter, marmalade or maple syrup.

Cornstarch (*maizena)* Powdered starch from the endosperm of corn kernels becomes a thickening agent when mixed with liquid.

Corn stew *(guiso de maíz)* Costa Rican corn stew takes two forms, kernels from several ears of corn simmered with squash, diced onion, garlic, salt, sugar, milk and butter (typical where I live); and cornmeal stew with garlic, oregano, onion and ground pork. There are all shades of grey between the two and both are garnished with fresh cilantro.

Empanadas *Empanada* literally means "baked in a pastry crust." *Empanadas* are typically hemispheres that range in size from quail eggs to loaves of bread. The most common size would just cover the palm of your hand. They can be savory or sweet and vary significantly from coast-to-coast and country-to-country. Standard Costa Rican turnovers are made with corn dough, baked or fried and filled with savories – meat, cheese, puréed beans, chicken or potatoes; or sweets – sweetened cheese, *chiverre,* coconut cream or pineapple. For variety, try Caribbean *pati* or Argentinean beef and gravy-filled pastries. In his book *The Art of South American Cooking,* Felipe Rojas-Lombardi relegates forty pages to *empanada* variations.

Hominy (*pozole*) Large white corn kernels, similar to those used to make *masarepa,* are "peeled" by soaking in a caustic solution which causes the kernels to swell and the skin to fall off. The swollen skinless kernels, hominy, are slow cooked with pig's feet, pork loin cubes, chicken parts, garlic, salt and chicken broth. In Mexico, ancho chili peppers are added, but not in Costa Rica. After hours of cooking until all the ingredients are tender, the chicken, pork and broth are served with an accompanying platter of condiments for the individual diner to add – slivered green onions, diced chili peppers, shredded lettuce, corn chips, sliced radishes, cilantro leaves, lime wedges and avocado pieces in any combination. The dish is often a weekend special.

Tamales *Tamales* are stuffed cakes of corn dough, *masa harina,* wrapped and steamed. In Costa Rica, they are an art form as well as a common food. *Tamale* making is a seasonal family affair. Multiple generations of family cooks assemble pork, vegetables and herb fillings in rectangular packets of freshly made cornmeal, wrap them in folded plantain leaves and tie them decoratively with reeds or twine. They are traditionally given to neighbors at Christmas, and steamed or simmered before eating. In Colombia and Venezuela, they are called *hallacas* and may contain raisins or olive pieces. In Mexico, they are wrapped in dry corn husks. Cuban *tamales* are fluffier and spicy.When the same ingredients are layered and baked without a wrapper, the result is *tamale* pie. Tex-Mex *tamale* pie usually is laced with red and green chili peppers.

Tortillas *Tortillas* are flat circles of *masa harina,* dough made from corn meal soaked or cooked in lime water. They are patted flat by hands that press and turn in one motion or they are formed in a metal press. They are the daily bread of Central America. In Mexico, similar unleavened thin pancakes are more often made from wheat flour than corn, though both types exist in both cultures. They are lightly browned on a dry griddle called a *comal.* Hot off the *comal,* they are eaten as is, wrapped around dozens of different fillings, deep-fried until crisp rounds or triangular chips, cut into strips or layered into casseroles. *Tacos, tostadas, chalupas, burritos* and a dozen other dishes are made with *tortillas.* What is in a name? If you order a *tortilla* off a menu in Spain or a *tortilla Español* in Latin America, you will get a potato omelette.

Garbanzos Chick peas or garbanzo beans are irregular cream colored spheres. These legumes are sold dry or canned throughout the world. In Latin America, they find their way into soups, stews, salads, as side dishes and toasted and salted cocktail snacks. Puréed garbanzos with ground sesame seeds, garlic, parsley and lemon juice make Middle Eastern *hummus.* They are a favored bean in pork stews worldwide, in Italian soups (*pasta fagiola, minestrone*), in Brazilian fritters, in Colombian tripe stew, in Israeli *falafel,* in stuffed Indian-style bread in Trinidad (*doble),* lamb *tajines* from North Africa, and leek soup in Australia, to name a few.

White and yellow potatoes *(papas)* With so many different size, shape and color of potatoes from the countries of the Andes, it is surprising how few are grown in Costa Rica. Local potatoes are thin skinned, usually yellow inside and firm, similar in texture and taste to Yukon gold. These properties make them perfect for soups, stews, potato salad and hashes (*picadillos),* but not for baking whole. As a side dish, potato is probably fourth fiddle for starch after rice, beans and yuca. Because of unusually high water content, these potatoes can be a challenge for mashing. I suggest that after you boil, drain and skin them, you return them to the heat in a dry pot to remove more moisture, before you add butter and mash them. If you want to add a dairy product, use cream instead of milk, and only sparingly or you will end up with potato paste.

French fries are ubiquitous and standard. They are typically served with packets of mayonnaise and ketchup. Baked potatoes never have thick crunchy skin. They are foil wrapped and the paper thin steamed skin is not worth eating. Hash browns and home fries exist nearly exclusively in American style restaurants.

Sweet Potato (*batata, boniata, camote*) Sweet potatoes (*Camotes* in Costa Rica, *batata* in Colombia, *boniatos* in the Caribbean) are a staple throughout Central and South America and the Caribbean. They are members of the morning glory family. In Central America, the most common variety has purple skin and pale yellow flesh. More common in South America is the kind with rusty red skin and orange flesh. The moist potato with dark brown skin and orange flesh from the southern U.S. is called "Louisiana yam," but is actually another variety of sweet potato. The Tico *camote* has thin skin and dry flesh. It crumbles fairly easily like starchy white potatoes after boiling or baking. Since it is neither sweet nor tasty, Ticos usually boil it, peel it, mash it with butter, cane sugar and salt and bake it in an oven-proof casserole, moistened with a little rum, brandy or orange juice. I like boiled and peeled cubes splashed with a little maple syrup and sprinkled with toasted black sesame seeds. Other local tubers are described as ingredients in *olla de carne,* beef and root vegetable stew.

Sweet potato chips (*camote frito)* Banana chips, yuca chips and sweet potato chips look like thicker white potato chips and are usually more flavorful.

Rice (*arroz)* Local rice is long grain and not very starchy. It is a staple mixed with meat, chicken, pork, seafood, fried Chinese style, mixed with beans, in soups and stews, and as sweet creamy pudding. Nearly every household seems to have an electric rice cooker. Shorter grain rice with more starch finds its way into risottos and ethnic sticky rice dishes. A side of white rice comes with most bowls of soup. Cantonese fried rice is part of the long list of rice dishes in non-Chinese Costa Rican menus, along with chicken, fish, seafood, pork and beef with rice. *Gallo pinto,* the national dish and most common breakfast dish, has two parts rice to one part black beans. Rice pudding for dessert is sweet and flavorful, owing to liberal use of cinnamon and a little clove.

Chapter 7
Meats

The meats of Costa Rica are beef and pork, with a smattering of lamb and goat. The locally grown cattle are pure bred or mixes of brahmas. Their meat is very good quality, but different from what North Americans are accustomed to - Argentina rather than Omaha style.

Let me introduce you to Argentine *bife*, because most Costa Rican steak houses are Argentine in design and cuisine.

Bife is the pride of the gaucho and the joy of an entire nation. Argentine beef may be the best in the world. Reared on little more than grass and sunshine, your typical pampas-raised specimen produces a somewhat leaner, chewier steak than its corn-fed American cousin.

At Buenos Aires steak houses like *Cabana Las Lilas*, headshots of blue-ribbon cows line the walls the way pictures of the Rat Pack did at Sardi's.

Argentina may be a vegetarian's nightmare, but it is heaven for the dedicated carnivore. No diner would accept anything but a superb steak, and even French-style restaurants could not survive if a thick, tender, juicy and perfectly-cooked fillet was missing from the menu.

A good *parrilla*, beef barbeque grill, has an *asador* -- an open fire of glowing coals around which a number of vertical metal crosses hold carcasses of goat, lamb and pork meat. These slowly rotate to get the most benefit from the glowing embers, and the chefs, usually in gaucho outfits, will come over from time-to-time to slice off portions as they are ordered by the customers.

South Americans dine very late, with international-style restaurants generally not opening until 8 or 8:30 p.m. and diners often arriving as late as 9 or 10 p.m. and finishing around midnight or later. Fortunately, *parrillas* in Costa Rica usually open at 6 and many are open from noon to three for lunch.

What often confuses visitors trying to select a meat course is that the local cuts may differ greatly from those found at an American, Asian or European butcher. Here is the code-breaker which will allow you to understand the strange, romantic-sounding names on the *parrilla* menu.

The finest cut of beef, and likely to be the highest priced -- though ridiculously inexpensive by international standards - is *bife de lomo* which equates to eye fillet. The most popular cut is *bife de chorizo,* a steak cut off the rib and somewhat similar to sirloin or porterhouse. T-bone steak has its equivalent in *bife de costilla*, and is generally enormous. Rib roast, known as *tira de asado,* is the second most popular cut. When grilled on the spit, this cut will be thick and short, if cooked on the char-grill it will be thinner and longer. Cheaper cuts not generally used for roasting in other countries -- shank, brisket or chuck -- produce a budget-priced steak known as *churrasco.* It is inexpensive, yet tasty. The *parrillas* will also offer grilled chicken *(pollo*), pork (*cerdo*), kidneys (*riñones*), sweetbreads (*mollejas*), and a marvelous Argentine sausage called *chorizo.* Ask for your beef "*bien hecho*" if you want it well done, "*al punto*" if you prefer it medium and "*poco hecho*" if you like it rare. The bottom part of sirloin porterhouse is known as "*vacio*" and the flank is called "*matambre.*" Fish is also frequently available at some of the better restaurants. Portenos also like offal and most menus feature lamb's testicles (*creadillas),* intestines *(chinchulines*) and udder *(ubre).*

The Brazilian variety is a newcomer to Costa Rica.

In Nova Brescia, in the south of Brazil, a statue of a man barbecuing meat sits in the center of the town square. Folklore accounts for the depopulation of the town in the past few decades, from 150,000 people to about 30,000 as a product of townspeople going to every city in Brazil and to major cities worldwide to open *churrascarias* and share barbecue culture for profit.

Brazilian grilled-meat-on-a-skewer restaurants have come to a handful of major cities in the U.S. and Europe, but, to my knowledge, this is Costa Rica's first. Instant success of A

Churrascaria Brasileira will probably spawn more for the future. It is a lot of fun and offers variety and large amounts of nicely seasoned grilled flesh without wasting half eaten slabs.

The system is simple. Diners sit at a nicely set table with a placemat that shows a picture of a cow with six labeled body parts from which cuts of beef are served and lists five other cuts of chicken, pork and beef that complete the sacrificial offerings to us carnivorous gluttons. All the tenderloins, sirloins, prime ribs, flank steaks, filet mignons, buffalo hump pieces, chicken shoulders, chicken hearts, lamb and *linguica* (Portuguese-Brazilian sausage) are brought to your tables for offerings of chunks, pieces or slices. You leave the table only for trips to the salad bar or to the starch table of mashed potatoes, white rice or beans cooked with pork dice.

You are served a wide variety of beverages of your choosing from ice water to flavored martinis and sample meats until you cry or moan "uncle." A peppermill shaped two-tone wooden piece sits on each table. As long as you keep the green side turned up, waiters will present you with a never ending procession of meats. When you want to rest or quit, turn the wooden piece over with the red side, as in stop, facing upward.

In Lisbon, London, New York, Chicago and all across Brazil, you are likely to get veal and fish skewers as well. The lamb and chicken offerings are traditionally marinated for hours before roasting. The fattiest pieces of all the flesh are chosen to keep them juicy. Some leaner morsels are bacon wrapped. The beef pieces are basted with salt water often flavored with crushed garlic during cooking. The most vulnerable pieces to drying out are pork and chicken. *Chimichurri*, a sauce of finely chopped cilantro and garlic suspended in oil, serves as a remoistening dip for dry tidbits.

Like their cousins from the pampas of Argentina, Tico cattle are grass fed. Compared to corn fed U.S. beef, ours is chewier and tastier and the cuts are a little thinner and a lot less expensive in comparable scale restaurants. In California, grass fed beef is currently trendy, more expensive and favored for more flavor and less fat. Paradoxically, more fat usually equates with juicier and more flavorful, although experts contend that grass fed beef has an additional appealing fresh earthy flavor of its own.

The names of cuts also differ on opposite sides of borders. Most simply, filet mignon is the same tender buttock steak. A fillet of the eye is called *bife de lomo* and can cost more than mignon. *Lomo* is sirloin, very flavorful and a little chewy. *Bife de chorizo* is the always popular rump sirloin or porterhouse cut off the rib. *Lomito* is tenderloin, a little more tender and a little less tasty. *Bife de Costilla* is a t-bone. *Churrasco* is a cheaper cut of meat, usually marinated, such as brisket, chuck, shank, or a lesser sirloin. It is frequently the most flavorful (to my palate) and toughest of all the cuts.

Baby beef is not veal, but rather a different sirloin from an 800 pound younger rather than a 1200 pound older steer. It is devoid of marble (very little fat) and tends to be bland, soft and dry. It is very popular, but to me the texture is like a mixture of pulverized beef and cooked cereal in need of more liquid. Can it be mushy and dry at the same time (ox y moron)?

The *parrillas* will often offer beef parts or products, *anchuras*, as appetizers or as part of a mixed grill for two people. Components often include intestines, kidneys, sausage, sweetbreads and udder.

Every December the aroma and squeals from rural Alajuela pig farms desist. The winds of Christmas arrive as if to freshen the air, and a local flock of guinea fowl vanishes about a week before Christmas. All over South America, but especially in Colombia, a ten to fifteen pound whole roast suckling pig is the centerpiece of the Christmas dinner table. Glazed hams are also becoming more popular south of the Rio Grande. There is no doubt in my mind that more pork goes for tamale filling in Costa Rica in December than for anything else. In my pueblo, as in the rest of the country, two or even three generations form a family assembly line to mass produce the plantain leaf wrapped packets of pork filled corn meal cakes. Neighbors give each other boxes of Christmas tamales and add a critique of preparation skills to the usual front gate gossip. “Cecelia’s spices are amazing....Martha left out the raisins this year.... Sandra ties the most perfect twine patterns....Josefina doesn’t use fresh corn, does she?”

What happens to the rest of the pig? The belly goes for bacon. The skin crisps in *chicharrone* cauldrons. The ribs are roasted and barbecued, often along with chickens over coffeewood fires, *a la leña*.

In the sixties, I lived in a Chinese neighborhood in San Francisco and bore witness to the adage that Cantonese people eat every part of the pig except the squeal. Cheeks, snouts, ears, tails, kidneys, livers, hearts, spleens, stomachs, skin, feet and intestines appeared in thick rice soups, clay pot stews, on dim sum platters, at banquet tables, in braised sauces over rice and on buffets of cold hors d'oeuvres. Dozens of puns emerged from that neighborhood playing on the words "offal" and "awful."

What happens to those nether parts here? In Brazil, feijoada, the national dish, is a black bean stew containing at least five different pig parts to gain respectability and authenticity. They include combinations of feet, necks, snouts, ears, tails, jowls, blood sausage and, rarely, intestines. Here in Costa Rica, I haven't seen stomach or intestine used. I assume they make their way into sausage, hot dogs and cold cuts. The tripe used in *mondongo* and *menudo* is from cows. A Brasilera friend bought frozen "cleaned" pig intestines for her *feijoada*, but still boiled and recleaned them before using them in the stew-pot.

In the southern U.S., chitterlings, or "chitlins", are made from pig intestines. They were part of the slave culture in which the masters gave their slaves only those pig parts they wouldn't eat. Pig intestines have a vile smell and require hours to clean and prepare. Now, they survive nearly exclusively as nostalgia food. In Salley, South Carolina, the annual Chitlin' Strut is a festival that attracts about 75,000 people. In Guatemala, I had a bowl of *revolcaldo*, pig offal stew including intestines and brain. It wasn't bad, but one of my sons noted that "caldo' meant soup-pot and "revol" was short for revolting. In Jamaica, there is a dish of beans and pickled pig tails. Methinks all food preferences are cultural.

Have you ever eaten *frito*? It is the same word as "fried" but is a common and much loved fiesta food served in dozens of pueblo festivals across Costa Rica. It is pig part and organ meat stew without intestines - a dice of heart, lung, liver, spleen, kidneys, ears, nose, cheeks, ribs, rind, neck, head and feet. Kidneys need to be pre-boiled and rinsed a few times before dicing. The dice is marinated in lemon juice, mashed garlic, oregano, thyme, sliced onion, salt and black pepper, for several hours or overnight. Dry and brown the dice in a skillet, put it in a pot with any unabsorbed leftover marinade, enough water to cover, optional diced aromatic vegetables - carrot, onion, celery stalks with leaves, sweet pepper, tomato, plantain, zucchini, cubed potato and *guineos*. It is seasoned with salt and *salsa Lizano* to taste. I thought the last ingredient was a cut up guinea hen. I didn't know why, but I guessed that was where the pre-Christmas flock went. My ear for Spanish led me astray. The cook who shared her recipe for *frito* with me said "*guineos*" – green bananas, not "guineas"-- guinea hens. The stew-pot is then simmered for about two hours until everything is tender (an extra half hour if you live at an altitude higher than the Central Valley). All the different meats, despite their disparate origin, become tender and tasty. If you are tempted to make it, when it is finished, refrigerate it overnight, remove the top layer of white fat, reheat, garnish with chopped cilantro and serve with white rice.

In the Veneto region in Italy, *frito misto* is a nearly comparable winter dish revered by old timers and eschewed by modern youth.

If you are offal challenged, you can go to the December *chicharrone* festival in Puriscal, west of Ciudad Colón, for festival food, arts and crafts, music and a horse parade. More pork? What is a cardiologist doing, writing about pork? What is the skinny about pork?

The truth is that pork is not "the other white meat." Neither is it poison for your heart.

Pork is a red meat. Redness is defined by the USDA according to the amount of a muscle substance called myoglobin. The US Pork Board began the "other white meat" ad campaign in 1987 Pork and beef have much more myoglobin than white meats chicken or fish. Veal has less than pork when it is very young. That pork lightens when it is cooked, is irrelevant. All meats carry saturated fats, the unhealthy kind. Poly or mono saturated fats are better for you. Artificially produced trans-fats are worse. Different cuts of pork can be lean or fatty. Pork tenderloin has similar fat content as skinless chicken breast. Boneless loin roast and extra lean ham are similar to sirloin chops in fat content, but bacon and sausage are much worse. Nice juicy pork chops are juicy because they have lots of fat, as are marbleized steaks.

What about pork ribs? When I make them at home, I boil off a lot of the fat before they go into the oven. It also makes them "fall off the bone tender." The largest ribs are Chinese country style with a generous chunk of meat attached. The red color is due to artificial dye. They are moderately fatty. Next come spareribs from the side of the animal. They are perhaps the tastiest but have more bone and less meat than the others. Ribs from the back, called baby-backs, have less bone and more meat. The tiniest with only a little piece of bone or cartilage are the Chinese dim sum variety steamed in black bean sauce. I love their flavor but they are about half fat. Fortunately for those with little restraint, the servings are tiny.

Ropa Vieja is scrumptious stew of tomatoes, onions, green peppers, potatoes, green olives, diced red chili peppers and shredded beef that melted in my mouth when I first ventured into a Latino restaurant at age 16. It was called "old clothes," since the meat was first simmered for hours, cooled in its juices, then shredded by hand like old rags and re-cooked before serving. I loved it then and still enjoy it now.

Chapter 8
Poultry

More than Chicken

Not hardly a chicken in every pot, but Costa Rica does have a chicken eatery or three in every hamlet. Beyond the obvious, there are often menu surprises. Soda J & M in San Rafael de Alajuela offers fabulous ribs *a la leña* (roasted over wood) as well. Rosti Pollo has a lunch time buffet and a nice tortilla soup. Power Chicken in Belén's Ribera Mall food court had paella for the bargain price of less than $4 per serving with salad every Friday, Saturday and Sunday. It may have been too much of a bargain. Power Chicken closed in 2007. Rock and Roll Pollo, despite its name, does not feature chicken alone. It is an American-Canadian sports bar and restaurant. Among its daily specials is a hefty plate of tender and tasty barbecued ribs St Louis style on Thursdays for a little less than $7 served with mashed potatoes and a salad. Even the Colonel at KFC now offers baked potatoes, a relative rarity here.

Roasted and fried chickens are everywhere. Roasted or fried chicken quarters cost about $1.50. Grilled breast (*petcha)* is a little more expensive and is served with a variety of sauces. Breaded and fried, it is called *petcha de pollo empanizada. Muslo,* dark meat thigh and leg are the cheaper by a tad than white meat breast and wing. Chicken with rice and chicken soup are common.

Turkey, duck, goose, quail, Cornish hen, etc. are frozen holiday imports only.

Chapter 9
Seafood

A sweet old man asked me if I had a Dick Tracy decoder ring to help him figure out how to buy fish in a Tico market or order it in a restaurant. With nothing to *show*, I resorted to *tell*.

Preparation:

Ahumado = smoked

Al ajillo = in a sauce of butter and garlic

A la plancha = grilled or broiled

Al horno = baked

Al vapor = steamed

Budin de pescado = fish baked in a pudding of sour cream, tomato sauce and grated cheese, usually layered with tortillas

Ceviche = small cubes of fish marinated raw (pickled) in lime juice with cilantro and diced red onion and red pepper

Colombiano = baked in coconut milk

Croquetas de pescado or buñuelos = fish croquettes or fritters made with bread crumbs, flour and/or mashed potatoes plus onions, garlic, salt and pepper, fried crispy.

Empanizada = breaded and fried

En papillote = inside a packet made of parchment or aluminum foil

Entero = the whole fish, scaled and gutted, and fried with the head, tail and fins intact

Entero sin espinas = the same as entero, but boneless

Escabeche = cooked in a vinegar and pickling spice-like sauce

Frito = fried

Rollo de pescado = fish sausage made with bread crumbs or potatoes, diced hard boiled eggs, cream and spices mashed together and boiled or steamed in cheese cloth, chilled and sliced

Salsa crema or salsa blanca = in a white cream sauce

Salsa de mariscos = in a seafood sauce, usually white with small shrimp, octopus, squid, baby crabs or clams in any combination

Salsa negra = served in or with a sauce of puréed black beans, often thinned with white wine and/or cream

Sopa de mariscos = pieces of filleted fish in clear broth, often served with white rice on the side.

Veracruzana = a sauce for fish of tomato, onion, capers and olives

Fish :

***Atún*, tuna.** The four kinds of tuna caught or bought here are, by size, 1) black tuna (atún negro), smaller than 15 pounds, 2) skipjack tuna (barrilete) about twice as large, 3) Yellowfin tuna (atún aleta amarilla) up to 300 pounds and 4) the even larger big eye tuna (atún ojo grande). Steaks, crusted in herbs and cracked pepper and seared with the inside rare are the most fashionable and tasty

***Bobo*, mullet.** Every fisherman has seen mullet jump clear out of the water in coastal rivers, bays and along beaches. They hardly ever bite on lures or bait, presumably because they are vegetarians. They are quite good smoked

***Bonito*, bonita**. Bonita are smaller, less prized cousins of both tuna and mackerel. They have dark oily flesh, suitable for canning. Dried and shaved bonita flakes are the essence of Japanese broth and sauces.

***Congrio*, conger eel.** In all likelihood, conger eel is not a single beast, but one of as many as 150 related species that inhabit all the world's warm and temperate oceans where there are lots of food fish and rocks. What they have in common is that they are long, large, devoid of scales, look more like a sleek fish than an eel, have sharp teeth and an upper overbite. I include them because you should buy some if they ever appear in a local market or on a restaurant menu. They are among the sweetest and tastiest of all fish. If you visit Santiago, Chile, try congrio in one of the seafood restaurants in the Mercado Central.

***Corvina*, sea bass.** Far and away the most common fish in Costa Rica, it is a bargain – similar but smaller and a little milder than the very pricey Chilean sea bass that is featured in fine restaurants in the States.

***Dorado*, mahi-mahi or dolphin fish.** Lean, firm, white, moist and versatile, it runs close behind congrio on my hit parade. It is beautiful in the water and a good fighting fish.

***Guaho*, wahoo, ono.** A gamefish from the south coast of the Pacific all the way to Hawaii where it is prized, it is very good eating.

***Guapote*, rainbow bass.** The featured catch in Lake Arenal, catch and release after securing one in the fish box for lunch. It is delicate and delicious.

Halibut. Not commercially fished here but just as good as its Canadian cousins. A friend catches them fairly often near Golfito.

***Jurel*, amberjack and big eye trevally**. It is edible, but not valued.

***Marlin*, marlin.** Most commonly found in fish counters in markets, marlin ceviche and fillets are quite tasty and cheap.

***Mero*.** The grouper may be a monster of the deep reefs. Although it is not a common food fish in Costa Rica, it makes moist tasty fillcts and steaks.

***Muchaca*.** A common river fish with too many bones, locals near Tortuguero often make soup out of it. Despite the inconvenience of separating the flesh from the bones, it makes lovely ceviche.

***Pargo*, snapper.** We have several varieties of this very good eating red or yellow fish. Many upscale restaurants feature it with or ahead of corvina.

***Pescaito*, tiny fish or whitebait.** Eaten whole, floured and fried or in omelettes worldwide.

***Pejerreyes*, sardine or anchovy sized fish.** A little bigger, therefore usually stripped of backbone and head before frying.

***Pez espada*, swordfish.** Firm steaks are tasty, but dry out quickly if overcooked.

***Pez gallo*, rooster fish**. Catch and release.

***Pez vela*, sail fish.** Catch and release.

Picuda, barracuda. Good smoked and decent grilled.

***Robolo*, snook.** More fun to catch than to eat, but the smaller ones are pretty tasty when fillets are lightly breaded and pan fries. Snook is not often smoked in Costa Rica. The delicious smoked snook, prized in South Africa, is not snook at all, but actually a kind of barracuda.

***Salmon*, salmon**. Not local, but quite popular, Salmon is imported from Chile and Washington.

***Sierra*, mackerel.** Oily and dark fleshed along the back, but less so than Atlantic varieties - Spanish, king and chub mackerel, it is best prepared Japanese style, fillets with skin intact, covered with sea salt on skin side and crisped close to hot flames or grill. This Pacific variety is often cooked over simple fires along the beaches of Mexico, scaled, gutted, rubbed with salt and garlic, skewered until the skin is crackled and served with a tortilla and wedge of lime.

***Tarpon*, tarpon.** Catch and release.

***Tiburon*, shark.** If bled when caught and washed well, many types are good eating, prepared like swordfish.

***Tilapia*, tilapia.** Fillets in the markets are from this farm raised delicate fish used for ceviche, grilling and frying. Tilapia Park just east of Turrucares town center is a great place for kids to catch fish from an artificial pond. Line and bait are less than a dollar. Scaled and gutted fish go for market prices. Open weekends and holidays.

***Trucha*, trout.** Introduced to mountain streams fifty plus years ago in southern Costa Rica and farm raised at higher altitudes, they are usually pan fried with the skin on.

***Vieja*, red perch.** A freshwater river croppy type good for frying or grilling.

Other Seafood:

Clams *(almejas*). The two most common types of clam are the sweet brown shelled razor clams (*navajuelas)*, best when steamed, and the tiny Manila morsels found in soups, stews and seafood sauces.

Black clams (*chuchecas)*. These charcoal grey gastropods make elegant *ceviche*. Their firm flesh and rich taste remind me of cold-water abalone.

Mussels *(mejiones)*. Blue-black mussels seem to inhabit rocky coasts everywhere, and arrive fresh in all seafood markets. Costa Rica is no exception. They don't seem to come steamed, only in seafood soups, stews and sauces.

Crabs *(congrejos)*. Local crabs are very small and hardly worth the effort to dissect in search of meat. Their presence in seafood soups and stews is as a flavoring agent and decoration.

Shrimp *(camarones)*. From tiny "pinkies" to "jumbos", shrimp are on most menus grilled in garlic butter, fried in cornmeal crumbs and/or shredded coconut, steamed, in white cream sauce with or without coconut milk, in salads or in cocktails. The small ones make popular *ceviche*. Shrimp with rice, *arroz con camarones,* is a Tico favorite.

Lobster *(langosta).* Spiny or rock lobsters are in great demand for exportation. Therefore, they are pricey and not always available. By local custom, they are nearly always split longitudinally and grilled. The result is tasty but invariably a little overcooked. You might try to get the chef to steam them, *al vapor,* but many are reluctant. Even a little tough and dry from grilling, they are quite nice. In local unpretentious restaurants, a lobster dinner with fries and salad costs about $10. In upscale restaurants that cater to tourists and expats, expect to pay three times the price.

Squid *(calamares).* Despite great popularity in Mexico and South America, squid dishes are less common in Costa Rica. Battered and deep fried squid is common in Italian restaurants and sports bars. Squid and rice, *arroz con camarones,* is the other major presentation.

Octopus *(pulpo).* Octopus is ubiquitous and delicious in Costa Rica. It is a major ingredient in seafood stews, soups, sauces and *ceviche*. Fabulous octopus *carpaccio* can be found in a number of elegant Italian restaurants. Octopus cocktails and salads are also available on occasion.

Oysters *(ostiones).* Oysters on the half shell are expensive by local standards. I haven't seen oyster *ceviche* or oyster stew closer to the equator than Guatemala to the north or Peru to the south. My guess is that there are two reasons: local waters are too warm so they have to be flown in on ice to stay alive at great expense and that Ticos have never developed a taste for them.

Chapter 10
Dairy Products

Costa Rica produces excellent milk and milk products from grass-fed cattle. The standard containers are 2 % fat which means that a little more than half the fat has been removed. The taste is very good. It is clearly dated for freshness and refrigeration is not a problem. In days long past, Ticos relied on sweetened condensed milk or unsweetened evaporated milk. Both still are used, particularly in dessert making and in coffee or hot chocolate instead of cream. Indeed, the country's most famous cake uses all the milk forms in the standard recipe and bears the name ***tres leches*** – three milks. Another popular sweet might be called *dos leches* – two milks, but instead it goes by ***dulce de leche*** – sweet milk. Equal amounts of condensed and evaporated milk are slowly simmered for about half an hour until the mixture thickens and caramelizes to the color of straw. Like caramel candy, it is a children's favorite.

Local cheese making surprises visitors for its variety and economy. As in all of Latin America, fresh salty white cheese is a staple. In addition, local companies make cheddar, chèvre, emmenthaler, feta, gorgonzola, Gouda, manchego, mozzarella, palmito, parmesan, processed American, smoked provolone, Swiss and Turialba. No, it is not as good as quality imports, but some of it is decent. Palmito is like string cheese but it strips off in flat ribbons and is much more flavorful.

Local yogurt, cream cheese, heavy cream and sour cream are fine. The sour cream, *natilla,* deserves mention. It has a light consistency and pleasant tartness like a sour cream-*crème frâiche* mixture. When exposed to air, it turns slightly pink, but remains edible.

Ice cream, *(helado)* Vanilla, rum raisin, strawberry, blackberry, tutti frutti, chocolate, peanut and coconut seem to be the common flavors. Generally good quality and low prices make it a favorite. Milkshakes, sundaes, banana splits, ice cream cakes and ice cream sodas can be found in the fancier chain outlets, along with frozen yogurt.

Chapter 11
Herbs and Spices

If you were to combine fusion, international and Nuevo Latino restaurants in Costa Rica, you might have a list that includes 40% of the upper-end venues. Their recipes probably include nearly all the herbs and spices of the sophisticated culinary world from allspice to za'atar. Typical Tico home cooking, however, uses a limited number as listed below.

	Common	Occasional	Rare
Achiote	XX		
Allspice	XX		
Anis			XX
Basil		XX	
Black Pepper	XX		
Caraway			XX
Chile Pepper		XX	
Cilantro	XX		
Cinnamon	XX		
Clove	XX		
Coriander			XX
Cumin	XX		
Dill		XX	
Fennel seed			XX
Garlic	XX		
Ginger	XX		
Lemongrass		XX	
Marjoram		XX	
Mint	XX		
Nutmeg	XX		
Oregano	XX		
Paprika	XX		
Parsley	XX		
Rosemary		XX	
Saffron			XX
Taragon	XX		

	Common	Occasional	Rare
Thyme	XX		
Turmeric		XX	
Vanilla	XX		

Chapter 12
Sauces

Avocado sauce *(guacamole)* Locally, avocado is mashed, dashed with lime juice and seasoned with a little diced sweet red pepper and onion, salt and cilantro leaves. The Venezuelan version, *guasacaca,* adds hot pepper, oil and vinegar. In Colombia, avocado sauce becomes *ají de huevo,* hot pepper eggs. Mashed avocado is mixed with mashed and diced hard-boiled eggs, chili pepper, vinegar, cilantro and scallions.

Béchamel, mushroom, tomato sauces and a host of vinaigrettes are the same as they are in North America.

Chilean sauce *(salsa chilena)* Tomatoes, onions, lemon juice, beef stock and oil are blended into a creamy dressing for cold dishes and for a side sauce with cooked meats, hot or cold.

Creole sauce *(salsa criolla)* This sauce of tomato, onion, garlic, sweet pepper, lime or lemon juice, oil and vinegar is blended into mayonnaise consistency and used to dress broiled or roasted meats and cold dishes.

Garlic sauce *(salsa de ajo)* Note that *ajo* (garlic) and *ají*(hot pepper) in one of the next items are very different words. *Al ajillo* means cooked in or dressed with garlic butter and *ajiaco,* an unrelated word, is Cuban and Colombian meat and vegetable stew.

Green tomato sauce *(salsa de tomatillo)* Only in Mexican restaurants or canned on supermarket shelves, can you find Mexico's favorite sauce in Costa Rica. *Tomatillos* are tart tasty little green tomatoes that grow in husks and never turn red.

Hot pepper sauce *Salsa de ají* is a hot pepper sauce in Colombia and Ecuador. In Mexico it is called *ixni-pec, môhlo de pimento* in Brazil and Chile's red pepper sauce is *salsa de ají Colorado.*

Mayonnaise Mayonnaise, alone or mixed with ketchup, seems to be the dressing of choice for Ticos on fries, hamburgers, hot dogs, sandwiches, salads, *ceviche,* fried fish or shrimp and fried chicken.

Orange sauce (*salsa de naranja)* Though not very common, orange sauce in Costa Rica is usually made with scrumptious tart Seville oranges. It usually is served with pork, chicken, fish or duck.

Pesto Classic Italian pesto comes in jars, plastic packs and cans. It is common in Italian restaurants. The local variation substitutes cilantro, ground peanuts and lime juice for basil, pine nuts and lemon juice.

Salsa cruda *Salsa cruda* is a sauce made from uncooked ingredients. Tomato, onion, sweet pepper and cilantro leaves are chopped into small pieces, but not blended smooth. Salt, pepper and a little sugar give it a flavor reminiscent of North American jarred "Chili Sauce."

Salsa frita *Salsa frita* is a sauce wherein the components are cooked in hot oil.

Salsa oscura *Salsa oscuro* is a dark opaque sauce as opposed to a clear sauce – *salsa clara,* or a white sauce – *salsa blanco.*

Salsa picante Be it a red hot liquid like Tabasco or local equivalents (Alfarro, Lizano) or diced red chili peppers and onions in vinegar, *salsa picante* is hot sauce.

Salsa verde See green tomato sauce above. Green vinaigrettes made with cilantro are the local equivalent of parsley vinaigrettes elsewhere.

Chapter 13
Beverages

Batidos Similar to smoothies, *batidos* are made in a blender from fresh fruit, ice, and milk or water. If the fruit is tart, the drink is sweetened. Blackberry, pineapple, guava, passion fruit, *guanabana,* strawberry, *cas* and melon are but a few of the flavors available in season.

Beer *(cerveza)* German style beer comes from local breweries Bavaria and Imperial. It may not be up to snuff with Belgian, Dutch or Czech beer, but it is superior to many North American brands. Here, beer comes with a glass of ice cubes. Local dark beer is *Bavaria oscura.* Beer may be available on tap. Imported beers are common.

Carbonated drinks If you ask for soda, you will get club soda. Coca Cola, Pepsi Cola, Sprite, Seven Up, Canada Dry, Everest and Fanta are the major players. Dr. Pepper, Orange Crush and Hires Root Beer are occasional residents on supermarket shelves.

Chicha de maiz and **Chicha morada** Fermented corn is the basis of *chicha,* a punch drink which can be golden, slightly alcoholic and beer-like. The Peruvian version uses purple corn and the drink, *chicha morada,* looks like a deep burgundy wine cooler with bits of diced fruit floating on top, like *sangria. Chicha de maiz* is a punch using local pale yellow cracked corn as a base.

Coffee Costa Rican coffee is rich, aromatic and cheap. Many brands can be brewed very strong without any bitterness. The Arabica beans grow well on shaded slopes from 2500 feet to about 5500 feet. The Colombian government sued Costa Rica in International Court in The Hague because of bumper stickers that read “Juan Valdéz drinks Costa Rican coffee.” They lost. Ticos are rightfully proud of their coffee. Most of them brew it weaker than North American standards, and add sugar and milk. Local brands of good quality sell for about $2 per pound.

Fruit juices The fifty or sixty tropical fruits that are sold in Mesoamerican markets can all be squeezed, puréed or blended into drinks with or without the addition of sugar, water or milk.

Guaro *Guaro* is a colorless cheap but potent alcoholic drink consumed mostly by local creators of imaginative mixed drinks, weekend revelers and impoverished alcoholics.

Horchata *Horchata* is a blended rice, ground peanut and milk drink, flavoured with cinnamon, vanilla and sugar.

Maté This caffeine rich tea is made by steeping cured and crushed leaves of the *Ilex paraguayensis* (Paraguayan holly). Argentina's national beverage, it is sipped through a silver tube called a *bombilla*. *Maté* is bitter and the huge caffeine content makes hearts pound and hands tremble. The *maté* cup is a gourd that fits in the hand, adorned with silver and gold trim.

Milk Tico children drink white, chocolate flavored and red milk. The red syrup is sweet and called "kola," but it is not caffeinated. Costa Rica produces excellent milk. The standard containers are 2 % fat which means that a little more than half the fat has been removed. The taste is very good. It is clearly dated for freshness and refrigeration is not a problem. Goat's milk is sold locally and some old timers advocate mare's milk for newborns.

Pinolillo Toasted corn kernels finely ground give this drink a gritty texture. Add to the corn a little cocoa powder, sugar and milk to make *pinolillo*. More popular in Nicaragua than Costa Rica, Nicaraguans are sometimes called "*pinoleros*."

Resbaldera This "slippery drink" is made with rice and barley boiled in water, blended with milk and flavored with the same sweet red "cola" syrup that kids put in milk, cinnamon, nutmeg and sugar.

Rompope Canary-yellow eggnog in bottles has a little alcohol in it, usually rum. It is less common in Costa Rica than in Mexico

.

Water Public water is safe throughout the country. Untreated well water is rich in minerals that form water spots if allowed to dry on cars and windows.

Whiskey After *guaro,* local people seem to prefer rum, tequila and Scotch among the "hard" drinks. Excessive alcohol consumption is a national problem and drunk driving is particularly bad on weekend nights.

Wine Good Costa Rican wine is an oxymoron. The local sweet fruit wines leave a lot to be desired. Fairly priced Chilean and Argentinean wines are more than adequate. For a little more money, wines from Australia, California, France, Italy, South Africa and Spain are available. Many sparkling wines grace the same shelves.

Chapter 14
Restaurants

Five stars - Worth a special trip, Excellent

Bacchus

When Bacchus opened its doors in 2005, it became an instant hit. It received accolades from two publications and my dear friends, the very discriminating Costa Rica Women's Group Out to Lunch Bunch. We joined the parade and were surprised at the smooth execution of a challenging menu, service without the frenzy of newness and joy on the faces of the two charming host-owners, originally from Turino, and the diners. A new restaurant in a large space replete with excellent art on the walls is a very costly undertaking without a high probability for success. Where was the anxiety? Very impressive indeed.

We returned with friends a few months later and again to answer readers' questions about the spun sugar golden sombreros and baskets on and around some of the exotic desserts. Both visits were flawless. In the past few years, we dined there again several times and with a larger party for dinner. On all occasions, every dish met expectations. Extraordinary flavors? No, just solid, consistent, nicely prepared very good food. Neither were the presentations on a par with the desserts, but they were lovely, not ostentatious.

Devoid of radical changes, the menu continues to evolve slowly. One transient addition, the Mediterranean salad, speaks volumes for simplicity and perfection. A bed of crisp cool arugula supports about twenty warm and juicy shrimp and shaved Reggiano Parmigiano cheese, tossed with light citrus vinaigrette. Other salads ($5.50-5.75) include Caesar, caprese, Greek and smoked trout with an oregano vinaigrette.

French onion ($4.75) or Spanish gazpacho ($4.50) soups, eggplant parmigiana ($4.50) and filo pastry stuffed with chicken breast, mushroom, spinach, onion and gorgonzola are hot options as appetizers. The cold selection adds the following to the mix: corvina ceviche ($5.70), Norwegian salmon carpaccio ($5.95) or tartar ($6.50), steak carpaccio with balsamic vinaigrette and parmesan cheese ($5.75), octopus tossed with black olives and celery in a creamy sauce ($6.25) and a king size antipasto for a table of three or four ($12.50).

Pasta dishes fall into two categories, fresh and dry. The fresh group contains well made ravioli, fettuccini, cannelloni, gnocchi and lasagna; the dry are spaghetti, linguini, bucatini and penne. Prices range from $5.75 to $7.25. The house special linguini with smoked salmon in a white wine cream sauce is delicate and delicious as are potato and spinach gnocchi in a creamy gorgonzola sauce. For anchovy lovers, the spaghetti a la puttanesca fits the bill.

There is nothing wrong with the bread basket but I urge you to try an order of focaccia with rosemary ($3.50) with whatever starter you choose. Another gem of pure simplicity – paper thin pizza dough dusted with salt and rosemary, drizzled with olive oil, blistered in a hot oven. They are so good you might want to figure on an order for every two or three people in your party. The other focaccia, calzone and pizza choices offer nice combinations of fine ingredients for an average of $5.50 and fill two entire menu pages. Even after so many visits, I have yet to try a pizza because the pasta and main courses are so pleasing.

The seafood and meat main courses cost $8 to about $12 and include prawns, salmon, trout, duck, pork and steak in a variety of very nice combinations and presentations. The least expensive is an entire grilled trout with spinach salad and baked potato for $7.50. The most expensive is duck breast in a port reduction on yellow polenta with a ragout of mushrooms (12.75). Steak tartar is often a challenge. The beef needs to be coarsely ground to be tender without becoming a paste. The seasoning should be bold but not overpowering the steak flavor. Bacchus' rendition is simple, straight forward and perfect for my preference. The texture and taste of the meat, dressed in a nice Dijonaise mustard sauce, brings smiles to my old bearded face. It comes with cucumber slices and crisp fries($9). The salmon in tarragon butter ($9) is very nicely done, moist and delicately flavored. The house fricassee of large prawns, mushrooms and grilled baby zucchini in a garlic white wine sauce with spinach quiche is a justified favorite ($11.50).

Our usual scenario is to eat too many focaccia wedges with salad or appetizer followed by a pasta dish or main course. Invariably none of us has room for dessert, so we order one for the table with the appropriate number of spoons to taste. When there are four of us, the chef adds an extra fried pastry half moon filled with hot apple compote so we can have one each as part of "Ravioli fritos rellenos de compota de manzana verde, con salsa de toffee y helado de vanilla." A golden lacy spun sugar basket cradles the half moons, the ice cream and the caramel sauce ($3.75). The other six dessert choices are quite good as well.

All these goodies reside in a nice location. The old road from Escazú to Santa Ana is two way to the east and divides into two one way streets as it goes west. As you reach the divide from Escazú, turn right. From Santa Ana, left. Take the road north until it ends. The restaurant is around the corner to the left. Inside, past the desk, the décor is stunning, rustic oversized red painted brick floors, earth tone walls from pale beige on the garden walls to shades of butterscotch and papaya, oriental rugs, striking colors from the beautiful Max Rojas paintings and Burgundy accents on the tables. Cane ceilings, a two meter wide garden and wrap-around patio complete the tasteful environs.

Bakea

If I were to believe what other reviewers have written, Bakea on 7th Street and 11th Avenue in San Jose's Barrio Amón would be unparalled in our entire country. Frommer's Guide, the New York Times, Jeffrey Van Fleet's Three perfect Days in Costa Rica and Eliot Greenspan's guide glow effusively. Savvy Dining.com grades alphabetically and gave Bakea an A for food, service, hospitality, etc. with a C only for value. No other restaurant did as well. So off we four went, all with enthusiasm and I with a little skepticism. My skepticism was completely unfounded. What a jewel! Among Barrio Amón's old coffee baron posh residences, Bakea is right at home.

Inside the entrance, you feel as though you have crossed the threshold of the house of an art collector with a sharp eye for pleasing, if a little off-beat, modern art. Small, separate dining rooms branch off the corridor in both directions with one or two tables in each, adding to the feeling of privacy and personalized attention. One room is a cozy lounge, another leads to a small, street level al fresco ivy clad terrace. The corridor ends in the largest dining area, fronting the kitchen. The dominant piece of art is a whimsical painting of a table setting, a knife and fork surrounding a black shoe.

We shared our nonsmoking room with two diners at a second table across the room. Both tables had their own attentive server. With our drinks, we were served complimentary mushroom toasts to sooth us as we read and reread the menu's bountiful mouthwatering choices. We lingered over our selections, not for a lack of appealing choices, but for the frustration of having to skip so many enticing options.

We settled for smoked salmon carpaccio ($6) and Camembert triangles served with a sauce of blackberry purée and reduced port ($4.75) first, then thick pork steak in a vanilla flavored port sauce over roasted mini potatoes ($14), scallops in an incredible dark curry over saffron and mascarpone flavored risotto, ($14), grilled chicken breast on a bed of two colored taglierini bathed in an orange and ginger sauce ($7) and tilapia atop dark angel hair pasta sauced with a mango, coconut, vegetable curry ($12). All of the fabulous sauces were innovative, superbly balanced, yet never overwhelming the flavor of the main ingredient. Each of us left nary a drop on the plate.

Curries are spice blends that vary from family-to-family around the world and are as distinctive as signatures. For the scallop dish, the chef uses her uncle's spice blend that he ships from Durban, South Africa with a little balsamic vinegar and orange juice to make a simple, subtle, clean, intoxicating sauce that compliments the scallops and perfect risotto. Anything more intrusive would have diminished the other two mainstays. The ginger and orange sauce was more dominant, but perfectly suited to the less subtle and blander chicken and pasta. We shared a bottle of Chilean merlot and finished with a dessert sampler and rich coffee. With the addition of an extra ten per cent for seamless service, the bill for four reached $106. A comparable meal in New York or San Francisco, if you were so lucky as to find one, would cost three to five times the price.

My dilemma for a second visit was the number of guests. The more diners, the more courses to sample, but such exquisite preparations require a level of attention that becomes difficult in the noisy party atmosphere of a large group. I opted rather to return with only Joan, to savor another two main courses, a pair of appetizers and desserts. I would also forego my anonymity this once for a chance to talk to the chef.

We returned at the end of a week day lunchtime as a score of well dressed French men and women were attacking their main courses with gusto and murmurs of praise. Every seat was occupied except our corner table for two. We opted for the daily special, a bargain for a starter, main course and beverage for $6. Joan had a house salad with a delicate dressing of oil, a dash of balsamic vinegar and citrus zest. I began with silky pumpkin soup, upon which floated a drop of homemade cayenne pepper oil. Our main courses were grilled chicken breasts, done only moments beyond the disappearance of pink centers, tender and juicy, atop a ragout of portobello and porcini mushrooms and roasted sweet red peppers. The lick-the-plate sauce was mustard, honey, thyme, rosemary and rice vinegar perfection. We mopped up every last drop with lightly toasted herbed focaccio. Then came two remarkable desserts - Joan had caramelized figs with mild rosemary ice cream ($3.50), and I had hot out of the oven rich chocolate tart filled with mashed ripe banana, surrounded by macadamia nut brittle and adorned with a scoop of butterscotch ice cream ($5). The by-the-glass red table wine was a full bodied fruity Italian ($2).

Chef Camille Ratton-Perez came to our table before dessert. She is charming, articulate, youthful and as attractive as her presentations. She trained at Cordon Bleu in Paris, later joined their faculty, worked in a restaurant in Lyons and a patisserie in Aix before returning to her native Costa Rica. Her style incorporates those of Paris, the south of France, the greater Mediterranean basin, Costa Rica and the currently, very chic Basque region, plus select ingredients from French Polynesia, Southeast Asia, South Africa, etc. If it weren't for our system's maximum five star system I would give her a well deserved sixth and hang a gold medallion on a red, white and blue ribbon around her neck. There are many more expensive restaurants around, but none finer. How fortunate we are that she practices her art where we live. I can hardly wait to see what she does next when she changes her seasonal menu.

In 2007, three years after our first pair of visits, Bakea is thriving. The chef has her own cookbook on sale at the restaurant. She instituted sushi night on Wednesdays.

The new lunch menu contains a "light" set of offerings for diet conscious diners, replete with dietician details. Iced gazpacho comes with basil flavored croutons and diced vegetables ($4) and roasted red pepper soup is topped with eggplant caviar ($4.75). Eight paninis and eight gourmet wraps, all creatively combined, cost $4-4.50.

Seven salad plates with unique combinations that include roast beef, chicken breast, grilled tuna, goat cheese, fruits and vegetables cost $8 on average.

From the dinner a la carte menu, come an assortment of exotic appetizers that average $7.50 each. The least expensive ($5) is a velvety goat cheese cream of diced tomatoes and basil. The most costly ($15) is an antipasto of cold cuts, cheeses and vegetables. Pastas and risottos are all lavish combinations of great ingredients ($12.50-14.50). Two favorites are fresh pasta with rabbit in a perfect sauce of wild mushrooms and herbs and creamy risotto in a three mushroom sauce of portobellos, Paris mushrooms and porcinis.

Main courses include Parisian steak frite, red tuna in vanilla-soy sauce, medallions of tenderloin dressed in gorgonzola and chicken Bengali all for $10-16. New Zealand lamb chops served with cherry tomatoes candied in lavender honey is $23.

There is yet another menu, the seasonal menu that changes as often as monthly. The desserts are great. Yes, the prices have risen in three years. They have gone from below the norm for upscale locations to competitive. Bakea remains a great destination that is no more expensive than most other five star restaurants. The quality remains priceless.

She plans to open a bakery and coffee shop across from Auto Mercsdo on the Sata Ana – Belén road, by early 2008.

Telephone: 221-1051

Cerutti

Will the real Cerutti please stand up (and take a bow). Our first trip to Cerutti was shortly after we arrived in Costa Rica. I was impressed and dismayed. My host, a local business mogul, was mistaken for a Gringo since we were chattering away in English. He was given an English menu along with the rest of us. The restaurant is very expensive to begin with, but the prices were even higher than they were on the Spanish language rendition. He asked for and received the second version to confirm his suspicion. One of the daily specials was very similar to a usual menu item which he really liked. He touted it to the rest of us. Three of our six ordered it and enjoyed every morsel. He alone saw the bill. He paid with the forced smile of a poker player trying to win a bluff after shoving all his chips in the pot. The menu item was $18, the special $29, he confided to me at a later date. In 2004, when I wrote a food and restaurant column for AM Costa Rica, I received additional reader complaints about overcharges on wine that were at variance with the wine list, server recommendations to try this or that special for substantially more money than the dish the customer first asked for with nary a word about cost and a "padded" bill that may have been an innocent error. Not a single person ever complained about the lovely dining room, professional and attentive service or superb food. After a few exposés by reviewers, the shenanigans seem to have disappeared and Cerutti can take its place among Costa Rica's elite dining experiences, romantic, professional and delicious.

It is open for lunch and dinner every day but Tuesday with the same menu for both meals. If you savor privacy and intimacy, Monday lunch is least busy. Centrally located in Escazú, just up the hill to the left of Scotia Bank, on the left side of the road, there is parking down the driveway between it and the massive Chinese restaurant.

My wife and I chose a Monday lunch after a hectic week and chose to dine à deux. We were in the mood for romantic and it was.

A friend of hers knew of our plans and ordered wine by phone for us as her gift. The owner, server and assistant greeted us with warmth and respectful formality. Our orders received, the assistant brought us water, tuna canapés, delicious brown olives, warm crusty bread and bread sticks along with our wine.

Joan began with a hot appetizer, a thin omelet bathed in white truffle oil and slightly sweet Italian cheese sauce ($11). It was fantastic. Her main course of tagliatelle with porcini mushroom sauce ($16.25) was also very good. The pasta was al dente and sauce rich and earthy. I sampled both early and often.

I settled for one of the two daily specials – *corvina* fillet enclosed in parchment paper and aluminum foil along with thyme, tarragon, white wine, vinegar flavored onion slices and butter. Moist, tender, delicate and luscious, it was perfect. Piped mashed potatoes came on the side ($15.75, same as the menu price). A cappuccino ($3) brought the total to $57. Costly for Costa Rica and probably the most expensive Italian restaurant in the country, but for the elegance and a romantic interlude, it seemed well worth it on a drizzly Monday in October.

Telephone: 228-4611

Da Marco

It used to be called Ristorante Grand Canal. Its new name is Da Marco after the chef, Marco De Nando.

Since it was my third and final trip to Da Marco before writing my original column, I chanced discovery and engaged the chef in conversation on our way out. Contrary to what a waiter had told my wife a few weeks before, the chef was from Verona, not Genoa. He proudly showed us a print of an ancient amphitheater in his hometown hung next to the kitchen door.

My assessment: charm, very good food, large portions and moderately priced, particularly when compared to friend Jorge's or my first choices for 2004.

The indoor and outdoor eating areas are both more rustic and comfortable than formal or elegant. The two-tone earth color tile floor and pale walls reflect soft light from the blue-grey Venetian glass fixtures. Antique prints and contemporary Grand Canal paintings cover the only wall that isn't glass looking out on garden. The waiters were relaxed, friendly and attentive. Dress was casual. The other diners all appeared pleased to be there. Each seemed to smile with approval at the platters of food as they were carried to other tables.

Is it romantic? Yes and no. If romantic to you means regal with grand floral arrangements and violins, no. If it means charming, cozy and conducive to intimate conversation, then, by all means, yes.

Marvelous steaks, large and tender, as good as any steakhouse offering we have tried and less expensive than most. I particularly liked mine draped in melted gorgonzola for $7. Sixteen different rich risottos including one made with squid and its ink complement choices of 27 pastas.

Of the pastas, only taglierini with jumbo shrimp or lobster cost more; the remaining 25 range from $4 to $6.50, including ravioli and gnocchi. The meat dishes cost from $5 for chicken in a pesto cream to $9 for steak in brandy or porcini mushroom sauces. Seafood dishes begin at $6 for corvina a la plancha and top out for lobster or jumbo prawns at $11.

Thirty or so pizzas range from $4 to $6. The ones with prosciutto di Parma or seafood are $6 to $ 10. Also: six salads - $2.50 to $4, six carpaccios all for $7, 15 reasonable antipasti and desserts that I never had the capacity to try.

By now, you might know that I like eggplant and anchovies. So, among my favorites were an appetizer of paper thin slices of eggplant in a tomato parmigiano sauce ($3) and al dente penne with a rich putanesca (in the style of prostitutes) sauce of tomato, capers, black olives and real anchovies ($4). A friend loved the salmon and avocado fettucini. The closest thing to a criticism was that the portion size of the mixture of Italian national cheeses was too small for everyone to taste each of the four varieties. Other portions, especially the pastas, were very large.

As we were leaving a large event, someone overheard that we were going to Da Marco for dinner. “May we join you?” “How about us?” Twenty three of us arrived nearly simultaneously, without reservations. Fortunately it was on a weekday evening during a downpour. They accommodated us graciously and efficiently. The food was superb. We all had our piping hot meals in front of us in about forty minutes. Bravos for the entire staff.

After many more visits, Da Marco has become my favorite combination of outstanding food, seamless service, great value and very comfortable surroundings.

Location: From the highway to Ciudad Colón heading west, turn left at the flashing yellow light just past where four lanes narrow to two, towards Piedades. On the right side as you climb the hill you will see the building and its sign. Enter to the right of the building and park past the gatekeeper for a hotel.

Telephone: 282-4103

Di Bartolo

How was it possible to extol the virtues of a single Italian restaurant when we are blessed with so many? My first excellent Italian meal was at Pecora Nera on The Caribbean coast. Other exemplary Italian dining experiences in addition to La Pecora Nera have been at the following restaurants: the always crowded and reliable Sole e Pepe; Tutti Li with its Palermo pizza, homemade pasta and cannoli; Da Marco in Piedades with its fine chef from Verona — my current (2007) favorite; Il Pepperoni in Belén — decent food and the best chocolate ice cream in the land; Il Retorno with a fine chef back at the helm; Bacchus, instantly a hit, in Santa Ana; and elegant Cerruti in Escazu. Yes, I missed a few.

Di Bartolo, number 1 at the end of 2004 had no garden, no view, no valet parking, no flowers, no music and no open kitchen. It was hidden in a minuscule u-shaped mall named Formosa Mall in Guachipelin, on the main road, about 800 meters north of the Escazú intersection, across from a pet shop. Accolades for chef and owner Carlo Di Bartolo. His café Di Bartolo stood taller than the prodigious competition in 2004. His restaurant has held fast since and remains among the top few. My wife favors his veal dishes over the expanding and improving competition.

The design is remarkable. Three shallow store fronts in a cramped parking lot have been altered to make a charming three-room restaurant. The chairs are wrought iron backed with pale green soft cushions. The tablecloths are textured ivory. The china and walls carry through the same colors. In the room with the charred wooden opening to the pizza oven, even the attractive still life paintings carry forward green and wrought iron elements and apple red to match the design on the plates. The flatware is large and sleek. The oversized water and wine goblets appear to be quality crystal. Pasta and entrée plates are transparent blue and silver and dessert plates opaque white. Adjacent to the fine art selection are enough framed proclamations of merit to do justice to the Wizard of Oz. The dark wooden wine bottle display cases add to the decor.

Carlo is from Syracusa in southeastern Sicily, once second only to Athens in the Greek empire, and still a grand city, an ancient and modern mélange with a proud culinary tradition. Ever accommodating, he welcomes diners with his soft smile, blue-gray eyes and perfect English. For all of his years in Guachipelin, he continues to win awards and the highest rating of any Italian restaurant in the country: five forks from the government.

Cuisine begins with ingredients. We were served nothing less than garden perfect vegetables, fine cheeses from gorgonzola to parmiggiano reggiano, crimini mushrooms tempered with dried porcinis from Italy, fresh hearts of palm, tender veal from Europe and truffles. The generous menu begins with cold first courses; eight salads, five excellent carpaccios, shrimp, salmon or mushroom cocktails, antipasti, mixed plates and more, 23 in all and all large enough to split, 11 other hot first courses include gratins of mushroom and asparagus, eggplant parmigiana, bruschettas and focaccios Nearly half of the 20 pastas are homemade, including the raviolis, gnocchi and lasagnas. Three are creamy risottos. The exceptional risotto with mushrooms and truffles is a shade less than $11. The same dish with roast duck was a daily special for $28.50. One guest appraised the risotto without duck as the best he has ever eaten, and he dines all over the world on a regular basis. The tagliatelle with seafood is full of great stuff: tiny scallop-shaped bivalves, tender octopus and large crisp prawns and enough crushed red pepper flakes to add zest. The ravioli dish of triangles stuffed with sage, truffles, cheese, butter and mushroom on prosciutto is probably the most celebrated menu item.

Specialty meats include steaks, lamb and duck. Add 16 thin crusted pizzas and 10 artistic desserts and an entire page of daily specials, and you have a sumptuous dining experience. The pizzas contain all the usual players plus Italian cold cuts, real sausage, buffalo mozzarella, smoked provolone, smoked salmon and Greek olives. Among the desserts are a pastry filled with pine nuts, pecans and almonds, another filled with almond cream and Amaretto and a classic apple tart.

With a few days notice, Chef Di Bartolo offered to make my favorites, Sicilian deep fried rice balls - *arancini* and *cannoli*, the signature dessert of Sicily. One special, veal scaloppini, was as good as I have ever eaten and melt-in-the-mouth tender. Pan-seared tuna was a tad dry, not quite sashimi quality, the only minor flaw of the day.

Even the homemade ice cream, fresh fruit and yogurt based, dressed in strawberries and blackberries, showed painstaking preparation and attention to detail. Good coffee — even the decaffeinated — and a nice selection of Italian wines by the copious glass.

The servers are bright, neat, attentive, yet unobtrusive. Waits between courses allow for leisurely relaxation without impatience. The clientele are well dressed and obviously affluent, yet visitors in shorts and t-shirts were treated with respect.

The prices are high for Costa Rica, but a bargain compared to comparable offerings in any other culture. The prices are a little less than Cerutti, but higher than the other upscale Italian restaurants.

Hours are noon to 11 p.m. Monday to Saturday and noon to 6 p.m. on Sunday.

Telephone: 282-2800

El Grano De Oro

Close friends and family stay at our house in the country when they come to Costa Rica. For those with whom we are less intimate, we recommend El Grano De Oro Hotel. It is on a quiet treelined street (Calle 30) a little less than two blocks north of Paseo Colón and a short walk to La Sabana Park and its art museum. This 1900 coverted plantation mansion had 35 cozy affordable rooms prior to its recent remodel/expansion, and a staff reknowned for its hospitality. It oozes charm out of every cranny, antique, sconce and tropical plant. It may be the perfect place to start a honeymoon trip around the country. I warn all prospective guests, however, of two caveats. First, there are a lot of stairs, and second, the restaurant is so good and so romantic, you may never care to eat anywhere else.

When I wrote a weekly food column and restaurant review for A M Costa Rica, readers inundated me with their preferences and El Grano De Oro garnered the most accolades. The cuisine is a marvelous fusion of traditional old European style with tropical seafood, fruits, nuts and vegetables.

Among readers' favorites were camembert cheese drizzled with a sauce made from fresh local blackberries, Mediterranean salad, a pair of filet mignons sandwiching gorgonzola, seabass crusted with macadamia nuts in orange sauce, tenderloin with reduced brandy sauce and fresh pears, tilapia in herb sauce, macadamia pancakes for breakfast and the famous El Grano De Oro Pie, made with layered chocolate mousse, Bavarian cream and coffee mousse. Since the 2007 makeover, the menu has changed somewhat and the prices are a little higher. Still the prices are lower than nearly all the other grand restaurants in town.

The lovely indoor restaurant off the main lobby is a fine choice. The lush jungle-like garden court is gone. The new garden restaurant will take a while for the plants to mature. The comfortable U-shaped banquettes and tasteful adornments make the new restaurant very attractive and comfortable.

Open every day from 6 AM to 10 PM

Telephone: 255-3322

Jürgen's

Now in its eleventh year, Jürgen's is a great restaurant with an imaginative menu. Presentations are bold and beautiful. Ingredients are fabulous. Sauces complement, not dominate.

Jürgen F. Mormels opened his restaurant in 1997 with two decades of experience in the local market and an eye for classic recipes, perfect service and comfortable artistic décor. The restaurant became a member of the Châine des Rôtisseurs, an exclusive catering service and an importer of truffles, caviar and more than a hundred different wines from all the major wine-producing areas of the world. Talented Victor Jiménez ascended to the role of chef and deserves praise. Its complementary past reputation has been "old world European ... a clubby hangout for leaders of the state ... a conservative menu ... French." In my estimation, it is much more, combining classic techniques with tropical produce.

For starters, let me suggest sea bass and salmon *carpaccio* served with fresh dill and olives ($9), London club salad ($5), classic French onion soup *gratinée* ($7) or oysters Rockerfeller ($ 14.50, only served at dinner).

In addition to very well executed specials of lamb and prawns that we ate one holiday eve , I can recommend the surf and turf of beef tenderloin, fresh fish and shrimp in béarnaise sauce ($19.50), Chilean *churrasco* served with baked potato and a tortilla basket full of bean salad ($17.50) and grilled tenderloin with your choice of three sauces, Parisienne mushroom and butter, béarnaise, or green pepper sauce ($16.75).

From the sea, *corvina* "Veronica," broiled seabass in a white wine sauce with grapes and apples ($14.50), tilapia in Dijon mustard sauce ($13) and prawns Provençal ($25) are tempting. Or from the boot, how about *gnocchi* in truffle cream sauce ($11) , *fettuccini al pesto* ($9) or chicken stuffed spinach and cheese, dressed in a mushroom tomato sauce ($13.50).

The restaurant is part of the boutique hotel, Hotel Jade, on the quiet tree-lined boulevard, 250 meters north from the large Subaru dealership in Los Yoses, west of the San Pedro roundabout.

Leave room, if you can, for an elaborate dessert, if only to share. With so much fine food and drink, is the atmosphere conducive to lingering and savoring? Absolutely. The chairs are cushioned and backs upholstered. Colors are relaxing earth tones. The walls are decorated with elegant, but mellow, works of art. The music is soft and serene. Even the ceiling is latticed. Fresh flowers and lovely table settings frost the cake.

The service is worthy of special mention. It is very attentive, but never intrusive. The waiters are very knowledgeable and helpful. You never need ask for a waterglass refill or appropriate utensil.

Hours: Lunch Monday to Friday noon to 2:30
Dinner Monday to Saturday 6pm to 11
Internet site: www.hotelboutiquejade.com
Telephone: 283-2239

Le Chandelier

A marvelous old mansion in San Pedro – Los Yoses is the site of this romantic and tasteful French restaurant. Multiple small dimly lit rooms adorned with ceramics, art and antiques add to the feel of intimacy. Charming waiters are helpful, professionally genteel but not stodgy or pretentious. We celebrated our tenth wedding anniversary *à deux* in flickering candlelight. With our beverage, house wine by the glass, came small plates of excellent pâté on a plate with minimal decorative greens, peeled grapefruit section and small warm rolls with creamy butter. The elegant but not gaudy presentation presaged all the dishes that passed on their way to our or a nearby table.

We then ordered a pair of specials not on the menu, rack of lamb for my wife and half of a roast duck in passion fruit sauce for me. Next came another unsolicited surprise, salads of romaine lettuce and finely sliced herbs and onions, dressed with velvety delicate vinaigrette. Rising from the greens was a dramatic single crisp fried greaseless banana chip - paper thin and as long as the entire fruit. It harkened the feather in Yankee Doodle's cap.

Her lamb was, in her words, "the very best" she has eaten in Costa Rica despite admirable competition from the likes of Beirut, Lubnan, Jürgen's and L'Ile de France, all of which were quite good. My Long Island duckling, was boned and a little over-roasted but not dry. The benefit of extra oven time was crispy skin. The sauce was a wonderful slightly tart compliment to the tasty duck. It paired better with the duck than most sweet sauces of orange, apple or cherry. Stuffed green tubular squash with a potato purée cap completed the savory lovely dish. Courses were well spaced. We had luxurious interludes to savor the evening without ever approaching impatience. Desserts were crème brûlée and a liqueur tasting of berries and violets called "perfect love" for her and chocolate mousse and tawny port for me. The brûlée was good, smooth under a torched crisp but not burnt top hat. The mousse was made with Swiss chocolate, rich in flavor and barely sweetened (Owner Claudio Dubuis came here from Switzerland many years ago). The texture was perfect. Below it was a small scoop of rich vanilla ice cream, on the side lighter than foam Chantilly cream. Mousse is so common worldwide and so nearly uniform, it may seem like a stretch to rhapsodize about a single rendition, but we both agreed that it was the best either of us had ever devoured.

The special main courses were more expensive than most of the menu comparables. With complimentary pâté and salad courses, we skipped appetizers despite delicious sounding offerings such as escargot in puff pastry or onion soup with a camembert gratinée. Other main course options included an enormous chateaubriand, jumbo shrimp, salmon and my gourmet friend David Fogg's favorite dish in all of Costa Rica, steak with four sauces. The total bill was less than $80.

A New York Times reviewer once called Le Chandelier the "classiest" restaurant in Costa Rica.

From the traffic circle under the peripheral highway in San Pedro, head west along the service road of the highway past the large ICE building. The road ends at a fence a block later. Take the mandatory right followed by the first left, and the well marked restaurant will appear on the left side of the street two blocks ahead.

Lunch 11:30 -2:30, dinner 6:30 – 11
Telephone: 225-3980

L' Ile de France

The charming Hotel Bergerac in Los Yoses is home to the classical French restaurant L' Ile de France. The restaurant, a bastion of traditional haute cuisine, reserved charm, elegant accoutrements, consistency, formality and a very good wine list, performs admirably under the auspices of long-time chef Jeane Claude Fromont.

He also performs well. His trips from the kitchen into the diningroom to greet regulars or revered guests fill the room with smiles, hugs, cheek kisses, animation and an aura of so-happy-to-see-you pleasure. His starched, spotless white jacket assuredly hangs on a hook by the kitchen door to be donned only on the way out.

The hotel is on a quiet side street in the embassy neighborhood of Los Yoses. To enter the restaurant, you walk through the gate and small garden, up a few stairs to the right of the lobby entrance. Considering the proximity of the tables to each other, the tastefully appointed room is remarkable serene. Little conversation rises above the mellow soft music, a mixture of old French ballads and lyrical classical, except when the chef is holding court. Then, a cacophony of delighted French voices compete with Ravel and Debussy.

The candle-lit tables were full on both weekday visits, yet there seemed to be no pressure to move people along to make space for a second sitting. The waiters moved effortlessly in narrow spaces through and among the diners, causing minimal distraction. Old hands, I presume. They were unruffled and helpful even with the most trying patrons, exhibiting considerable knowledge of ingredients to help with course and wine selections.

During two visits with a different couple each time, I was fortunate enough to taste six different appetizers, seven main courses and five desserts. The positive side: all the presentations were flawless, the flavors well prepared in traditional manner and the ingredients exceptional, including salad greens and baby vegetables.

What was lacking? In all honesty, nothing. What I missed, however, was a little flair, some risky combinations, integration of tropical produce or even a hint of Mesoamerica in the excellent, but very predictable cuisine. My guess is that if we had the patrons vote, I would be in a very small minority seeking a telltale sign that we weren't dining in France – possibly a minority of one.

The blanquette de veau was tender in a proper mushroom cream. The daily special of duckling in orange sauce was moist, and the sauce delicately balanced between mild citric acidity and sweet. Steak in a green peppercorn sauce arrived to the exact doneness ordered. It was tender and flavorful. Large prawns, dressed in garlic and tomato, were done expertly so as to avoid overwhelming the delicate prawn flavor. Nor were they overcooked. Similar adeptness was evident when neither salmon nor prawns stewed in a basil sauce were overdone.

There are about a dozen different ways to prepare Coquilles Saint-Jacques. Most often, scallops in a creamy white wine and mushroom sauce are served in scallop shells with a hint of brown crust atop the dish from a brief final trip under the broiler. Alternately, many restaurants serve the dish in a ramekin or puff pastry shell. Since coquille means shell, I am always a little surprised when a ramekin is used. There is nothing wrong with the choice. Similarly, the absence of a trip under the broiler is not wrong. One subtle difference for which I praise chef Fromont is the choice of tarragon as opposed to thyme as the dominant herb in the wine sauce. The barely perceptible licorice flavor works very well with the sweetness of the scallops.

The homemade rabbit pâté, with a hint of cognac flavor, was yet another success. The escargot was classic. We devoured an entire basket of good French bread salvaging every last drop of garlic butter.

The wine choices both times were fine: a white Cote du Rhone and a red Carmen Reservado 2000.

No letdown with the desserts. Profiteroles, fruit tart and crepes in orange sauce drew murmurs of satisfaction.

The question of value always arises when the price is in our maximum range. The answer is dependant on so many variables. Expensive, yes, but not prohibitive. Virtually identical food in a similar restaurant in Paris or New York would cost at least three times the price

Is it a worthy destination for special occasions? Yes, depending on the occasion. It may be a little formal to be romantic and a little staid for frivolity.

Congratulations to chef Fromont and his staff. I suspect that they have mastered exactly what they want their restaurant to be, a flawless, seamless traditional French culinary experience rather than an adventure.

Sample prices : rabbit pâté $7.50, country salad $7, escargot $9, Coquilles Saint-Jacques $10, traditional onion soup gratinée $7.75, chicken breast sauté $12, duckling in orange sauce $19, duck confit $18, veal stew in mushroom sauce $14.50, steaks $16-17, lamb chops $25, fish dishes $13-14, salmon and shrimp $19, shrimp alone $22 and mid range wine $19-35 per bottle. Thus, an appetizer, main course, a bottle of wine, dessert and coffee will cost about $50 per person.

Open Monday through Saturday from 6PM to 10PM.

Telephone: 283-5812

Park Café

What would you say if I told you that Merryl Streep had come to Costa Rica and was acting in the Little Theater, that Seji Osawa was the new conductor of the Costa Rican Symphony or that Tiger Woods had left the PGA tour to play and teach at Los Reyes ? You might laugh. You might think that I have gone over the edge. Well, don't laugh when I tell you that a world famous chef with three previous restaurants that garnered two Michelin stars in London, another Michelin star in Cannes and Conde Naste's inclusion in the world's best 65 restaurants in Marrakech, has a restaurant in San Jose. Yes it is true. Richard Neat was on top of the international culinary world when he came to Costa Rica to be with Louise.

Louise is the vivacious, articulate and charming ex-pat who runs a fabulous Indian, Indonesian and British antique gallery in Sabana Norte. Her antiques include large columns carved out of wood more than 100 years old, formidable hoary doors, tables, tranquil Buddhas, ornate chests and a wide variety of smaller pieces. They are exhibited around the perimeter of a lovely garden under a roof, sharing space with seating for about 25 lovers of fine cuisine for Richard's art form, gorgeous plates of international medleys.

Thank you, Louise for giving the gourmands of Costa Rica such an opportunity, and thank you Richard for performing your mastery in our presence. May the two of you have a lasting relationship here in Costa Rica.

The menu consists of only eight to ten choices, all elaborate fusion tapas, a little larger than the typical Spanish variety, about the size of a nouvelle main course. All eight cost about $10. One will suffice for a light lunch. Two might be necessary for a heartier appetite. Each presentation is worthy of a digital camera shot. To my utter delight, I got to go to Park Café with eleven women, members of the Women's Club of Costa Rica's "Out to Lunch Bunch", who honor me by inviting me along to their monthly forays into the restaurant world. Lucky me, I got to see nearly all the menu items and sample bits of at least half.

Among the sighs of pleasure, were questions about this sauce and that garnish that required four of us to taste half a teaspoon of *babaganoush* sauce, to decide if the extra little kick was from raw garlic, *wasabi* or horse radish. We never reached consensus, but loved trying. The plate in question was tataki* of tuna, seared on the outside and barely cooked inside served with the purée of *babaganoush* and shrimp coated with a light tempura batter amidst paper thin roasted herb leaves and vegetable strips. The most popular order among the women was brochette of shrimp with Thai mango salad and crispy fried calamari rings. Second was smoked salmon, asparagus and a shot glass of *gazpacho*. Sweet velvety cold corn "soup" was the sauce under a filet of pork that created a marriage of heavenly flavors. Other offerings combined braised veal tongue with homemade pasta and mustard sauce, wild mushroom ravioli with a sauce of basil and asparagus and, for dessert, a plate of five tiny original tastees. The ladies particularly liked the caramel soufflé with roasted banana and a delicate thousand layer strawberry pastry.

Of course there is a grand assortment of fine wine and creative alcoholic beverages to accompany the plates.

My wife and a close friend share the same birthday. Four of us went to Park Café the night before they closed for Easter week, to celebrate. Richard outdid himself by creating some new dishes out of perishable great ingredients that might not have survived the holiday. We gladly partook in his experiments, which were sensational. His charm and boyish glee accompanied the masterpieces to the table. Some may reach the ever-evolving menu. To add to the unforgettable evening, he served a surprise candled cake with an astonishing array of desserts coupled with a late harvest dessert wine.

If you desire comfortable elegance in a romantic setting with world-class cuisine at affordable prices, try Park Café. You won't be disappointed.

To get there turn north off the road that flanks the north side of the park. The restaurant sits about 150 meters on the left. Reservations are recommended.

Open for lunch and dinner

Telephone: 290-6324. Fax ; 296 5720.

E-mail: richardneat@hotmail.com

* Tatki of tuna is a roll of sushi-grade tuna, coated with freshly ground black pepper corns, seared and seasoned with a sauce that often includes, ginger, soy, sesame oil and anise.

Tin Jo

Tin Jo is one of my favorite restaurants in Costa Rica. It does so many different things very well, that each time I go, it seems like a new adventure. The food emanates from nearly all of Asia and each dish is at least as good as its counterpart in restaurants specializing in just a single cuisine. Tin Jo doesn't offer as much variety of Indian dishes as Taj Mahal, but the four curries, *samosas* (potato fritters) and *pakoras* (vegetable fritters in garbanzo batter) are nearly on a par. In similar fashion, Bangkok offers many more Thai choices than Tin Jo, but none compare for flavor or presentation. The sushi assortment is stellar. Add to these offerings four *teriyakis,* nine Chinese stir fries, three sizzling rice dishes, three kinds of *mu shu*, two sweet and sour sauce dishes, *satay*, *guo tie (*pot stickers), an array of Chinese and Thai noodle dishes, *cha giao (*Vietnamese spring rolls*),* Philippine *adobo,* two menu pages of vegetarian choices, mouth-watering specials and many more, and you can imagine why it differs from visit to visit. Just choosing a small bowl of soup to start, presents challenging decision-making – hearty wantan, tangy hot and sour, Japanese *miso shiru,* Thai chicken soup with lemongrass and coconut milk or Thai seafood soup. Among the Thai and Chinese salads, there is even a Costa Rican classic.

Fine Chinese restaurants often serve seafood or other delectables in edible baskets. Tin Jo's are made from two kinds of Costa Rican root vegetable matchsticks, an outer layer of *yuca* and an inner layer of *tiquisque*. Fried to golden crispiness, they are nearly as tasty as their contents.

I have fallen into one rut at Tin Jo. Despite a well chosen wine list, and wine offerings by the glass ($4) and half liter ($13), I always order a half liter of ice tea with lemongrass and ginger. The other ice tea offerings are tempting – jasmine and passion fruit, mint and tamarind, basil and lemon, Indian *chai*. Even the table water is mint hinted. The waiter starts you off with complimentary nibbles (fried noodle pieces and sliced cucumber and red pepper plus a dipping sauce) while you change your mind about what to order as you turn each page.

If you don't plan ahead and leave a little room for dessert, you will miss out on the likes of tongue-tingling sorbets, ginger figs, passion fruit cream tart or lychees over ice. Most dishes are $7.50 -$15.

Care for more variety? You can sit in the Indonesian room with its kites, masks and bamboo placemats; the beautifully simple Japanese room with rice paper light fixtures and faux *shoji* panels that slide open, exposing the children's playroom off the Chinese room; the "Rest of Asia Room," with black woven reed place mats and burgundy napkins, weathered frescos near the ceiling by the entrance depicting Thai musician and dancers and Laotian shadow puppets; or the Chinese central room dominated by two large colorful modernistic masks on the far wall, which, on closer scrutiny, are made up of golf balls, tees and other links things on the right, and a mélange of brushes, paints and other art supplies on the left. They represent the original owners and their hobbies, golfer Joseph and artist Rose.

Their daughter, Maria, and her husband Robert run the restaurant. They are among the most generous and caring people anywhere, supporting the arts, giving to worthy charities, and, prior to returning to Costa Rica, helping needy people all over Asia. Robert speaks nearly every language in Asia in addition to his native English and, of course, Spanish.

From the floor manger Johnny, to the waiters and doorman, the staff is courteous, pleasant, helpful and very attentive. Despite grace and perfection on all accounts, Tin Jo's elegance is soft, understated and very comfortable.

There is a parking garage two doors past the entrance.

Avenue 11 between 6th and 8th streets.

Open every day at 11:30AM. Closes at 10 PM Sunday-Thursday, 11 PM Friday and Saturday and 3-5:30 PM weekdays.

Telephone 221-7605

Restaurants omitted because of cost

This small group of restaurants caters to upscale resort goers and people on expense accounts at prices well above the norm for all the other culinary choices, on average more than $50 per person for appetizer, main course, dessert and coffee. Although they may deserve four or five stars each, they haven't been reviewed since they are out of the range of easy affordability for most diners, despite the fact that they cost less than comparable venues abroad.

Capital Grill in San Antonio de Escazú

Di Mare in the Four Seasons Resort

El Mirador in Jacó

La Laguna del Cocodrilo Bistro in Tamarindo

Mirador Valle Azul in San Antonio de Escazú

Nuevo Latino Los Sueños Resort

Papagayo in the Four Seasons Resort

Four Stars – Very Good,

Even by International Standards

Bohemia

We are blessed with a wide assortment of Peruvian eateries from humble sodas to fancy emporia. The least fashionable (euphemism for "a little grungy"), and probably the least expensive of the lot, Inti Raymi in Alajuela serves decent food. Of the three Machu Picchu venues, Santa Ana is the smartest followed by San Pedro, but the original in a bad San Jose neighborhood off Paseo Colón seems to be the most fun, more raucous, least formal and the food seems be a skosh better, probably because of added Damon Runyonesque nostalgia. Both Inka Grills and Chancay in Itskatzú are good but the blue ribbon for first place has to go to Barrio Escalante's Bohemia.

Inside the entrance, you are in the foyer of a posh old mansion, at the base of a grand stairway. Off to the right is the bar and restaurant, understated elegance. Between the street and front door and in the back are areas for al fresco dining.

The food goes beyond standard Peruvian with imaginative ingredients and presentations. Traditional cuisine incorporates all kinds and colors of potatoes and corn unknown to outsiders, with hot chili peppers, Spanish, Chinese and Japanese overtones and Latin American variety. At Bohemia, regional accents are also honored. Tastes are enhanced to lofty levels and presentations are stunning.

The plates, platters and bowls are heavy ceramic vessels in earthy colors, befitting large portions for hearty diners. Robust flavors are a match. While you digest the menu, sip on a sangria-like purple corn and diced fruit drink, seasoned with a little clove and cinnamon. It is called *chicha morada*. You might even nibble on a warm mini-*croissant* or dinner roll while selecting a first course. In coastal Peru, starting with *ceviche* is almost a ritual like saying grace. Unlike our Costa Rican version, it packs a little heat and comes surrounded by sweet potatoes, sliced onion and Andean corn. Options other than *ceviche* of sea bass include shrimp, octopus and squid alone or in combinations.

A Japanese influenced variation on the *ceviche* theme is Peruvian *tiradito,* thin strips, not chunks of fish, marinated in lime juice garlic, cilantro and salt, served with corn but without onion or sweet potato. Sea bass, salmon, octopus or any combination are the *tiradito* option .

The appetizers are filling, so you should talk your dinnermate into ordering a *causa,* the cold mashed potato pie first course that rivals *ceviche* in popularity, particularly in the heat of lowland Peruvian summer. What tops the potatoes are any of the following: mixed seafood, octopus and black olives, sea bass and shrimp.

Some like it hot, particularly in the mountains. *Huancaina papas* are warm potatoes covered with creamy white sauce enlivened with chili peppers. Another warm appetizer is shrimp *ceviche flambé* flamed in Vodka. Other starters include carpaccios and Caesar salads.

Of the two soups I have tasted, *parihuela* and *chupe de camarrones,* both are delicious and filling. The former is similar to Mediterranean seafood soup from Italy, Turkey or France, but with Peruvian heat and spice, lots of good seafood and a wine accented broth. The latter is a richer orange colored thicker soup. The color derives from shrimp shells sautéed in butter, the texture from cream, egg and cheese; plus barely cooked corn kernels and green peas, a poached egg and half a dozen large shrimp. I haven't tasted the rice, risotto or pasta dishes, but regulars love them.

Main courses of fish, shrimp, steak and chicken are all very well executed and attractively presented. My wife's favorite is a mound of mashed yellow potatoes on a bed of incredible mango-ginger sauce, topped with six large shrimp called *camarrones Bohemia*. A popular chicken dish both here and in Peru is *aji de gallina* – red chili pepper chicken, shredded in a cream sauce with nuts and cheese. One of the steak dishes is *chufa* in origin, Chinese Peruvian (also called *chifa* or *chaufa).*

The tenderloin sauté is a multinational stir fry of steak strips in red chili pepper, soy sauce, tomatoes and onions.

For dessert, their *suspiro* is delicate and superior. The coffee is rich, but not bitter.

The waiters are professional and helpful. The restored mansion setting is lovely. Patrons are well dressed and almost reverent. More expensive than the competition, it is well worth it. First courses average about $7, soups $6-10, seafood pastas $10-11, main courses $9-20 and desserts $4.

The restaurant is in the middle of the block on the north side, five blocks east of Santa Teresita Church in Barrio Escalante. Street parking only. Open every day for lunch, closes at 5 PM on Sunday, 6:30 to 10:30 Monday through Saturday.

Telephone: 253-6348.

Café Mediterráneo

The absolute epitome of a popular café, Café Mediterráneo bubbles and bustles with animation, vitality, laughter, lots of people in small spaces, friendly harried waiters, substantial portions of well prepared nice ingredients and prices that are down to earth.

To get there, take the large street that runs west from La Sabana, the huge park and former airport, towards the American Embassy. Turn right (north) onto the small side street opposite Pali, the large supermarket. Immediately on your right is Café Mediterráneo, swarming like the entrance of a beehive. Inside, there is a nice little deli and a diningroom adorned with posters and typical café art. The clientele are yuppies and neighborhood-niks. Finding parking within a block can be a challenge.

Yes, the home-made pasta and thin crusted pizza alone are worth the trip, but a nice array of appetizers and main courses of fish, chicken, beef, pork and shellfish compete admirably with *haute* dinner houses that charge twice the price or more.

I asked a friend who lives nearby and eats there often to name a special dish or two, but I cut her short after she rattled off asparagus wrapped in prosciutto, lasagna, fettuccine al Fredo, pasta putanesca, pizza with porcinis, sea bass in seafood sauce and antipasto without taking a breath.

To give you a feel for costs, here is a sampler from various parts of the menu:

Minestrone soup $4, antipasto $8.50, Cesar salad $5, eggplant parmesan $5.50, pizza Marguerite, $5, caprese salad $6, calzone $6.50, porcini mushroom and parmesan pizza $8, spaghetti pomodoro $5, penne in pink vodka sauce $6, penne putanesca $6, fettuccini Alfredo $6, veal scaloppini with Serrano ham and smoked cheese $9, tenderloin of beef with green pepper sauce $10.50, chicken medallions in mushroom mustard sauce $9, corvine in white wine sauce $8, salmon in lemon sauce $9.50, jumbo prawns in Neapolitan tomato and oregano sauce $17, pecan pie with ice cream $3.50, creamy panna cotta with strawberries $3.

Neither romantic, nor the place to spend an evening or long lunchtime dining in serene leisure, it receives highest marks for café cuisine and authentic atmosphere.

Closed on Monday, It is otherwise open for lunch and dinner. The deli sells imported cheeses and *prosciutto.*

Telephone: 290-5850

Colbert

Jean-Baptiste Colbert (1619-1683) was minister of finance and commerce during the reign of Louis XIV. He was also the father of France's ship and canal building industries. Bordeaux burgeoned and La Rochelle and its shipyards essentially came to life with the maritime genesis. To this day, many regional culinary treats in French cookbooks bear the name Colbert — not only seafood and fish dishes, but also pumpkin and asparagus soup and escargot.

Joel Suirer was born in a town near La Rochelle 48 years ago. His mother claims that he began to help her cook soon after he learned to walk into the kitchen. An old hand, he entered cooking college in Tours at 15. He has been cooking ever since. Six years ago, he built his own restaurant. It sits on a barren windy hill, up Poas Mountain, 25 kilometers from Alajuela. Just 10 kilometers short of the volcano, take the right turnoff to La Paz Waterfalls and Vara Blanca. Six kilometers straight down the road, 400 meters past the La Paz marker (do not turn), Colbert looms naked except for beds of impatiens, behind a sign that emphatically declares ABIERTO in red. The other side of the sign, CERRADO, never faces the road except in the middle of the night. Suirer cooks three meals a day, seven days a week.

Up the long flight of concrete stairs, you enter a large, rustic diningroom with rough hewn beams, a central brick fireplace, many humble tables and few diners. The tablecloths are burgundy with white napkins and place covers, watched over by new wildflowers.

Fresh baked crusty loaves and a cheese display near the door add delicious aromas to the wood fire that burns when the clouds descend from the mountaintop, which must be often, since the trees are covered with bromeliads and other epiphytes. The room is glass enclosed on all but the kitchen side. Hummingbirds feed in sun or gloom. Maps of Costa Rica and France, a three fork La Nación review from four years ago and few prints hang from the walls. Brandies, aperitifs and digestifs sit across the room from a display of wines from Bordeaux and the Rhone Valley to Spain.

Tabletop signs proclaim the daily specials, smoked salmon appetizer, a cheese board, roasted pairs of quail, rabbit in a mustard-tomato sauce, baby goat in beer sauce and *pejibaye* soup. Complimentary tastes of pork pâté, Joel's mother's recipe, topped with a small slice of homemade cornichon or slices of cured Bayonne ham came to the table with warm crusty bread and sweet butter.

Our group of four ordered them all plus a baked-to-order puff pastry vol au vent topped with mushrooms and hearts of palm in a smooth savory cream sauce for our one vegetarian. The *pejibaye* soup was rich but not to excess. Too much cream reduction may render this purée too rich in other venues. No complaints on the other dishes. The rabbit was tender and sauce, classic. Crisp cooked *chayote* cubes and boiled small potatoes were perfectly uniform in size shape and doneness, the mark of a very caring and skillful kitchen. Salads were crisp, simple and well dressed with house creamy vinaigrette dressing. Crêpe Suzette and profiteroles disappeared without a trace. On another occasion, our experiences with chicken crêpes and pork slices in a Valencia orange sauce were as good.

On a third visit, I arrived for breakfast. The morning spread was less sophisticated but decent. The warm bread and rich coffee were just rewards. Afterwards, I blew my cover for the chance to ask the chef some questions and to see the kitchen, which was immaculate. After 27 years in Costa Rica with a Tica wife, he is a relaxed charmer with none of the Gallic pretentiousness I have seen in other French kitchens. Also missing are the kitchen staffers (except for a single prep person), tuxedoed waiters, patronizing greeter and haute prices. What an unusual, refreshing throwback experience.

In the age of celebrity French chefs on book tours, talk radio and television, trying to run multiple restaurants from afar, always seeking more stars from reviewers, we find Chef Suirer who bakes bread, makes his own fruit preserves, cooks all the meals and often helps greet and serve, with old fashion grace and humility as if we were guests in his home. There is no star system to do him justice. The notable well staffed kitchens on Paseo Colón and Los Yoses can out-fancy him with pomp, crystal, fine china, starched uniforms, wall hangings, costlier ingredients and florist arrangements. I doubt that any of them could match his work ethic and dedication to his restaurant and its patrons or his modest prices. He does the name "Colbert" proud.

When next I take visitors to Poas or La Paz, I always bring them to Colbert. After more than a dozen visits, not a single major disappointment.

Prices: Hot and cold appetizers, soups and fresh plates of pasta are all less about $4. Main courses: chicken and pork less than $4.50, fish less than $8 and steak and shrimp dishes about $9.50. Desserts are $2-4.

Telephone: 482-2776

Essencia

Chef Jose Lopez is a native son and local favorite. He left home to study French culinary artistry, returned to head a classic kitchen only to have the owner close the restaurant and leave the country. After stints on luxury liners, he partnered with two talented young men who are rising-stars in the boutique hotel business. Their combined efforts have created a romantic jewel in a gorgeous setting – the restaurant Essencia in Costeza Amarilla Art Lodge and Spa.

As you head west along the highway past Escazú and Santa Ana, the road narrows to two lanes, passes a flashing yellow light, descends a hill and crosses a small bridge. Almost immediately after the bridge, turn right into the entrance. As you cross a quaint second bridge and enter the parking area, notice the glorious vegetation and the mosaic emblem illuminated by flickering tiki torches. When you enter the art nouveau sanctum, take your time and notice the details from sconces, to lithographs, to sun catchers, to bold paintings, to 60's Bohemia and lovely antiques. To call itself an art lodge seems less pretentious when you are there.

The dining areas are subdivided into three levels in a horseshoe around the garden and are further broken up into more intimate partially separated spaces. Under an umbrella, a table sits in the garden. The table tops are mosaics and settings lovely.

Not to be outdone, the food is presented with superb artistry on a variety of colors and shapes of plates and stoneware. The servers are attentive and genteel. Ice water, two kinds of bread and aioli and hummus come to the table with a visually beautiful menu of paired sheets of transparent plastic enclosing pressed dried leaves and little sleeves with individual menu items inside.

The menu offers an eclectic variety of fusions. Among the long list of starters are Norwegian *graavlox*, Bavarian white sausage in brandy and Dijon mustard, yellow-fin tuna *Carpaccio Nikkei* with arugula and sweet garlic aioli, tuna and salmon marinated in a reduction of balsamic vinegar and soy sauce served with Israeli couscous and truffle scented liver pâté with sweet peppers, caramelized onions and a pistachio crust ($6.50-8). Well worth a try are Thai summer rolls, rice paper round logs, filled with savory shrimp and mushrooms, set on three complementary liquids, green herb essence, red chili oil and brown balsamic vinegar reduction.

Among my favorite main courses is a dish that epitomizes creative melding from different cuisines. Hawaiian-style mahi mahi oblong tenderloins, probably caught locally, are crusted with Japanese panko crumbs, fried to a crisp coat, dressed with reduced Chinese Hoisin sauce and served on a cold bed of *pad* Thai noodles. Many complex fusions go too far and don't work. This one is fine. From Brazil, comes *moqueca de carnarao,* shrimp sautéed in red pepper and cilantro seasoned coconut milk served on a bed of *faro*. Local snook is bathed in Thai curry and served over Japanese whole wheat noodles. Polynesian tuna over wild rice has an unusual vanilla and soy sauce. Pork tenderloin also comes with wild rice and a nice brown sauce that is called *mole poblano,* but doesn't taste like my memory of that Mexican sauce made with pumpkin seeds, unsweetened chocolate, smoked chili peppers and more. Other choices include New York strip steak in a red wine-mushroom sauce, Chicken *satay* in peanut sauce, Chilean salmon with mango chutney and marinated chuck roast with balsamic honey sauce ($11.50 – 14).

The desserts are equally creative and some combine two separate entities adjacent to each other on the same plate ($6.50).

Nice pairings include beggar's purse of crisp *filo* sheets forming a sack, filled with caramelized apples and toasted nuts, plus a crêpe with toffee sauce and strawberry mousse paired with key lime pie.

In the two years since the restaurant opened, Chef Lopez has fine tuned his dishes from merely good, to very good. Still, the cuisine has not quite achieved the excellence to which he aspires. Perhaps in time.

All in all, Essencia is a marvelous place to share a romantic, well prepared and beautifully presented creative meal.

Telephone: 203-7503 Hours: 6AM to 10PM except 9PM Sunday

E **Il Retorno**

Growing up in New England, I knew three brawny tall men named Alaimo, an all-Ivy power forward and two highschool linemen. When I met Tony D'Alaimo, the ebullient and acclaimed chef at Il Ritorno, I did a double take – short, mustached, not athletic and a look alike for the comical ceramic salt and pepper shaker holder on each table. His outgoing charm won us over in short order.

From where we sat, I could see past the wood burning pizza oven into the kitchen. Tony worked like a whirling dervish. As he completed each order, he strode into the dining room like a proud bantam rooster and greeted each doctor, lawyer and senator by title and name. He received warm greetings, handshakes and an occasional hug in return. Speaking of "return," Tony returned to Costa Rica from Peoria, Illinois on May 25th, 2003, a day his many fans remember happily.

When he finished his culinary studies in his home city of Florence, Tony opened a tiny restaurant a few yards from the banks of the river Arno. He called his eatery Il Ponte Vecchio after the famous bridge over the river. Hope of fame and fortune called him to Greenwich Village in New York, to Thompson Street, only a few blocks north of predominantly Sicilian, Little Italy. He survived in Il Ponte Vecchio II despite more intense competition, distrust of Northern Italians by the locals and harsher critics than anywhere else I know in North America.

Next stop, San Jose, Costa Rica and Il Ponte Vecchio III. Here he achieved an excellent reputation and quite a fan base for preparing Northern Italian cuisine. When the Caterpillar Corporation wooed him away to Peoria, Illinois, his many devotees were crest-fallen. When he returned (hence the name, Il Ritorno) he had to overcome a site that had floundered under a parade of changing owners and chefs. It took a while, but his fine restaurant is once again among Costa Rica's most popular.

Il Retorno sits on a busy hilltop corner on the east side of San Jose, in front of a traffic light, under an unmistakable green, blue, red and orange awning. The main multilane road from San Pedro, has a left fork just past Kentucky Fried Chicken. Take that fork down the one way street that passes the restaurant, continues west into central San Jose, and becomes 8th Avenue. Two blocks down from the fork, your eye can't miss the awning. The entranceway is lined with celebrity photos and accolades for Chef Tony. The inside is awash in light from windows on two sides and mirrors on the other two. The ceiling above the central chandelier and one wall panel are actually eggplant purple. Would you believe that the chairs are slip-covered in two different patterns? One has vertical red and ivory stripes, the other a pale plaid of green, yellow, red and white. The table clothes are dull maroon and wheat. The other walls are pale brick and wood. Despite what it sounds like, the combo works. The interior designer was as courageous as the first person who ever ate an oyster.

The food is very good and quite different. Closer to Swiss than Sicilian or even Neapolitan, the food doesn't send up garlic warnings, nor are there flakes of crushed red pepper floating atop excesses of olive oil. Not much oregano either unless you order sea bass in oregano – garlic sauce topped with flavored breadcrumbs ($10), the nice exception that makes the rule. Sauces are creamier, thinner and crisper than most other Italian style dishes in Costa Rica. It seems that Chef Tony prefers light white wines for cooking to heavy red burgundies or *Chianti.*

The multiple veal dishes are more thinly sliced and are not breaded and deep fried into oblivion. Only one of seven (six main courses, $8-9, and an appetizer) is even breaded at all. The one veal appetizer was a first for me. Veal in tuna sauce is quite popular in Italy, but I have always opted for something else because the combination never sounded appealing. Three thin pale veal slices, spread lightly with a sauce of tuna and caper purée ($5), made a most interesting marriage. The sauce resembled *hummus* flavored with fine white wine vinegar, rather than typical canned tuna and salty capers. The delicate flavor and different textures exceeded my meager expectations.

Pastas and thin crusted pizzas are excellent. The homemade raviolis are cooked *al dente*. The meat filled version in a tomato meat sauce makes the case well. The meat is salted minced beef, minced veal and a little red pepper purée, giving it the appearance and flavor of corned beef pâté. It sounds strange but it works even better than the diningroom décor. The sauce is pale creamy fresh tomato red with tiny bits of meat and a lovely clean earthy flavor ($6.50). The most expensive ($7.75), and among the most popular of the pages of pasta dishes, is homemade fettuccini sautéed in seafood, porcini mushrooms and fresh asparagus.

Beyond the oregano-garlic sea bass, are other sea bass, salmon and tilapia dishes made with butter, white wine, brandy, cream, black olive and lemon combinations. A mixture of shrimp and mussels in a spicy marinara sauce is the delicious solo red sauce dish. They are all $10-11.

Of the six chicken breast dishes ($8), all have white wine in the sauce and only one has tomatoes. None are garlic or oregano flavored. Asparagus, mushrooms, broccoli and artichoke hearts are ingredients in some of the sauces. Light touch, nicely executed.

Four filet mignon choices ($9.50 – 11) come with green pepper, amaretto, porcini mushroom or prostitute style sauce. The first three sauces are creamy white sauces containing butter and either white wine, brandy or amaretto. *Putanesca* is a red tomato sauce with garlic , olives and capers. My friend and premiere Costa Rican columnist, Jo Stuart, prefers Tony's steaks to all others. She might also be persuaded to share the origin of the name of *putanesca* sauce, as whispered to her by her mother.

The dozen or so appetizers, salads and soups ($4-5.50) are well prepared. Favorites include the Roman salad and spinach soup.

Add a daily main course and pasta special for the sake of completeness and a page of desserts.

Two desserts worthy of special mention are *Mousse de Torrone con Choclato Caldo* and *Crepe d'Arancia, Cointreau e Gelato* ($3.50).

The former is a frozen mound of nougat mouse, bathed in dark chocolate sauce with nougat pieces sprinkled over the top and around the base. The latter is a crepe napped in tart orange sauce, my all time favorite, balanced by a scoop of creamy vanilla ice cream.

Hours: Noon to 2:30 & 6:30 to 10.

Telephone: 263-6239

La Luz

Every restaurant has a story. Few have the drama of La Luz.

Only little more than a decade ago, Costa Rican architect Ralph Ruge created a futuristic looking Spanish Colonial masterpiece, the Alta Hotel. Everyone who has ever driven the old road from Escazú to Santa Ana knows the vastness and beauty of the view of the valley off the steep slope of the north face. Alta sits below the road and looks out over gardens, a pool and the valley below. From reception, the main corridor winds down five sets of five stairs each amid fabulous art and crafts with such high ceilings that one feels like a visitor down an Andalusia ancient walkway. At the bottom sits the restaurant.

La Luz is a visual feast. Earth tones on the walls and on the hand painted beamed ceiling and a floor of rare glistening hardwood set the stage greenery and the non-stop vista. The tables are set with blooming orchids, aromas of bread baking and soft jazz or light classical music caress all of the senses except taste. Waiters move by gracefully carrying plates that are beautifully presented. Diners smile and speak softly, nearly reverently.

The food story began only a decade ago. Sherman Johnson emigrated from California and established a kitchen of California cuisine and Asian fusion. La Luz was an instant success. After two years, he returned to the states and left Stefano Delgrano in charge. Chef Delgrano came from the Modena area of Italy, home of the world's most famous balsamic vinegar. He came from a long line of chefs. Having learned Johnson's approach, he expanded it to fuse European and North African cuisines into the existing menu. La Luz was featured in Conde Nast as one of Central America's best and received five forks, the highest rating from La Nácion. Sadly, the renowned chef fell ill and died.

The new young chef who had risen from the kitchen ranks on site, also died at the tender age of twenty-six. In the summer of 2006, Carlos Zúniga came home to his native Costa Rica after several years of cooking in New Jersey and Staten Island. His teacher/master had been from New York's Inter Continental Hotel. In subsequent months he learned the eclectic worldwide menu, striving to recreate consistency rather than change. Few of the regular patrons noticed enough change to comment. Chef Zúniga is a pleasant man and I wish him success. May he outlive his predecessors and achieve the stature of Chef Delgrano.

The menu is challenging. The delivery is a little disappointing. The food is good but not up to par with the ambience and artistic presentations. On one occasion under the previous young chef, all three fellow diners who partook of the elaborate Sunday brunch felt that their main courses fell short of the menu descriptions. So too, did I have a "classic" Caesar salad recently with less than crisp romaine, croutons that had lost their crunch (moments under a broiler or in a hot dry skillet would have sufficed), whatever amount of anchovy was in the dressing, its flavor was AWOL and the Parmesan was bland domestic. Moroccan chicken came to the table with perfect crunchy threads of fried vegetable strands sitting atop the dish. They were as thin as Asian rice noodles. The sauce had a hint of heat, less than I would prefer, but probably just right for Costa Rican taste. The additions of tarragon's mild anise-like overtones and sweetness of papaya chutney and citrus to the sauce were great. With a little more *harissa* and cumin, it would have retuned my happy palate to Morocco. The chicken breast was a little overcooked and hard at the edges. My final course fit the experience to a tee. Mocha flan arrived on a short bread cookie with sculptured pieces of rich chocolate and whipped cream, on a milky sauce; beautifully presented and fairly tasty, but neither imaginatively flavored nor unusually good.

I plan to return often because the totality of the dining experience is quite satisfying, particularly on a Saturday night when blues and jazz singer Sasha Campbell performs.

After Hurricane Katrina, a famous New Orleans chef spent a few weeks at La Luz while his restaurant was being resurrected. He left a handful of additions to the menu.

Chef Carlos Zúniga is doing well considering the enormity of his challenge.

When he left Costa Rica at age 18, none of these dishes from the La Luz menu had ever been seen here and probably were unknown on Staten Island:

Jumbo shrimp and avocado cocktail in *wasabi* and soy cream $7.50

Portobello mushrooms filled with spinach and gorgonzola cheese, glazed with a reduction of balsamic vinegar and strawberries $5.75

A Middle Eastern mixed platter for two of *hummus, dolmadas, babaganoush, falafel, tzaziki* and more $13

A hand molded tart of feta cheese, sun dried tomatoes and caramelized onions in a cilantro and honey vinaigrette $5.50

Seafood gumbo $5.50

Blackened rib eye $21 or fish $19.25

Pork tenderloin in a reduction of teriyaki sauce and balsamic vinegar $16

Marinated lamb chops served over German *spaetzle* seasoned with sweet and sour tamarind curry $17

Turkey breast glazed with passion fruit and served over *spaetzle* pasta with bacon and pears.$19.25

Crab ravioli in a Vodka tomato sauce $15

Open daily 7AM to 3PM and 6PM to 10PM

Telephone: 282-4160

La Pecora Nera

My first truly memorable Italian meal in Costa Rica was at La Pecora Nera, just south of Puerto Viejo in the town of Playa Cocles. Four of us were dazzled by eight dishes, half appetizers, half main courses, that were all very well prepared, comparable to the best fare in San Francisco, our previous home. Father and son chefs put on quite a show in the open kitchen a four hour drive away from the capital and population center of Costa Rica.

The thatched roofed open air restaurant surrounded by dense tropical vegetation is down a long driveway past another restaurant. It looks pleasant and pristine, but hardly resembles the usual five-star restaurant. Even the menu can deceive and disappoint. It looks limited. Despair not. The loquacious enchanting owner/chef/maitre'd/ waiter will perform his magic. While waving his arms in delight, he will tell you the evening's special Tuscan hit parade in exotic detail. Four of us were dazzled by eight special dishes, half appetizers, half entrees, that were all very well prepared, comparable to the best fare in San Francisco, our previous home. The cost was about $ 15 - 20 per person. Chef Ilario Giannoni put on quite a show in the open kitchen. On our second visit, we stuck to menu items, mostly pizza and pasta for less than half the price.

Any visit to the Caribbean coast south of Limon should include a meal at Pecora Nera as a priority. Then, and only then, should you consider the Caribbean specialties in a host of modest cafes and sodas in the area.

Open Tuesday through Sunday noon to 10PM

Telephone: 750-0490

Machu Picchu

In the past few years, Joan and I have dined in about a half dozen Peruvian restaurants, most of them attractive and most of the food tasty and satisfying. Before coming to Costa Rica, I used to frequent only a single Peruvian restaurant in San Francisco, Fina Estampa on Mission. I loved the seafood stews and soups, the tongue blistering hot sauce and the purple corn and diced apple cinnamon flavored drink, *chicha morada.* Unfortunately, the rest of the cuisine eluded me until we settled here. Step-by-step the spicier ceviches, cold potato appetizers, pickled strips of grilled beef heart (*anticuchos*), potent pisco sours, caramel and meringue *suspiro limeño* and many other dishes have imprinted my brain in the "Oh, this is very good" center.

All my old time resident friends have reminisced about the days when the only Peruvian restaurant was unglamorous Machu Picchu off Paseo Colón and was clearly one of finest eateries of any kind in the entire country. When a local friend confided almost apologetically that she still returns frequently, despite the absence of glitz, glamour or romantic trappings, she added that the great food, reasonable prices and familiar friendliness have survived changing times. With this recommendation in mind, I chose to take three house guests from California with us to Machu Picchu, three unpretentious wholesome people who had all loved a prior trip to Colbert in Vara Blanca. I doubted that they would be put off by the lack of fresh flowers or candlelight at Machu Picchu.

The five of us, Fred, Marsha, Charlie, Joan and I ordered too much food, unaware of the very large size of the portions, devoured it all like gluttons and had a ball. It was great. With Tom and Rico, two other California house guests in tow a week later, we returned for lunch. The Menu was the same at lunch as at dinner. Every nook and cranny was packed with animated diners who all seemed to greet the waiters by name, like old friends. Another fine assortment of tastes and textures arrived piping hot and aromatic. We ordered less and didn't suffer overload.

Between the two trips and among the nine of us, we sampled the following:

COLD APPETIZERS

1) *Causa Limeña*, a savory citrus mashed potato base with a chicken layer and a topping of Creole spiced onions and avocado. $3.50

2) *Causa Machu Picchu*, a creamy potato salad base topped with fried shrimp and pickled red onion leaves. $4.50

HOT APPETIZERS

1) *Anticucho,* pickled strips of beef heart grilled and served on skewers – the most tender and tasty version of this great snack that I have had. $3

2) *Tamalito Peruano*, small Peruvian style tamales, filled with chicken, peanuts and black olives and beautifully complemented by the hot habanera sauce on the table. $3

3) *Papa Rellena*, a spicy meat filled roasted croquette of mashed potato that Rico likened to "a good potato knish." $3

SALADS AND SOUPS

1) Spring Salad, a nice assortment of fresh vegetables including avocado, red peppers, onions, tomatoes and lettuce. $3

2) *Chilcano*, a mild, thin but flavorful white fish soup loaded with large pieces of sea bass, perfect for people who don't like robust spicy Peruvian dishes. $3

3) *Chupe de Camarones*, much bolder, spicier thicker soup with a stock thickened with milk and fresh white cheese, a fried egg and medium sized nice shrimp. $4

MAIN PLATES

1) *Corvina Machu Picchu*, sea bass fillet baked in a sharp white wine, paprika and cheese sauce and topped with large juicy shrimp and a potato. $7.50

2) *Corvina a la Florentina*, another dish on the delicate side for gentler palates of baked sea bass in a white sauce with spinach. $6

3) *Corvina Rellena de Camarones*, shrimp in sauce *Americaine* spooned in and over rolled sea bass fillets, well executed. $7

4) *Lomito a lo macho*, a surf and turf variant with tenderloin of beef covered with shrimp, octopus, mussels and a well spiced tomato based seafood sauce served with rice and potatoes, devoured with gusto and smacking lips. $8

5) *Brochetta Mar y Tierra*, surf, turf and chicken brochettes served with a fresh salad. Only the skewers were left on the plate. $7.50

6) On neither occasion did we try the rice or pasta dishes, but with such a strong Chinese influence on Peruvian cuisine, I may try a *Chufa* (Chinese) plate next time. One of the three large seafood platters designed to be shared arrived at a nearby table amidst audible gasps of delight. Several chicken and steak dishes also looked very appetizing. Both of our visits ended with a dessert of *suspiro lemeño* and a spoon for each of us to leave our palates caressed in caramel $1.75.

The *chicha morada* drinks and *pisco sour* were great. The choice of wines covers most of Europe, Chile, Argentina and California. There are nine cocktail choices from Peru and eleven others from the rest of the world. With nearly two dozen aperitifs and liquors, several different beers, seven coffees and a host of non-alcoholic drinks from which to choose, you will never be thirsty.

None of the hordes of happy diners that pack the place seem to care about the non-existent elegance. They come for the hearty, well seasoned, consistently fine food, efficient friendly service and reasonable prices. We plan to return.

A block and a half north of Paseo Colón - Kentucky Fried Chicken corner on 32nd Street between first and third avenues.

Mon-Sat 11AM- 3PM & 6-10PM

Telephone: 222-7348

There are two other branches of Machu Picchu, both quite modern, pristine and purveying the same fare. One is in San Pedro – telephone 283-3679. The latest addition is aside the highway that runs from Ciudad Colón to La Sabana. It opened in mid 2006. Beautiful décor, easy safe parking, views of the Santa Ana hills and valley and the same wonderful food are the attractions. It is located on the north side of the main road between Multiplaza Escazú and Santa Ana.

Telephones: 203-7660 or 203-7657.

Rouge

Behind the Biblioteca Nacional, on a small blocklong street sits a magnificent old chateau numbered 1525 back of its elegant wrought iron gates, old lamp reproductions and Moorish tile fountain that is now a flower box.

The library sits on what once was part of Parque Central, in front of the chateau. This jewel houses two restaurants from a central kitchen presided over by a young chef, Christophe, whose credits include Paris' Four Seasons. Behind the chateau is a back entrance facing the large one-way, east-west street with the entrance just beyond the railroad overpass on the left and a parking lot on the right.

The sign by the back entrance says "Rouge," the name of the bistro. The high end fine dining restaurant faces front. It is a lavish location for special events. Connecting the two are a comfortable lounge and glass wall into the kitchen. Exquisite museum quality contemporary art and antique furnishings from the old chateau add to the overall charm.

The less formal bistro is itself a thing of beauty built around a recessed open ceiling patio dressed in river rock, water hyacinths and other greenery.
The tile floors are made to replicate the river rock appearance. The color scheme of dark adobe walls, pale olive green trim and yellow wheat seat cushions and table runners illuminated by sconces and candlelight is soft, sensuous and romantic at night. During the day, the diningroom is awash in bright filtered overhead sunlight. The flower petal noiseless black ceiling fans fill the space with gentle breezes. Bamboo placemats top the handsome wood tables. No more candles, just thin stemmed balloon water goblets, heavy modern silver cutlery and simple china.

The bistro menu is adventurous, extremely well executed, artistically presented and remarkably reasonably priced for the surroundings and plentitude of rigorously trained waitstaff.

Jose G. Salom, the gerente general, seems to have spared neither expense nor effort in this creation.

Our first meal in Rouge was at night. It consisted of a shared appetizer, separate main courses and a shared dessert and coffee.

The first course was a superb and different version of fried calamari. The squid rings were tender and crisp, unbattered and well seasoned with paprika and spice. They sat on a bed of greens dressed in beet flavored vinaigrette. For the calamari, which rested in crisp paper-thin rice flour crêpes (krupuk), aioli with just the right amount of garlic, was a perfect match.

Joan's tuna dish was crusted, seared yet deliciously rare inside. It came on a cluster of polenta cakes that complimented the tuna flavor and texture very well. I had tenderloin of pork, roasted to tender perfection with apples and fennel bulbs. The sauce appeared to be a balsamic deglaze of the meat's juice and caramelized apple and fennel. The three flavors were more than complimentary. We ate in near solitude. The only other couple within earshot rhapsodized over the duck main course. I intended to try it on our second visit. We jousted for our shares of a small perfect cup of crème brûlée, with crispy top and smooth velvety interior, not too sweet.

In a matter of only two weeks, we heard that the word had spread and Rouge was full most nights, so we opted for lunch. The menu was totally different. A daily tasting menu for only $7.50 featured a choice of two appetizers, two main courses, dessert and tea or coffee. Even without candlelight in the brightness of midday, we felt pampered by seamless cordial service, soft music, comparably gorgeous presentations and, of course, very well prepared food.

It was Friday and the menu was appropriately from the sea. The two starter choices were fried calamari and seafood soup. The calamari was battered lightly this time and served with tartar sauce rather than aioli. The greens were watercress rather than romaine. The vinaigrette and crisp rice flour crêpe were similar.

The seafood soup was creamy chowder, tasting of and laden with Neptune's tender morsels. Joan opted for salmon, moist and tasty, over a bed of spinach fettuccine in a slightly sweetened balsamic sauce. She was pleased. I had grilled mahi-mahi (*dorado*) with white butter sauce on a bed of Asian-style vegetable noodles. Our final course was a wide mouth, long stem flute filled with layered mango mousse and strawberry sorbet, topped with fresh strawberries and mint. Rich coffee ended a memorable lunch for two for less than $20.

On third and fourth visits, with another couple each time, there was a hint of inconsistency, marring an otherwise fine dining experience.

On the other days of the week, the appetizer choices include gazpacho with pesto, lentil soup with prosciutto, avocado soup, squid salad, Cobb salad and quail egg salad with tapenade and pesto tomatoes. Among the main courses are steak with blue cheese sauce and stuffed potatoes, tuna with fried polenta, and pork tenderloin with apples and fennel bulb like my first dinner.

Desserts include chocolate mousse, crème caramel, floating islands and their marvelous crème brûlée. The a la carte lunch menu includes main courses, soups, salads, sandwiches and pastas, all composed with tasteful combinations of fine ingredients.

The dinner menu contained choices of five each of elegant appetizers, salads and soups for about $4-6 and five pastas for a little more. Main courses ranged from $6-14 with an average of about $8 and included chicken, duck, seafood, beef, pork and vegetarian options.

Open 11:30AM to 11PM weekdays, 6-11PM Saturdays, closed Sunday

Telephone: 248-9337

Sunspot Grill

This gorgeous al fresco dining location, under purple awnings and umbrellas with matching tablecloths, at poolside in the Makanda by the Sea hotel and resort, has been the ideal spot for honeymooners and lovers. The cuisine of chef Roger Campos was at least co-star, if not the outright star. Unfortunately, he has moved on. The transition may not have been seamless, but recent reports have been positive. We gave Sunspot Grill four stars on past performance and will re-evalute it in the future.

Telephone: 777-0442 Open 6-10PM daily with reservations

Taj Mahal

When I surfed the net a few years ago, Taj Mahal, on the old Escazú-Santa Ana road, one kilometer east of Centro Comercial Paco, was the only Indian restaurant in all of Central America. Now it has a second location in Panama City on the same street as another Indian restaurant. To date (mid-2007), it is the only primarily Indian restaurant in Costa Rica. Fortunately for us, it imparts the sense of a wealthy home in Rajasthan and nearly authentic, nicely presented food. The combinations of cumin, cardamom, turmeric, ground almonds, cashews, chili peppers, anis, fenugreek, lime, onion, tomato, lentils, potato, mashed peas, spinach, cauliflower and garbanzos are real enough. Only the heat on the tongue and lips is missing. The reason is obvious. Ticos generally shun hot, spicy food and there are ten times as many of them as there are ex-pats. Assuming that half of the ex-pats like incendiary foods, Taj Mahal has to appeal to the twenty times larger clientele to survive. You can always ask for more heat in the preparation of your dish if it is neither deep fried nor in a white cream sauce.

A sophisticated well traveled Tico friend who abhors cayenne or chili pepper rhapsodized about a dish called *pollo muglai,* so I tried it. It is creamy and white so I couldn't order a spicier version. It was sweeter and milder than I might have liked, but it was marvelous. The sauce combined sweet cream, coconut milk, tempered egg, ground pistachios and bits of dates or raisins. Tender juicy chunks of chicken made a good marriage of complementary tastes. There was an additional aromatic that I couldn't identify. Since the chef from India spoke little Spanish or English, I may never know, but my guess would be roseflower water.

Before you order from the bilingual menu, one of the helpful friendly waiters will bring ice water, a complimentary *papadam* (a paper thin crispy large wafer made from lentil flour) and three sauces – mango chutney, tamarind and mint flavored yogurt. The menu contains more than 100 items.

First course options include *pakoras,* fritters in garbanzo batter, that are usually filled with vegetables ($3.50), but at Taj Mahal they come cheese, fish, or jumbo prawn filled as well ($ 3.25, 5.50 and 13.50); *samosas,* mashed potato and peas in pastry triangles ($2.75); *aloo tikka*, a pair of fried mashed potato patties ($2.75); a mixed platter of *samosas,* vegetable and fish *pakoras (*$ 6.25) and choice of four soups ($3.25 – 3.75).

From the *tandoori* beehive oven in the backyard, come *nan* and *roti,* white and whole wheat flour Indian bread, simple, buttered, garlic flavored or stuffed with cheese or meat, and sixteen main dishes of chicken, beef, fish, cheese, lamb and prawns baked in yogurt, spinach, tomatoes and a host of herb combinations in bowls or on skewers. Most of them cost $9-10 except for prawn, lamb and combination plates for $13-16.

The eighteen vegetarian main dishes ($7-8) include *palak paneer (*also called *saag paneer* in other parts of the world), cottage cheese and spinach; *malai kofta,* cheese croquettes in a creamy cashew sauce; mushroom *malai,* mushrooms in creamy tomato sauce and golden *dal tarka,* yellow lentils cooked in cumin, coriander, turmeric and pepper and garnished with cilantro. Pea, potato and cauliflower combos are the basics for the more common other offerings. Seven seafood (fish or prawn) dishes are either *tandoori* baked, set in creamy cashew sauce or served as a curry ($9.50-11). Chili fish ($9.50) is not too mildly seasoned, particularly if you order it "*picante*". Chicken ($9), beef ($9) and lamb ($12) dishes get similar treatment. All the rice dishes are made with Basmati rice, long grained and nutty. Prices range from $3.50, cumin flavored, all the way up to $13.75 for prawn dishes and $14.50 for lamb.

To end on yet another high note, consider a cup cardamom flavored sweet tea, *chai,* with rice pudding, *keer,* that has much more flavor than our own because of almonds, cashews and cardamom.

The restaurant proper consists of an upper and lower diningroom, a patio with a bar and three covered backyard spaces, one of which shares a roof with the *tandoor*i. A peacock and peahen strut among the outside tables.

Colors matter only insofar as whether or not they succeed. Imagine lilac, mauve, papaya, lime green and dark forest green coexisting. They do, and successfully. From gauze curtains, to solid colored table-clothes and napkins, to fabric ceiling hangings to brightly colored walls, the scheme exudes India.

What Taj Mahal gives us is so much more than what it is missing to be "authentic Indian", that we should celebrate its presence.

Noon to 11 PM everyday except Monday
Telephone: 228-0980

Three Stars –Good, won't disappoint

A Churrascaria Brasileira

My friend and food cognoscenti, Bob Waddington, bakes wonderful crusty bread, lemon meringue pies, German chocolate cakes and sourdough English muffins from his own starter. He told me about his favorite salad bar at the Brazilian restaurant, A Churrascaria Brasileira. It is a little surprising that, what I agree to be a better than usual salad bar, sits in a haven for ultimate carnivores.

Churrasco is Brazilian or Argentinean barbecue. The Argentinean variety is so common here that it needs no further elaboration. The Brazilian variety is a newcomer.

In Nova Brescia, in the south of Brazil, a statue of a man barbecuing meat sits in the center of the town square. Folklore accounts for the depopulation of the town in the past few decades, from 150,000 people to about 30,000 as a product of townspeople going to every city in Brazil and to major cities worldwide to open *churrascarias* and share barbecue culture for profit.

Brazilian grilled-meat-on-a-skewer restaurants have come to a handful of major cities in the U.S. and Europe, but, to my knowledge, this was Costa Rica's first. Instant success of A Churrascaria Brasileira spawned two more similar venues in a year and a half. It is a lot of fun and offers variety and large amounts of nicely seasoned grilled flesh without wasting half eaten slabs.

The system is simple. Diners sit at a nicely set table with a placemat that shows a picture of a cow with six labeled body parts from which cuts of beef are served and lists five other cuts of chicken, pork and beef that complete the sacrificial offerings to us carnivorous gluttons. All the tenderloins, sirloins, prime ribs, flank steaks, fillet mignons, buffalo hump pieces, chicken shoulders, chicken hearts, lamb and *linguiça* (Portuguese-Brazilian sausage) are brought to your tables for offerings of chunks, pieces or slices. You leave the table only for trips to the salad bar or to the starch table of mashed potatoes, white rice or beans cooked with pork dice.

You are served a wide variety of beverages of your choosing from ice water to flavored martinis and sample meats until you cry or moan "uncle." A peppermill shaped two-tone wooden piece sits on each table. As long as you keep the green side turned up, waiters will present you with a never-ending procession of meats. When you want to rest or quit, turn the wooden piece over with the red side, as in "stop," facing upward.

In Lisbon, London, New York, Chicago and all across Brazil, you are likely to receive veal and fish skewers as well. The lamb and chicken offerings are traditionally marinated for hours before roasting. The fattiest pieces of all the flesh are chosen to keep them juicy. Some leaner morsels are bacon wrapped. The beef pieces are basted with salt water often flavored with crushed garlic during cooking. The most vulnerable pieces to drying out are pork and chicken. Chimichurri, a sauce of finely chopped cilantro and garlic suspended in oil, serves as a remoistening dip for dry tidbits.

So how does our restaurant compare? It had no rival in Costa Rica when it opened, but it would not do too badly against competition abroad. In Brazil it would be fair. Some of the fare is a little overcooked, therefore dry (the chicken and pork as expected). All the meats are well seasoned and quite flavorful despite the fact that salt is the only condiment. The salad bar is quite nice with quality cheese, olives, pasta salad, fresh hearts of palm, quail eggs, garbanzos and well chosen fresh greens, tomatoes, onions, peppers, purple cabbage etc. and toast points spread with garlic butter. The sweet red pepper house dressing, Russian dressing and chimichurri are fine. The meal has a fixed price of $12 including service and tax. I have yet to have the capacity to try any of their desserts except to taste a nice mouthful of flamed caramelized bananas with cinnamon and ice cream called *gato de botas*. It was good.

The interior is tastefully appointed in modern tones, cocoa and forest green. The waitstaff is helpful, courteous and well trained. The overall experience is jovial and satisfying. Go when you have an empty stomach and lots of time to enjoy it in leisure. A Churrascaria Brasiliera is just at the entrance in front of the semaphore of the large happening new Centro Commercial La Ribera in San Antonio De Belén (home to Supermercado, La Brasserie and Ichi Ban Japanese restaurant as well). It is closed Sunday evenings.

Telephone 239-1532.

Within a year, two very similar Brazilian restaurants opened, Fogo Brasilero in Sabana East and La Fogueira in Plaza Itskatzú. The former has the largest salad and appetizer bar.

Both are more expensive than the original. No two people seem to agree on whose meats are the best.

Beirut

You might surmise, that after vacationing in New Zealand and Australia, Joan and I have had our fill of the least common of all Tico meats, lamb. Not so.

In search of another option to savor my favorite red meat, I took my wife and a friend to Beirut for its ballyhooed slowly roasted lamb ribs and shoulder.

A long-time local, originally from Lebanon, told me about the dish while visibly salivating at a United Nations function in San José quite a while back. I never forgot the look of rapture she wore while describing the lamb.

Beirut sits on a corner 200 meters north of Rosti Pollo in Sabana Norte. The effusive owner/chef loves to extol the virtues of seasoning lamb with 11 different herbs and spices and roasting it for five hours until it all but falls off the bones. When queried, he admitted to using garlic and three kinds of onion. I also tasted sumac, and he nodded when I asked him.

My follow up question was whether he used a typical Lebanese herb mix called *zahter* (or *za'ter* or *zaater*). Again he nodded yes. "I can't divulge the recipe," he countered ." It is from my grandmother." Well, zahtar contains thyme, marjoram, sesame seeds and sumac. Add three kinds of onion, garlic, salt and pepper (probably Syrian red pepper called *flefle halibi*) and we have 10. The 11th herb, I would guess to be oregano.

The three of us shared a combination appetizer platter (*mezze*) for two ($18) and followed it with individual orders of roast lamb ($15) and a single portion of *kneffe* ($3.50) to share among us along with cardamom-flavored coffee ($1.50). Add a glass of lemonade, tip and tax and the total was just under $80. Not a cheap lunch, but an enormous savory (as in both "tasty" and "to be savored") feast.

The mezzes included whole pitas and fried pita pieces, stuffed grape leaves, stuffed cabbage rolls, olives, lebne — yogurt creamy cheese, *babaghanoush* — a garlic eggplant puree, *hummus bi tahini* — garbanzo and sesame seed puree, *falafel* and *tabooli.*

The main course obscured an underlying large platter with a mound of tender lamb chunks and slices covered with a thick gravy-like paste of the 11 flavor enhancers and virtually no fat; *fatuch* — a toasted pita salad, roasted potato and a lentil and rice pilaf. The mini-cups of cardamom coffee were perfect after so much delicious food.

We tried the *kneffe* only because we had had a dozen or more different desserts of the same name in Syria 12 years ago, and were curious to see the Lebanese variation. It was unique, another of Grandma's secret recipes — a rich cheese custard layer topped with toasted cornflake crumbs, bathed in syrup flavored with rose flower water.

Intending only to sample a bit, we licked up every last drop.

The rest of the menu offered less expensive meats, poultry, appetizers and desserts, all of them, I have been assured by a regular diner, well-prepared.

Open Tuesday thru Saturday for lunch and dinner.

Closed after 5 on Sunday and all day Monday.

Telephone: 296-9622.

In the Middle East and North Africa, sumac seems to supplant citrus, vinegar and tamarind as the souring agent of choice. It is only mildly astringent, minimally piquant and has a nice fruity and slightly smoky flavor. It is also used for all kinds of GI upsets. I use it sprinkled on chicken, lamb, beef, pork and even fish before grilling or roasting and to season olive oil for dipping (heat the olive oil and sumac briefly to mix). I use it liberally for roasts and slow braises, but my all-time favorite lamb dish is a combination of processes that I learned in Syria and from an Iraqi chef in San Francisco.

Favorite Lamb Recipe

Have the butcher butterfly a seven or eight pound leg of lamb so the meat comes off the bone as a single roughly rectangular piece of nearly uniform thickness.

Marinate the meat at least overnight or up to two days in two cups of red wine, one cup of pomegranate juice, half a cup of lime juice, a minced onion, a few sprigs of rosemary and four cloves of mashed garlic. Pat dry and rub the surface to coat with a paste made by mixing a tablespoon of sesame oil with a tablespoon of zahtar or comparable mixture of sumac and marjoram.

Broil for only a few minutes on each side on a rack above a pan close to the heat. The paste will smoke and burn a little. Don't fret. Broiling time will depend on the thickness of the meat. I slice into a corner every few minutes to avoid overdone lamb.

As it starts to go from red toward pink inside, remove the meat. Sprinkle with salt on each side and let the lamb rest for ten minutes. Slice thin against the grain as you would a London broil or a beef brisket.

The easy version of a sauce for the meat is to reduce the marinade to half by boiling, when the lamb is removed, to deglaze the broiler pan with another half cup of the red wine, to combine the two, simmer while the meat is resting and serve on the side in a gravy boat.

For a richer sauce, you may have the butcher cut the lamb bones into chunks and you roast them dark brown in a pan with a few carrots, several ribs of celery and a large onion. Add the ingredients, including all the caramelized bits stuck to the pan, to a pot of water. Mix in a tablespoon of the marinade and simmer for at least two hours, until the volume is reduced to about a pint of liquid. Strain the sauce, deglaze the broiler pan as above, combine the two liquids and heat and serve in similar fashion.

Serve with *couscous* or roasted potatoes and a vegetable of your choice.

Grilled eggplant, onion and red pepper slices go very well. You might want to follow it with a light salad of tomato, cucumber and feta dressed with lime juice, oregano, salt and pepper and topped with a few toasted pine nuts or almonds.

I like a glass of full bodied rich red wine with it, such as a cabernet from California (Sterling), Chile (Frontera) or South Africa (Hamilton Russel). And most importantly, invite me over when you make it.

Sumac is available in several Costa Rican markets as a dark, rust colored powder. The red whole dried berries are scarce, but appear from time to time. I haven't seen zahtar here yet. You can substitute maracuyá (passion fruit) juice if you can't find pomegranate. If you are curious about other sumac recipes and have ethnic cook books at home, it is spelled *sammak* in Arabic countries, *sommacco* in Italy, *sumach* in Germany and *zumaque* in Spain.

Café Mundo

The neighborhood, the street and Café Mundo exude charm, charm and more charm.

The first order of business is finding the restaurant among the winding small streets of Barrio Amón. Head east on Avenida 5 past the INS building and Jade Museum. Take your first available left, two blocks later. Follow the wind of the streets north until you face a one way coming towards you at the corner of Avenida 9. Park on the right side of the street if a spot is available. After you make a mandatory left, parking is worse. At that intersection, Hotel Esquina de San Jose is on the near corner and the unmarked Café Mundo is on the opposite corner. Enter the gate in the pale green wall and you are confronted by al fresco diners, a small fish pond and an old garden of lush trees, vines and thick bamboo. Up the stairs in the entrance, a chalkboard announces the daily special of salad, main course and cold drink for about $4. An example one Monday for lunch was small pieces of pork in a rich golden sweet and sour sauce served in a large mound with a comparable hemisphere of rice and a generous portion of beet salad. The choice of included drinks were iced tea or lemonade.

The dark wallpaper and banquettes create an old fashion café ambiance.

You have your choice of three different patios or two rooms with or without smoking.

The cuisine is purported to be international, but it is about half upscale Tico with steaks, chicken and fish dishes, and half Italian with a grand array of pastas and pizzas. The one outlier is vegetable tempura, which, although perfectly fried in a tasty grease-free batter, is not at all Japanese. The excellent dipping sauce of guava, vinegar and soy oil is also Meso-American rather than miso-Asian. During weekday lunches, the place is packed with well dressed diners who have walked to the café from nearby offices. Most of them seem to know each other. The majority order the daily special which appears on the table in about ten minutes. Three kinds of bread – slightly peppery multi-grain, white cheese and Italian olive – with crisp crusts come with butter and an olive oil vinegar mix.

My favorite from the Italian side of the menu is eggplant parmigiana, and from the other side, juicy chicken breast (two large halves) in a creamy porcini mushroom and honey sauce with rice and vegetables ($6.75). A dessert to dream about afterwards is called "three layered Bavaria." Indeed it had five layers and some streaks of reduced raspberry sauce on the plate. From bottom to top of the multicolored cylinder the layers are dark chocolate cake, brown cream, lighter brown cream, ivory colored cream and dark bittersweet chocolate sauce. If you offer tastes to fellow diners, the plate will probably return empty.

For my wife and me, two visits and similar orders both times – a shared appetizer, a main course each from different halves of the menu, two non-alcoholic beverages, a shared dessert and a bill for $ 25 -30. Every dish was artistically presented, nicely seasoned and generous in size.

When the famed chef left for the US, regulars moaned. He is back and the moans are now from satisfaction and overindulgence.

Closed Sunday. Dinner only on Saturday (5PM -12). Lunch and dinner (11AM to 11PM) Monday through Thursday.

Telephone: 222-6190

Casa Luisa

Casa Luisa was actually her home. Luisa Esparducer raised her two daughters there. Despite the fact that her entire family now lives in Spain, she continues to hold down the fort and prepare some of the finest Spanish food in Costa Rica. Her style reflects her native Catalan roots and influences from all of the Spanish Mediterranean. Her restaurant still has the warm feeling of a home. When her kitchen labor abates, she comes to the table to treat you as a dinnerguest in her diningroom, rather than as a faceless, nameless patron of a restaurant. Her informal earthy style is infectious. If you are receptive, you can feel like an old friend in short order.

In Catalan tradition, she uses only the finest ingredients. When the lambs are so large that the flavor begins to approximate mutton, lamb dishes disappear from the menu. Her choices of salad greens are exacting. Flavors are rich and pure - garlic, paprika, extra-virgin olive oil, Jerez sherry vinegar, Modena Balsamic vinegar, salt and pepper. They work beautifully with oven roasted tomato, eggplant and skinned red pepper strips. Rabbit, pork, duck, beef and fresh seafood need no other additions to taste marvelous. She does use a little Dijon mustard in her lovely sherry vinaigrette salad dressing.

Bread and butter? Not at a Catalan table. *Pa amb tomàquet* is the traditional way of eating bread, rubbed with garlic and tomato, and sprinkled with salt and pepper. Alternatively, she serves bread spread with a creamy aioli, garlic flavored freshly made mayonnaise. Grilled lightly, they come to the table bathed in delicate olive oil. Authenticity demands a little excess in the oil. If its presence doesn't bother you, you will have a hard time not eating the entire plate of fresh or toasted rounds before your first course arrives.

I love gazpacho when it is crispy, flavorful and so fresh-tasting that your mouth tingles. Hers does exactly that. One of my biggest disappointments when I first dined in Spain was the addition of cream to southern Spanish gazpacho, rendering it akin to old cold cream of tomato soup. Nor do I like a covering of soggy croutons, salad size vegetable chunks and hard boiled egg pieces. Hers is simplicity and perfection.

On our first visit, I ordered mixed paella and was again delighted. It was not a bed of fluffy white rice colored with turmeric or saffron, cooked in broth and topped with green peas. It was rich, dark and loaded with prawns, squid rings, tender octopus pieces, mussels, pork and chicken drummets in a classic Catalan sauce, *xanfaina* - a vegetable stew of onions, peppers, tomato, and eggplant. The result was caramelized and a little oily, a perfect rendition of the Catalan version.

On our second visit, we shared an order of eight battered shrimp served with aioli, *bunuelos de gambas*. Joan had a duck half, roasted to well done tenderness, yet with crispy skin and very little residual fat. It was sauced with a thick marvelous dark brown reduction of red wine, pan drippings, mushrooms and dried plums and served with slices of roasted potato. I had rabbit in a typical white wine picada sauce loaded with tender little bits of diced onion, ground almonds, flat leaf parsley and a little garlic, served with a plate of thinly sliced grilled eggplant, zucchini and small artichokes. Both items were very satisfying and presented in an appealing way.

Among the other menu items are more Catalan classics. *Canelons Rosini* ($7.75), a main course, are like Italian cannelloni, but the pasta is stuffed with a variety of meats and baked in béchamel topped with Parmesan cheese in Catalunya. *Escalivada* (c3000) is an appetizer, charcoal or oven roasted eggplant, red pepper and onions, smothered in olive oil, and sometimes chopped garlic. Luisa serves it with tomato-anchovy toasts. There are also roast suckling pig, seafood aplenty, steak in Roquefort sauce ($11.75) and an entire page of tapas. There is a choice of desserts that we have yet to try because we are always too full. Sangria and a variety of Spanish wines are available.

The setting is very homey. Polished wooden floors, many small rooms, colorful wall hangings, furniture and a toilet in a room with a full bath contribute to the ambiance of a family nest. The small protected garden in the back is a lovely al fresco choice. The waiter and waitress are very helpful and efficient.

Although the prices are hardly bargain basement, they compare favorably with other Spanish dinner houses we have tried in the Central Valley, unless you go to very expensive specialty side of the menu. Tapas are $1.75 – 7.50 with an average of about $4.50. Main courses are about $6-11. Our meals of a shared appetizer and two main courses with nonalcoholic beverages cost $25 and $37 on our first two visits and included paella, duck and rabbit. Much more expensive are an entire suckling for about $100 (probably serves four or five) and Beluga caviar $165. Broiled lobster is $24, giant prawns a little less and a broiled seafood mixture containing both is about $35 (enough for two). We returned with friends on a third occasion for a delightful tapas party to celebrate Don Quixote's two hundredth birthday.

To find Casa Louisa, turn south on the street adjacent to the nearly pyramidal large Contraloria building in Sabana Sur, across the road from the park. Four hundred meters later, turn left one short block after the traffic light. Casa Louisa is the purple and papaya colored house in the middle of the block on the left.

Closed Sunday, otherwise open for lunch (12-3) and dinner(6-11). Telephone: 296-1917

Chalito's

Clearly the least fancy of any of the three star restaurants is Chalito's. You are not likely to pass it by chance. The paved road through the hamlet of Las Vueltas turns to gravel a few hundred meters farther west. The bar and restaurant, open only from Friday lunch through Sunday dinner, is a happening place catering to people from La Guácima, Los Reyes and Las Vueltas. One couple from Escazú often joins a regular Friday night group of about a dozen ex-pats from the US, Canada, England and Trinidad.

Typical of a hundred other small town Costa Rican restaurants, there are no outer walls except on the side of the kitchen and bar. The parking lot is basically the adjacent lawn. Until 2006, there was not even a sign out front.

Virtually everyone is on a first name and cheek kiss basis with everyone else including the waitresses.

Why venture off the beaten path for Chalito's? For the essence of authenticity, for the kind of Tico warmth and hospitality that upscale foreign restaurants often lack, for huge portions of delicious food and for prices geared to local working people.

In addition to the usual mix of fish, shrimp, steak, chicken and pork dishes, there are a handful of Peruvian specialties – two soups (*chupe, cazuela),* three or four potato based appetizers and four *chaufa* rice dishes. *Chaufa* is the descriptive word for Peruvian style Chinese food.

Favorites include pasta with mushrooms or shrimp in cream sauce, steak smothered in onions, seafood *marescada,* fish fillets in a variety of nice sauces, fried chicken wings and *chalupas*.

The bar prices are also well within even modest budgets.

To get there, go west from the center of La Guácima, straight past the turnoff to Los Reyes and the butterfly farm, through a cluster of tiny businesses and the school, and it will appear on the right side of the road. If you reach the end of the paved road, you have gone too far.

Open for lunch and dinner Friday, Saturday and Sunday

Telephone: 439-1029

Chinese Cultural Center's - Casa China

The vast dim sum houses of Canton, Hong Kong, Shanghai, Saigon, Singapore, Vancouver, New York City and

San Francisco glare lipstick red, gold and often fluorescent blue white. The diners tend to be animated. Women pushing carts of food shout out their wares in high-pitched sing song, one or two different dishes per cart.

With as many as a hundred different varieties of dim sum, an army of servers zigzag past the tables, trying to appease the grandpa up front who can't get the attention of the woman in the back hawking duck feet or horse neck clams or the matron who demands the last portion of sliced pig's ear. Plates, cups and glasses clink and clatter. The sensory overload has at least two babies crying at all times. These food frenzies run from early morning to early afternoon with lines of hungry people filling sidewalks, numbers clutched in their hands.

With only about 1% Chinese in Costa Rica's population, you might not expect even a scaled down version of the real thing. Fortunately for us, Casa China, the Chinese Cultural Center's restaurant, is as authentic as it gets – chatter, clatter, an occasional crying baby and all the other sensory teases. The intoxicating aroma of five spice, garlic, soy, roast pork, steamed chicken and baked buns envelopes the vast space. Star anise and black bean steamed chicken feet, ginger flavored riblets, sliced pig's ears, garlic chive and shrimp dumplings fill the carts daily along with the standards.

Some readers may remember when the plates and steam baskets cost 45 cents apiece in Hong Kong or San Francisco. In our changed world, Casa China's dim sum prices of $1.40 to $2 a plate are a real bargain, probably little more than half the price elsewhere.

Small bowls of soup cost about the same, except for roast duck soup which runs about a dollar more. They also have my favorite soup. Perhaps it is an acquired taste, but typical rice porridge called *jook* or *congee* in Asia and in Chinatowns in the Western World is my favorite morning comfort food. Medium grained rice is boiled in broth for a few hours until it starts to break down into a velvety gruel, white pepper and ginger are frequently added along with the diner's choice of preserved egg, pork, fish, seafood, chicken or pig parts. Toppings include a dash of sesame oil, roasted peanuts, green onion and crispy noodles. At times, unsweetened doughnuts are torn into pieces and mixed with the *jook*. The steamed rice dough is fluffy, the fried wonton skin crispy, the baked desserts moist, the dumpling skins thin and tender and the fillings savory with traditional flavors. For the most action and the largest selection, go with the crowd on Saturdays from 10 to 3. Restaurant hours are from 8 a.m. to 11 p.m. every day and the staff professes to have dim sum at all hours on all days, but if you go with the masses, the ingredients will be fresh and the choices many.

The rest of the menu is 90% Chinese and 10% Tico. In addition to standard appetizers, noodle and rice platters; wantan, hot and sour and chicken vegetable soups; sweet and sour spareribs and pork and a host of fish and shrimp dishes, there is a page of wonderful house specials. Among them are the following: two hot pots – one of mixed meats and tofu ($9) and one of slab bacon and Asian radish ($6), two edible pastry nests – one filled with cashew prawns and crisp vegetables ($9) and one filled with pieces of stir fried meat and orange sauce ($7), two tofu dishes, Kung Pao chicken ($6), half a roast duck ($15) and the best rendition of Singapore style rice noodles I have had in Meso America. On the menu it is called stir fried rice noodles with shrimp and roast pork in a curry sauce. It also is loaded with bean sprouts and thin slices of onion.

There is no banquet menu despite the number of tables for ten. Family menus begin with four courses for two people for about $9 per person and become progressively less expensive. Five courses for six people are about $7.50 per, and six courses for a party of eight drops a little below $7.

Portions are very large and presentations are simple. No dazzling food art here. It wouldn't fit with the décor, or lack thereof. According to a waitress, the cavernous diningroom had a makeover about four years ago. It is hard to tell. From floor covering to ceiling there is no memorable color, scant wall hangings and two handsome light fixtures with dull yellow bulbs, definitely not a setting for romance. The yellow exterior is brighter, but shabby looking. No problem for me. I love the place for its authenticity and great food and low prices. The cavernous restaurant with less than pristine de facto decor is on Calle 25 between Avenidas 8 and 10 across the street from the towering Ministerio de Ambiente y Energía. If you are heading toward the eastern side of San Jose on Avenue 10, there is a hill to climb after a large modern gas station. Most cars slide into the right lane to turn towards Zapote at the top of the hill. If you stay in the left lane and turn left at the top where everyone else is going right, the restaurant will appear on the right side of the street as you turn.

Open 8AM to 11PM daily.

Telephone : 290-1247

Club Cubano

There is something special about ethnic clubs and their restaurants. They were everywhere in the 30's, 40's and 50's. They were Portuguese, Slovenian, Lithuanian, Ukrainian, Polish, German, Chinese, Sicilian, French, Italian, Norwegian, Swedish and many more. We are blessed to have at least three: Casa Espagna, despite its waning cuisine, Casa China with its marvelous *dim sum* and Cubano Club in Guachipelin, on the road from the Constru-Plaza exit of the highway, north only a few kilometers, past St. Mary's School, on the right side of the road.

The exterior has a throw-back look. The children's playground is falling apart. Inside either of the two front doors, you enter ethnic nostalgialand, a cavernous refectory with about two dozen tables aligned in four rows, with a bandstand at one end and the kitchen at the other. A bar along the far wall is populated with friends who greet each other by name and with hugs and handshakes. Particularly nice here in Costa Rica, where, at times, skin color seems to matter too much, these Cuban ex-pats seem to be diverse and color blind.

A collage of Cuban travel posters serve as a backdrop for the bandstand. Pictures of politicos and older members adorn another wall. Windows front and back and ceiling fans keep the place cool. There is nothing colorful, dramatic or modern about the décor. It is, however, comfortable and clean. Tablecloths and napkins are red, white and blue. Plates and glasses are functional rather than stylish.

The food has a nearly homemade quality, hearty, nicely seasoned and generously portioned. Among my favorite dishes are the stuffed potato appetizer ($1.40), an orange size deep fried ball of mashed potatoes filled with savory chopped meat; *ropa vieja* ($7.50) or "old clothes," a deliciously seasoned very mildly spiced shredded beef stew with onions, garlic, tomatoes, peppers and green olives in brown sauce; tenderloin in vermouth sauce; jumbo shrimp in garlic butter ($9.50); *lechon asado* ($7.25), white succulent roast pork, unprocessed with skin and a layer of fat left on, roasted in a slow oven, basted in a garlic/sour orange juice/oregano *mojo,* served with yuca, rice and a salad; and *picadillo habanero* ($7), a potato, garlic, tomato, onion and ground beef hash, Havana style.

Other appetizer choices include soups ($3.50-$50), salads ($3.25-$5), croquettes (65 cents) and Cuban-style *tamales($*1.75).

Other main courses include fish ($7-$9), three seafood *mariscadas* ($7), chicken dishes ($5-$6.50) and pork ($6) and beef ($13) tenderloins with sauces of onion, pepper, vermouth red wine and creole.

The dessert choices are the usual Costa Rican cast of characters. The coconut flan is tasty.

Venison is not on the menu, but they have it from time to time ($14). If your only experience with venison is a piece of tough, dry, gamey meat, you will be very surprised. Here the meat is as tender as pot roast simmered for hours in rich brown gravy, moist, tender and not at all gamey. Beware a few splintered pieces of bone. All dishes are served with lovely dense Cuban bread and garlic-rich aioli. Be sure to save some of the bread to mop up the gravy. *Patacones,* white rice and a small salad are the usual side dishes. The venison at El Indio Hatuay was more expensive and not nearly as good. Before it went out of business, El Indio offered Cuban food for a while which also didn't compare. The only competition is La Gua Gua in Plaza Itskatzú, which a few friends prefer. Indeed, it is more up-scale, modern and more expensive. Most of our friends and I prefer the home-kitchen flavors, warm service and old Havana ambience at Cubano Club.

On Thursdays and Fridays at lunch and dinner they have a buffet for $10, with Spanish food including *paella* and about eight other choices. Cuban dancing happens from 9PM to 1AM on Thursday and Friday nights. They are open daily from 11am until 10pm.

Telephone: 215-2001

Donde Carlos

A block down and a short block to the right of Spoon in Los Yoses, Donde Carlos sits, a modern architectural sentinel over a residential corner. The Church of Fatima, a hundred meters south, marks the other end of the same block.

Two stories of picture windows, clad in horizontal beige draperies, look out over tall papyrus at the well-groomed schnauzer and collie fenced in across the street. When the wind is right, smoke from the *parrilla,* the traditional Argentine oven, sends scents to them of caramelized steaks and chops. I can't see them drool, but I can imagine.

From our non-smoking seats on the first floor by the window, I inhale the same essence of marinated and abundantly seasoned charred meat that escapes from the brick and stucco parrilla adjacent to the entrance. With the corner of a white linen napkin, I dab away the drop of moisture from the edge of my mouth.

The diningrooms are smartly done in black, gray and white against aged brick. The chef and crew wear starched white uniforms and toques. The waiters are attired in black pants, dark blue-gray or lighter blue shirts and below-the-knee butcher aprons that tie around the waist. Brushed chrome wine racks and ceiling spots reflect precise composition. The first floor diningroom is for non-smokers. Upstairs, there are two more dining rooms and a terrace. Old photos and smart prints cover the walls.

Like their cousins from the pampas of Argentina, Tico cattle are grass fed. Compared to corn fed U.S. beef, ours is chewier and tastier and the cuts are a little thinner and a lot less expensive in comparable scale restaurants. In California, grass fed beef is currently trendy, more expensive and favored for more flavor and less fat. Paradoxically, more fat usually equates with juicier and more flavorful, although experts contend that grass fed beef has an additional appeeling fresh earthy flavor of its own.

The names of cuts also differ on opposite sides of borders. Most simply, fillet mignon is the same tender buttock steak. A fillet of the eye is called *bife de lomo* and can cost more than mignon. *Lomo* is sirloin, very flavorful and a little chewy. *Bife de chorozo* is the always popular sirloin or porterhouse cut off the rib. *Lomito* is tenderloin, a little more tender and a little less tasty. *Bife de Costilla* is a t-bone. *Churrasco* is a cheaper cut of meat, usually marinated, such as brisket, chuck, shank, or a lesser sirloin. It is frequently the most flavorful (to my palate) and toughest of all the cuts.

Baby beef is not veal, but rather a different sirloin from an 800-pound younger rather than a 1,200-pound older steer. It is devoid of marble (very little fat) and tends to be bland, soft and dry. It is very popular, but to me the texture is like a mixture of pulverized beef and cooked cereal in need of more liquid. Can it be mushy and dry at the same time (ox-ymoron)?

The parrillas will often offer beef parts or products, *anchuras,* as appetizers or as part of a mixed grill for two people. Components often include intestines, kidneys, sausage, sweetbreads and udder.

The menu at Donde Carlos is dominated, as expected, by steaks and beef parts. Token fish, chicken and pork dishes, appetizers, soups and salads and desserts complete the offerings.

Starters include several carpaccios, shrimp cocktail, grilled provolone, breaded mozzarella, sweetbreads, udder, intestine, black pudding and kidneys. The soups are cream of asparagus or tomato, onion gratiné and beef broth with sherry.

We came attired in our carnivorous habits and were not disappointed. First trip: charred sweetbreads, a huge hunk of baby beef for Joan and a very flavorful churrasco met expectations. The main courses came with a crispy skinned baked potato dressed with herb butter and a salad of chopped lettuce, tomatoes and sweet white onions.

To adorn the meat and salad, we had table choices of good quality light olive oil, red wine vinegar, superb chimichurri, green äioli, mildly picante salsa and a crock of hot chili remoulade. The only disappointment was a soggy Caesar salad devoid of romaine in a bland watery dressing. The Caprese salad was great.

We had the mixed grill for two on our second occasion. Once again we were served platters with salad and browned skin crispy baked potato. Between us, the waiter placed a heated serving tray of two sirloins and ample of each of the *anchuras* except for udder, which was unavailable that day. In addition, I had a blood sausage called black pudding.

In keeping with parrilla tradition, the *anchuras* were barbecued over hot charcoal to a light char on all surfaces and abundantly seasoned. No mistaking these sweetbreads, kidneys or small intestine pieces for French or Italian sautés.

The steak choices range from filet mignon to *churrasco*. Portions are generous with an average cost of $12. The mixed grill for two was $17.50. Appetizers averaged $4, soups $2.50, salads and desserts $4.

For a steak dinner, appetizer and dessert, it will cost about $20 per person without wine. The wine display is impressive, dominated by Argentinean reds (three Trapiche reds for $14 per bottle), but including choices from Chile, France, Spain, Italy, Australia and California.

My favorite French dessert is a Normandy apple pancake, a thin crisp crust, finely sliced and caramelized apples and a splash of Calvados (*tart tatin)*. Mario Serrano, the talented Tico chef at Donde Carlos, makes a nearly comparable excellent apple pancake with the substitution of Cointreau and Spanish sherry for Calvados.

With a dozen or more Argentine steak houses from which to choose, there are many similarities in style, scope and price. To date, one of the top choices, less expensive than most, and a cut above many of the others, is Donde Carlos.

Open for lunch (11-3) Monday through Friday, dinner Monday through Saturday (6:30-11) and Sunday noon to 7PM

Telephone: 225-0819

Don Rufino

One of the natural wonders of the world has to be the nearly continuous eruption of Arenal Volcano on the occasional night devoid of cloud cover. Freight car size chunks of iridescent magna vault into the air after a crescendo of chugging sounds from the bellows that is the mountain. Rivers of molten lava dash hundreds of yards down the mountainside before the color goes from orange-red to grey.

From La Fortuna to Lake Arenal, dozens of hotels offer cabins or rooms with picture windows that face the pyrotechnics. Visiters usually spend at least one night before going west to the lake for windsurfing or fishing, on to Monteverde's cloud forest or out to the Pacific beaches.

So many restaurants, so little creativity. If you are satisfied with standard chicken, pizza, pasta, *gallo pinto*, burger, ribs and steaks, La Fortuna has an option for you every block or two. The heavily advertised German and Swiss venues farther west are mediocre at best. If you crave more, try Don Rufino diagonally across the street from the gas station in the center of town.

The décor of the happening bar and restaurant is less eclectic than the bold international menu. Art deco, a nice impressionistic painting of a queen and court member graces the back wall and the paper placemats. Quality photos line the wall farthest from the street. The script on the placemats and menus honors the pioneer founders of La Fortuna, including the grandfather of the current owner.

The Colombian chef has a flair for dramatic and appeeling presentations, nicely seasoned quality ingredients, large portions, great variety and a case of serious hyperbole when it comes to naming menu items. Nonetheless, his fare is worthy of the accolades that make him so popular with upscale locals. He trained at Cordon Bleu, but not in Paris, in Colombia.

We visited twice with a total of eight diners, including a chef, a sommelier, a vegetarian and an Indian food fanatic. Every course from appetizer, to salad, to soup, to pasta, to steak, to chicken, to seafood, to dessert got approvals or raves. The diner who ordered "*tandoori* chicken" got an attractive sesame coated chicken dish served in a pineapple shell with a mélange of pineapple chunks, sweet red peppers, cashews and more. Her initial upset that this chicken had never seen the inside of a *tandoori* oven, nor was seasoned with Indian spices, waned rapidly when she tasted what she labeled her "chicken misnomer," liked it and finished every last morsel of the large serving. "Istanbul chicken" was another sesame seed coated dish, served on a bed of mango and pineapple with a coconut sauce. Another satisfied diner. The sommelier thought the wine list was well chosen and prices reasonable. His Peruvian seafood stew ($17), *zarzuela,* came in a coconut shell, unlike his expectations, but nicely seasoned in a coconut cream sauce and redolent with quality marine morsels, including a small lobster. The vegetarian enjoyed fettuccini a la Huerta ($6), al dente noodles, slices of eggplant, medley of vegetables diced and fresh tomato sauce. The steak eater had juicy tenderloin medallions in a three pepper sauce ($16), done to perfection. Another carnivore gave thumbs up on his pork chops with caramelized apple ($12). My chicken Kiev ($12) was nicely prepared and characteristically unauthentic. Instead of herbed butter, the lightly fried and moist breast was stuffed with herbed cream cheese, bacon and almonds, and it was bathed in a luscious fruit sauce. No complaints leveled at the Caesar or Caprese salads ($4), French onion or *pejibaye* soup ($4), desserts, coffee or mixed drinks.

If you have kids in tow, they can have burgers and fries.

It is located diagonally across from the gas station in the center of town.

Open daily from 11 AM to 10:30 PM
Telephone: 479-9997

El Banco de los Mariscos, Santa Barbara de Heredia

"What is in a name?" sayeth the Bard of Avon. There are at least three other restaurants in the Central Valley with the same name and another called El Balcon de Mariscos. All they have in common are lower than typical prices for seafood.

In my humble opinion , El Banco de los Mariscos in the charming hilltop town of Santa Barbara de Heredia, ranks head and shoulders above the other four (San Jose, Santa Ana, Curridabat and San Pedro). It even compares favorably with venues that cost twice as much and reside by the sea.

Follow signs to the center of Santa Barbara de Heredia, about nine miles northeast of the airport, and head down the hill from the town square for about three hundred meters in the direction of Alajuela. A large red and blue sign on the right side of the road marks the private drive. Except on weekends when both large parking lots are packed, access is easy. My guess is that it seats more than a hundred and fifty people. The only time I ever saw it less than half full was a Monday lunch, and it was nearly half full. Spacious, airy, happy, busy – these are the adjectives that come to mind.

Incredibly popular despite its absence from all the major restaurant guides, El Banco serves large portions of very fresh seafood at prices well below the competition. Service is fast and efficient, and even attentive during peak hours. No tablecloths or fancy cutlery on the bare wooden tables surrounded by plastic chairs, but the indoor and outdoor vegetation and humming chorus of ceiling fans make it attractive. The tables are adequately spaced to afford privacy and ease of navigation. Empty tables are cleaned rapidly of lobster shells and backbones and heads of large whole fish, avoiding the look of an ossuary that plagues other large, busy restaurants.

Neither is the food fancy. Plating is simple and straightforward. Unless you specify to the contrary, your selection will come with fries and a salad. The main ingredient, however, is likely to be twice usual size and prepared well.

If you can eat more than most people, you might want to start with one of nine *ceviches* ($2-5), six salads ($3-6), seafood soup ($3) or marine party soup ($4).

My friend Jacques is not an adventurous diner, but he knows fried sea-bass from Playas de Coco to Limon. He thinks the *filet empanizado* at El Banco is the largest portion and as tasty as any he has ever had ($4.50). Most lobster dinners cost $30-40 in Costa Rica. Here they are $18 for three halves of medium sized lobsters that I guess amount to about a half pound of meat, served buttered, grilled, in garlic sauce or thermidor.

Among the favorites are boneless whole sea-bass deep fried crispy outside and sweet and moist inside, plain or with asparagus cream sauce (priced by weight). The mixed seafood plate sautéed in garlic butter ($8) is enormous and devoid of shells. The octopus in it is remarkably tender. Rice dishes with tuna, sea-bass, shrimp, octopus and chicken cost $4-6.

If Aunt Martha from Iowa mistrusts seafood, she can select from an assortment of beef, chicken and pasta dishes. And the prices for tight-wad Aunt Martha? How about fried chicken, tuna or chicken salad or a burger with fries for $2.75, spaghetti with a white mushroom sauce for $3.75, grilled T-bone or house tenderloin steak for $5? I can't vouch for any of them because all of my compatriots and I have always ordered seafood.

Ten different desserts cost about $5 each. Some day, I'll limit myself to a single appetizer so I can try a dessert.

They offer more than a dozen each soft and hard drinks including draft beer ($1.40).

Open daily from noon to 10 PM.
Telephone: 269-9090

El Establo

The western end of the Central Valley is horse country. On weekends denizens of equestrians fill the backroads with their exquisitely groomed high steppers.

Forelegs swing out laterally to initiate each stride, truly a beautiful gait to behold. Not surprising with the local love of horses, the proprietors of steakhouses adorn their establishments with bridles, saddles and all things vaquero-esque. My mental picture of the ideal has been tree lined pastures, a corral and stables at the end of a grassy road, with an open walled rancho and restaurant. Thanks to a tip from Amy of Ciudad Colón, my picture came to fruition.

El Establo, the stable, is a restaurant loaded with charm and a feeling of authenticity, despite its neon Marlboro sign and flat screen TV. It sits at the end of a narrow unpaved and tree-lined road past grazing horses and stables. The parking area is in front of the veterinarian's office. A canopied walkway leads into the dining room.

Next to the entrance, a display case exhibits steaks, chops and chicken breasts resting in marinades and the multiple salad ingredients that will accompany the meat from the grill to the table. The starch options are baked potato or rice. The meats remain in the marinade for five or six days. Rosemary, tarragon, garlic, onion, salt and pepper infuse the meats with mouthwatering flavor. Usually bland tenderloin becomes rich with taste, as do chicken breasts, pork, T-bones and imported black-angus rib-eyes.

The baby-faced chef prepares all orders to perfection on a large grill that sears in the juices as it caramelizes the exteriors. Doneness is precise. " Medium" is pink and juicy. "Medium-rare" is as red as it should be. All of the cuts are incredibly tender. The rib-eye is by far the most expensive cut ($17), more than twice the price of the "tenderloin special" ($8.50) or of the very nice "mixed platter" ($7.50) which includes a smaller, but equally tasty and tender steak, a plump and moist chicken breast and a nicely grilled tasty large sausage. The plate also includes a decent fresh salad served with olive oil and wine vinegar and an OK local thin-skinned baked potato in foil with sour cream and butter.

My wife and I went twice and loved the food, the ambiance and the friendliness of the proprietress, waiters and chef on both occasions. By our second visit we were treated like family. Even the fluffy grey and white house cat, Grace, came by to say hello. There were eight of us the second time, on a Sunday afternoon. The restaurant was busy. Three of the four women in the party had birthdays within 10 days of our meal. Not only did all eight of us have great, albeit simple, food, we had individual pieces of chocolate cake with a birthday candle flickering on each for dessert.

Wine by the glass is $2, soft drinks $1 and coffee $.85. The chocolate cake, $1.75, was better than average but not spectacular. Our group of three Ticos, two Canadians and three former U.S. residents all loved their meals. The thick juicy rib-eye was as good a steak as any of us had tasted in Costa Rica. Two of us had had disappointing experiences with expensive imported black angus rib-eyes in local American style steakhouses in the past.

We had in common, not only friendship and birthdays, but all of us are horse lovers. The décor of cowpoke pictures, bridles and a three-headed bola on the walls was pleasurable. The frosting on the proverbial cake, however, came during a walk among the stables, the pasture and corral after the meal. Marvelous old fruit trees and giant decorative vines framed the picture perfect setting.

Unfortunately, El Establo is only open from Friday through the end of Sunday afternoon (6 p.m.). Just before lunch on Saturdays, there is a horse show in full regalia, weather permitting in the corral adjacent to the restaurant. The total experience of pastoral beauty, stables and horses, comfortable informality, friendly people, excellent steaks, efficient execution of a simple menu and a glimpse into our world away from metastasizing glitzy mall culture make this place very special.

To get there, follow the highway that begins at Sabana Sur and passes Escazú and Santa Ana to Ciudad Colón. The road halts just east of town at the gas station with a "Do Not Enter" sign that forces you to turn. Turn and proceed as far as the bumpy little road goes, about 500 meters. Turn right again for about another hundred meters. The road forks. Just beyond the right fork is the entrance to El Establo. Inside the gate, follow the narrow road to the end and park alongside the corral. The canopy leads inside.

Phone: 249-2258

El Novillo Alegre

Che, the charming young owner of El Novillo Alegre, has built a popular restaurant empire in only a few years. Beginning with his unadorned grill and steakhouse past Sorretto's market in Escazú, Parrillada Argentina El Novillo Alegre, he now has opened two more places called El Novillo Alegre, another called Bariloche (where San Telmo was in Paco Mall, Escazú), a creperie (next to the new two story Auto Mercado, also in Escazú) and a Spanish restaurant, La Tasca (attached to El Novillo Alegre in Santa Ana where Bokaös used to be). He doesn't appear to be overextended. Décor in the newer places reflects tasteful attention to detail. His steakhouses are very popular, particularly the one in Santa Ana. They serve up good cuts of meat, well prepared and remarkably tender, at prices that are competitive with other high end steak houses. The $20 New York seak is their signature dish. It is large, tasty, juicy and tender. It comes with fresh and toasted bread, thin breadsticks, garlic-chive cream cheese, *chimichurri, pico gallo*, *vegetables and a baked potato*. Fish, seafood, pork, chicken, pasta and a variety of appetizers grace all the menus. The *empanadas* Argentinean-style, with olives, are juicy and tasty. The desserts include nicely poached pears in red wine and apple pancake. For wine lovers, the list is exemplary. Servers are well trained to be helpful, efficient and reasonably unobtrusive.

La Tasca was running remarkably smoothly by its second week in early 2007. Servers were helpful to diners unfamiliar with the cuisine of Spain. The food was respectable, portions large, ingredients fine, but neither very imaginative nor worthy of raves. To judge so early in its infancy, however, would be unfair.

Telephone: Santa Ana 203-4753, La Tasca 282-3042
Escazú 288-4995
Curridabat 254-0353

El Rodeo

Just a few meters south of the origin of the Belen – Santa Ana road on the western side of the road, sits the locally very popular El Rodeo steakhouse, hotel and new café. Inside the gates, parking is easy and secure in front of the beautifully appointed ranch house. On display inside are a grand collection of saddles plus bridles, whips, wagon wheels and all the trappings of a cattle ranch.

Service is prompt, friendly and efficient. Table settings include *chimichurri, salsa picante* and *pico de gallo* to slather on fresh bread or to dress the robust meats. I can't vouch for the appetizers or desserts, although they look appetizing on their way to other tables. The main courses are so large, most people, me included, cry "uncle" before the bottoms of the platters come into view. The steaks are always prepared as ordered. My favorite is the less costly, slightly tougher *churrasco,* tastier to my palate than the thicker, tender sirloins and tenderloins. They are all large and better value than most of the competition. Add a bevy of complimentary sides (rice, beans, veggies, potatoes) and you won't want more food for many hours.

On the same property, their new café, Grand Café, offers sandwiches, pastries, ice cream sundaes, nice omolettes, upscale coffees and decent hot dogs. Fred Jimenez, the co-owner, has recently completed La Fonda. an attractive new restaurant adjacent to Rio Segundo, the river that divides San Rafael from La Guácima.

El Rodeo is open every day from noon to 11PM.

Telephone: 293-2692

King's Garden

Déjà vu. Climbing the stairs inside the red and gold entrance, I feel the familiar heavy carpet beneath my feet, smell the essence of ginger, garlic and sesame oil vapors and look upward anticipating ornate phoenix and dragon motif amid five foot vases and shiny wooden lattice work. It is all there. It is my first visit to Kings Garden, but I have been in its fraternal twin establishments in Vancouver, San Francisco, Chicago, Boston and New York. It is as authentic as any traditional 1970's-80's Chinese restaurant could be, neither modern nor eclectic. I spy Chinese and non-Chinese Asian patrons. People are eating familiar looking food from my life before Costa Rica - Cantonese vegetable art, black bean sauces, broad *chow fun* and bean sprout dishes, and one of favorites *sing chow chow mai fun,* a spicy curry noodle dish, Singapore style, made with thin rice noodles, green onions, shrimp, roast pork and egg.

The restaurant is very large and spotless. The waiters are friendly and efficient. The service is uncharacteristically prompt. Judging by their helpful hints, they have years of experiencc with the chef and the cuisine.

Do you enjoy cornucopia menus? This menu has it all from Westlake beef soup to Peking duck, from Szechwan spicy *ma po tofu* to edible seafood baskets, from sizzling rice hot metal skillets to steamed ginger flavored fish. The chili pepper is under-seasoned in keeping with Tico palates, but if you ask for extra spice, there is no problem – excellent balance between heat, sweet and savory. For your curmudgeon of an old aunt who informs you, after you are seated, that she really doesn't care for Chinese food, there is a steaks, fried fish and chicken and potatoes page.

Ma po tofu is a favorite of mine, but less so here in Costa Rica. When it comes with a dinner roll, is devoid of chili flakes, substitutes ground hamburger for savory pork, tosses over-cooked peas on top, uses canned mushrooms and yellow onions, I even prefer *chop suey seco*. At King's Garden the *ma po tofu* is fabulous - tender velvety bean curd, savory pork, finely sliced and crunchy black fungus, savory brown sauce and diced tender chives with enough hot pepper to warm my mouth (I ordered extra heat).

A fellow diner orders egg rolls. Even these generic appetizers are crunchier, less oily and tastier than the usual competition. Even the typically unappealing (to me) sweet and sticky dipping sauce is less sticky (less cornstarch) and pleasantly laced with ginger at King's Garden. The homemade hot sauce is great.

My only caveat - if you want dim sum, don't settle for the leftover stuff in heater case. Choose something else unless you are offered fresh fare just out of the kitchen.

On my next visit, I have the best hot and sour soup I have had in Costa Rica and a plate of Singapore style thin noodles with six juicy shrimp, bits of roast pork and an authentic tasting splash of curry.

Prices are moderate, particularly pleasing in light of the quality ingredients. Though more expensive than neighborhood faux Chinese restaurants, the cost is a bargain compared to the fancier venues.

The restaurant is located across the beginning of the highway from the tall hotel Tryp Corobici in a strip mall, upstairs from Papyrus and Mas X Menos supermarket. The entrance is around the corner.

It is open everyday from 11AM to 11:30 PM.

Telephone: 255-3838

La Brasserie

What happened to Jacques Nicaise? Jacques is originally from the French half of Belgium, but he had been in Costa Rica for 22 years with a continuum of experience as a French chef and restaurateur. His newest venture was a delight despite its anti-romantic location. La Brasserie is in the middle of La Ribera Mall in San Antonio de Belén. It sits on a busy corner next to a supermarket, diagonally across the parking lot from the food court. The tiny space holds six or seven tables indoors, a handful more outdoors and it looks out at the parking lot through walls of picture window glass. The interior design is limited to a single tasteful mural, conical glass ceiling lights and modest covering on the seats of the chairs. Green walls and earthtone accessories soften the atmosphere. Still, the interior is made comfortable by the pleasant waitstaff, smart table settings and lovely aromas from kitchen and adjoining tables.

On our first trip, my wife and I split a fabulous gorgonzola, walnut, poached pear and crisp lettuce salad dressed with a mildly tart Balsamic dressing ($7). She added a second appetizer, a delightful house special toast, topped pizza style with a medley of roasted vegetables ($3). I ordered about the most expensive dish on the modest menu ($12.50), a large portion of *blanquette ternera (Sp), blanquette de veau (Fr)* veal cubes and mushrooms in a Béchemel sauce (Eng). It was fork tender and very nicely seasoned. It would have been perfect had the sauce been just a little less thick. Also on the plate were three miniature summer squash, a cherry tomato and a nice potato fritter. Joan had a decent glass of Chilean merlot for $3. We finished the delightful meal with coffee and oven warm walnut and chocolate – macadamia cookies. With an extra ten percent tip for fine service, we spent less than $40.

The next visit was on a weekday at lunchtime. Joan had classic simple Parisian steak *frites*, a pound and a quarter thick, juicy sirloin that was remarkably tender and tasty – cooked to perfection and served with crispy fries and a small salad for $9. I tried the daily blue plate special, three courses for $ 5.75 before Christmas 2006. We noticed that the name had changed to La Brasserie. Jacques' name was gone and so was he, off to Nicaragua people thought. His replacement is a veteran chef from Italy with considerable experience working in quality French hotels. He is slight of build, soft spoken. Naples was his home.

The first course was a fine cream of oven roasted tomato soup. Second came as well prepared seabass *a la plancha* as I have had. The simple sauce of lime butter and parsley adorned a moist fillet browned on the outside. Matchstick carrot and sweet celery root and white rice were the sides. Dessert was a piece of Christmas cake – a moist yellow cake laden with holiday fruits and soaked in just enough Colorado rum to lightly flavor it without overwhelming the other ingredients. Our bill was a mere $20 including tip, tax and non-alcoholic beverages.

On a third visit, we noted that the onion soup was a little lighter than Jacques', the *blanquette de veau* was the same. I hoped that the menu, which hadn't changed, would be executed in the future with no appreciable diminution in quality. The acid test for Chef Mauricio came a month later. To my utter delight, I am often invited to lunch with the "out to lunch bunch" from the Women's Club of Costa Rica. It affords me the company of some very special women and a chance to sample as many as a dozen different dishes (usually no more than half a teaspoon of sauce). In late January 2007, they reserved a long table for 14 and 23 showed up. We occupied the entire inside of the restaurant and needed to add a few tables from out front. With one waitress and two in the kitchen, I expected chaos. I was wrong. Every dish, about thirty five counting first courses and desserts, came to the table carefully plated and appropriately heated or chilled. Beverages were no problem either, even when different steamed coffees concluded the meal. The owner helped keep the baskets of crusty bread and herbed butter, and tumblers of ice water filled.

For my part, I marveled at the sauces and how very different they were one from the other. The orange sauce was a rich dark demiglace with tangy Seville orange flavor; the Provencal was a tomato based, herbaceous, finely diced ratatouille; the Bercy buttery, Meniere silky and Florentine perfect.

At the end of the miraculously seamless meal, the diners toasted the owner and waitress and applauded the shy chef and his Latino sous chef when they emerged from the kitchen.

Very nice cuisine, attentive service and quite a value.

Jacques left seven other restaurants in his turbulent wake. El Refugio, Chef Jacques, Arthur and a few, whose names I don't remember, are all gone.

Open lunch and dinner except Monday

Telephone: 239-5410

Las Tapas de Manuel

Worldwide, many cuisines offer small plates of tasty comestibles. None seem to do it better than Spain. Some wonderful Costa Rican restaurants offer small plates that are like *tapas* in size, but with eclectic international ingredients, e.g. Ginger in Guanacaste and Park Café in San Jose. For traditional flavors of Spain, my choice is Las Tapas de Manuel.

I suffer from two maladies, the early-to-bed-early-to-rise syndrome and gastric reflux if I go to bed in fewer than two hours after a hearty meal. Were it not for *tapas,* I might have starved in Spain, where the main meal of the "day" begins around 10 PM and often lasts past midnight. Once in Madrid, when we actually ate at their usual hour, I fell asleep at the table and turned *gazpacho* red when my own snort woke me with a start. Yes, I love *tapas* for their flavors, but also for preserving my self-respect. Spanish *Tapas* bars open at 6 or 7 PM.

It is hard to extol the ambience of a restaurant in Plaza Itskatzú when the view from the congested parking lot stretches from faux Australian on one side to Boobs on Parade on the other with a total of about a dozen restaurants in between. Passing through the portals does achieve the sense of Iberia. Rustic tiles cover the floor. Baseboards, pillars and the front of the bar are done in Barcelona mosaic. Wrought iron sconces, chandeliers and grill work; bold paintings that cover the gamut from classic figures to transcendental fantasy; and the liberal use of brick all combine to transport the diner across the Atlantic. The menu seals the transition.

Of the forty odd *tapas*, the prices range from $3 to $4.50 and nearly 2/3 are hot. The three more expensive offerings are delicious baby eels, as thin as spaghetti, in garlic laden virgin olive oil, imported from Spain; a platter of imported cheeses; and shrimp cocktail made with jumbos. If you can't quite hear the flamenco guitar music, at least you can taste Serrano ham, authentic *manchego* sheep cheese, anchovies, black olives, mussels in white wine, sausage in fava bean soup, thinly sliced lambs tongue in marsala mushroom sauce, *gazpacho*, artichoke hearts with pimentos and Spanish salami, codfish croquettes, rabbit and almonds in a sauce of reduced sherry and garlic, octopus or smelts in oil and vinegar and many more. The crusty European style bread is baked in house. Creamy *aioli* with only a hint of garlic comes with the bread.

In addition to the *tapas*, the menu offers regular meals, weekly specials, a kids page desserts and a wide assortment of beverages. On Sundays at I PM, the house offers paella Valencia style (seafood, sausage, chicken and pork on a bed of saffron rice) for $7.50. The regular menu offers shrimp bisque and onion soup gratinée in addition to gazpacho, and lentil soup on the weekly menu. Salads, pastas, beef, chicken and seafood dishes complete the offerings.

Service is remarkably efficient, so you needn't order more than one or two small plates per person at a time. As if you were in Spain, relax and savor with sips of good wine.

Open seven days a week at noon. Closed at 9PM on Sunday, midnight on Friday and Saturday and 11PM other days.

Telephone: 288-5700

Lo Spago

The name caught my eye. Had Wolfgang Puck come to Costa Rica? The way he exploded from LA to San Francisco, New York and Las Vegas I thought it possible for a moment. Then I read the smaller letters affixed to Lo Spago's name – Da Marco – the same name as the fabulous chef from Da Marco in Piedades? Yes, the man from Verona whose cuisine I adore. In this simple, less elegant venue wedged in a strip of businesses, that seemed to be just another of dozens of pasta and pizza places, Marco scores again. With his partner Ricardo Rossi Ferrini, a charming white haired gentleman from Florence, they have another winner. They opened in the fall of 2006 on the road that runs from the highway to Cruz Roja in Santa Ana. It sits just a hundred meters north of Cruz Roja on the east side of the road.

The interior is tastefully simple. A Laurel and Hardy poster and old photos of Florence and Venice grace one wall and mouth-watering graphics of assorted menu items, the opposite wall. The menu offers a panoply of starters and enough main courses to satisfy all, but the pasta and pizza are the intended attractions. My first lunch was what I expected to the simplest of pastas, *pasta putanesca,* noodles in the style of prostitutes. There are several tall tales about the name, but the most often cited is that a woman of the night could prepare this dish quickly, between clients, by opening a few small jars and boiling pasta on a hot plate. From the jars would come capers, olives, anchovies and a little tomato sauce.

At Lo Spago, the pasta was linguini, homemade and pale green from the addition of fresh basil. Cooked to perfection *al dente* (on the teeth, firm but not hard), it came with the usual ingredients, but each was of excellent quality, especially the fine, not overly salty anchovies. Perfect simplicity.

We shared a well made Caesar salad with nicely balanced creamy dressing, anchovies, shaved reggiano parmigiano and fresh romaine; gorgeous beef *carpaccio* dressed in arugula, the same shaved cheese, a squeeze of lime juice and a twist of the black pepper grater; and a thin crisp pizza of Italian sausage, onion, red pepper and tomato on our second visit. It since has become a family favorite that doesn't disappoint.

Three other visits affirmed consistency and quality. The cream of vegetable and tomato soup, mushroom and arugula salad and polenta with gorgonzola sauce drew raves as first courses among our guests as did the spinach cannelloni and an assortment of pastas.

Despite the youth of the waiters, they were efficient and attentive. The prices are competitive with other pizza/pasta venues, but few can match the quality.

Lo Spago is open for lunch from 12 to 3 and dinner from 6 to 10 every day but Tuesday. Parking and access are easy.

Telephone: 582-2121

Lotus

Lotus is serene and pristine. From handsome floral carpets to light chartreuse walls adorned with lovely Chinese prints, from soft music to polite waiters, the mood is gentle. The food is authentic, unlike the majority of Chinese restaurants in our country, which court local palates with dinner rolls, gallo pinto and extra sugar. The chef, Jose Fang, was a professor of culinary arts at a college in Guangzhou before coming to Costa Rica with his wife Lili Zhang who tends the caja, and their children.

Presentations are simple and attractive. The overall impressions of the fare are conservative, genuine, labor intensive, carefully prepared and satisfying. I particularly like their renditions of hot and sour soup, steamed dumplings, seafood basket and mushu. The waiters are attentive, replacing cluttered plates with clean ones, replenishing hot tea and ice water and offering assistance. Prices are a little higher than the local competition.

The restaurant is less than 100 meters past Escazú's Del Centro Comercial Paco, on the same side of the road as it heads toward Santa Ana.

Open 11-3 & 5-10 Monday through Friday, 11-10 Saturday & Sunday

Telephone: 228-8105 & 228-8091

Lubnan

When my wife and I care to reminisce about our glorious visits to Syria and Lebanon, back in the days when it was possible, we head for a bountiful table bathed in the same sweet smells with Middle Eastern décor and music, down Paseo Colón to **Lubnan.** Authentic is the word that best describes the tasty food.

The mezze feast for two people includes 16 dishes that tease the palate and fill the belly with fabulous variety. Meats include juicy chicken kabobs, chicken livers in a luxurious sweet tomato sauce, *za'atar (zattar, zachtar)* flavored beef kabobs, ground beef flats, meatballs filled with beef and grains and fried croquettes of wheat and beef and lamb *schwarma (chawarma)* in a yogurt sauce.

Grains and starches are bulgar wheat, lentils, garbanzos, flat breads and rice alone or in combinations. Add cabbage and grape leaves stuffed with rice, lemon and beef; gherkin cukes in yogurt; Lebanese yogurt cheese; *hummus* and *tahini* topped with olive oil and paprika; perfect crispy falafel; tomato, mint and parsley *tabouli*: and a basket of fresh pita bread, and there is little room left on the glossy natural wood tables.

The spices are a balance of dry - cumin, coriander, sumac, *za'atar*, salt and pepper — and wet - garlic, onion, lemon and parsley. The tally for all of this for two with tip and tax, about $21.50. Two course meals average about $8.

For lamb lovers, the menu also includes juicy lamb chops done to pink perfection and tender lamb kabobs. My favorite salad is simplicity itself, Middle Eastern bread salad, *fattush* (*fatoush*). A standard lettuce, tomato, cucumber salad is dressed with garlic flavored citrus vinaigrette and tossed with crispy browned pieces of pita and sprinkled with sumac. Other choices include vegetarian dishes, raw ground beef mixtures and stuffed okra patties.

The dessert list is short, two pastries and a warm baked sweet cheese. The baklava and cookies are fine, but the star is the baked cheese dish. They all go well with the authentic coffee, ultra-fine ground dark roast cardamom flavor with an obligatory layer of black residue covering the bottom of the copper pitcher.

Like many restaurants in Lebanon and Syria, the décor suggests the inside of a brick and adobe fort with regional themes reflected in the wall prints. One of the prints is of a belly dancer. To see the real thing, reserve one of the twelve tables for Thursday night at 8 p.m.

The revolving hemp paneled front entrance adds a nice touch as do the beaded ceiling fixtures. Behind the main dining room are a bar and a room ideal for private parties.

The ownership and chef are Lebanese. The waiter is efficient, courteous and helpful.

If you arrive early, particularly at lunch time, you can usually park in one of the three spaces in front of the front door.

Very good food and good value.

Open Tuesday through Saturday for lunch (11-3) and dinner (6-1AM).

Telephone: 257-6071

Mangiamo

Kudos to the owners of Mangiamo for the willingness and ability to make major changes when their grand new restaurant stumbled. It is now well worth a visit. The venue is high tech with impeccable good taste. Chinese red walls and wine cabinets, neon blue recessed lights and blown glass are beautifully resplendent. Polished metal barstools and ducts, granite tabletops, leather banquettes, wrought iron and pale wood floors create the feeling of a modern Milanese high fashion, trendy club and bistro.

Shortly after it opened, I went there for a simple plate of pasta one lunch hour. There were more waiters than customers and the former looked a little nervous with good reason. I felt sorry for the owner(s) and decided that I would never review it formally. I was sure that it wouldn't survive and I wanted no part in contributing to its demise, especially in light of the obvious great care and cost of creating such an attractive space. The menu was so ambitious that I envisioned a Paul Bocuse army of apprentices, slaving away from early morning to meet expectations. The prices were substantially higher than the nearby competition, and out of the range of all but a small minority of folks who frequent the Santa Ana to San Antonio strip. Few locations in all of Costa Rica were home to more new restaurants than the mile or so north of the San Jose to Ciudad Colón highway next to the Forum, heading towards San Antonio de Belén. Ignoring Itzkasú, Santa Ana and Escazú, just along that mile, among the restaurants were three Japanese, two other Italian, a large pizza franchise, two Mexican, a sports bar, a large Tico soda, a roast chicken chain outlet, three cafés that serve pastries and light lunches, a deli, and a sandwich franchise. A new Italian seafood restaurant came and went along the strip in less than a year. A favorite of mine, a quaint Japanese restaurant, also went under. A new Argentinean steak house arose out of the ashes of a lavish Mediterranean restaurant.

On my first visit, a plate of pasta was undersauced and so badly overcooked that the noodles were mush. To add insult to injury, I was charged an extra $4 above the already substantial sum, the evening price for a noontime repast.

But lo these many months it stayed open, often with empty or near empty dining rooms (there is a second floor dining room as well, also beautifully appointed and ideal for private parties or meetings). So I returned reluctantly, assuming that a warning to our readers was in order.

WHAT A TRANSFORMATION! What a pleasant surprise! The menu is varied enough to be interesting but manageable. The prices are much lower and in keeping with the upper end competition (euphemism for "still expensive but a decent value"). The food is very good. The pasta is al dente. The sauces taste Italian. The plates are nicely presented. The quality of the ingredients is super.

After a third and equally pleasing visit, I asked a proud , smiling waiter about the chef and if he were new. The original chef was indeed gone. His replacement is a charismatic and charming Tico named Martin with the slender hands and long fingers of an artist. He paid a gracious visit to our table at the behest of the waiter. He is married to an Italian woman and worked in Navara, a city west of Milan, for two years before coming home to Costa Rica to try to help resurrect Mangiamo. Before leaving for Italy, he worked at Ponte Vecchio in San Pedro.

The table settings are pleasant. The diner is greeted with a basket of evenly toasted garlic cheese rounds and a bowl of warm fresh tomato sauce for dipping. The sauce is excellent and reappears on a number of different dishes. The attentive waitstaff refill ice water glasses and pour bottled beverages without having to be asked. They are well versed in the ingredients of the dishes and seem to really enjoy describing them and serving them.

The dozen or so starters include very nice Caesar and Caprese salads, smoked salmon, capriccio and fried calamari in the $5-7 range. An antipasto platter of buffalo mozzarella, grilled eggplant, prosciutto, Genoa salami and fresh basil is $12. The soup options ($3.50-5) include Tuscan white bean, *stracciatella* (chicken – spinach –eggdrop), minestrone and seafood.

Among the different pastas, gnocchi, raviolis and risotto, there are more than two dozen choices, all less than $8 except for two seafood and pasta dishes at $10 and 12. The chicken, fish, baby beef and veal dishes generally range from $8-10 with the following few very high end exceptions: two stuffed and/or layered chicken extravaganzas for about $14, jumbo shrimp dishes for about $18, roast duckling in orange sauce for $24 and a four chop rack of lamb for $34.

Many pleasant surprises include the addition of truffle oil to the capriccio dressing and mushroom cheese risotto, real Italian sausage in the sausage meat Bologna-style spaghetti, nice quality cheese atop the two parmagianas (grilled eggplant and tender veal) along with the same fresh tomato sauce and decaf coffee with full body and flavor for those of us who enjoy a cup after dinner but don't want our sleep interrupted.

A nice dessert change of pace is torron ($2), a white mousse drizzled with chocolate sauce and topped with pieces of nougat.

When the venue next door folded, Mangiamo opened an excellent satellite pizzeria, La Pizza, for less expensive alternatives.

Via Lindora is across the street from India Imports, a few hundred meters north of Auto Mercado in Santa Ana. There is ample parking and attentive security. Outdoor dining is also an option.

If you are among the denizens of diners who were disappointed when Mangiamo first opened, you might well be pleased if you were to give it a second chance.

Hours: 11-3 and 6-10 Tuesday thru Thursday. Friday 11-3 and 6-11. Saturday 11-11. Sunday 12-5. Closed Monday

Telephone : 282-0214

Oporto

Joan and I spent a month driving from Madrid north and west into Portugal, then south and east back to Madrid. The only parts of our itinerary that were fixed were the occasional nights when we got to stay in old castles, having made reservations months before. Run by the governments of Spain and Portugal, these *posadas* were amazingly affordable for regal elegance and history. I planned an entire day in the caves of Oporto, tasting vintages from the Dauro Valley, the world's most prestigious Port vineyards, the day before we went to an historic castle to stay two days. "The best laid plans...." I never imagined that all of Portugal would close for Columbus' birthday, our day in Oporto. We bought a bottle of port in a Seven Eleven look alike that we could have gotten anywhere and sipped it in our chateaux that evening.

When an acquaintance told me that his favorite restaurant in Heredia was called **Oporto,** I fantasized a second chance to sip good port after a hearty Portuguese meal. Alas, there is nothing Portuguese about what could indeed be Heredia's best restaurant. Two years ago, three sisters, who had never had a restaurant, opened a large and lovely one. In all fairness, they are not neophytes if you consider that one is a nutritionist and the other two studied food science in school.

Oporto is on the main road that runs from the Cariari autopista exit to Heredia. It is on the right side of the road just before you reach Heredia proper. The recipes are theirs. They trained the staff to prepare them according to their specifications. The entrance is through an iron gate into its private secure parking lot. Inside, a chalkboard lists the current specials that change every Tuesday. The stairway leads to lovely banquet facilities that could easily accommodate 50. The central skylight illuminates a Plexiglas pyramid in the center of the room, which, in turn, shines down through the ceiling of the first floor onto a fountain surrounded by potted palms and olive marble columns. The color scheme is gray and forest green below and lighter upstairs. Inside the main floor, more than a dozen pastries greet you from inside glass showcases in front of a large bar. The diningroom is split-level, non-smoking above, smoking below. Bathed in soft light, the setting exudes charm equal to the greeter's and an understated comfortable elegance.

As you begin to read the menu, the speed of the attentive service makes itself obvious: warm herbed biscuits, flavored butter and goblets of ice water appear in minutes. The menu advertises itself as international, but appears more Tico and Italian with a few North American additions. Pastas, steaks and fish dishes dominate.

On our first visit, Joan and I chose from what we guessed to be the less predictable offerings. She opted for the house pâté ($2,50) and jumbo shrimp fried in a coconut batter with mango dipping sauce ($10). I chose New England clam chowder ($3), a special listed as *sopa de almejas*, and baby back ribs ($6). Oh, what Gringo choices. For dessert we shared the house Oporto Torte ($2) which was unremarkable.

The pâté was rich and creamy, liver based, and served with toasts and blackberry jelly. The chowder was fair, a little salty and thin. Joan enjoyed the jumbo shrimp which were crispy and crunchy without being greasy, lots of coconut in the batter and well complemented by the mango sauce. Although, I prefer jumbo shrimp less sweet and simpler, this rendition might be as good as this dish gets. It came with a crunchy potato croquette and vegetables.

The ribs were a rack of eight, falling off the bone, tender, nicely seasoned, with standard barbeque sauce on the side. It came with a nice salad and potato croquette. Both courses were large and a challenge to finish. During our meal, 30 or so matrons descended the stairs from the banquet room nearly all carrying Styrofoam leftover boxes, suggesting that their portions were also very large. The "torte" was a slightly dry white cake with cream between the layers and dark chocolate frosting, not bad, but a little surprising for a featured dessert among so many visually appealing options.

Subsequently, we shared a very reasonable executive lunch special of tender thin steak covered with grilled onions, served with rice, cooked chayote and zucchini and a fruit drink ($3.75), and a marvelous hot sandwich of melted cheddar, turkey ham and poached pear on an egg twist roll ($3.50). Another diner had bountiful ravioli in a white cream sauce. The place was jam packed with white collar workers and well dressed young people eating everything from medium bowls of soup to large plates of salad to multi-course feasts. Our second dessert was an excellent hot pecan pie, creamy vanilla ice cream and a drizzle of caramel sauce ($2). Despite the large crowd, service continued to be unfrazzled, friendly, efficient and prompt.

Oporto deserves its popularity. It has a quality that the patrons belong, that they are not faceless transients passing through a meal, but rather, animated, nearly exuberant extended family members, especially the lunch crowd. The evening crowd is a little older and a little more sedate, but also has the feeling that most of the customers are cousins. Such status usually accrues exclusively to a family-run restaurant and only after decades. It is not the Mount Olympus of gourmet cuisine, but it does deliver attractively presented solid fare with some creative touches in a very comfortable setting by an accommodating staff at prices that are decent for the quality and volume.

Open every day but Sunday from 11:30 AM until 9:30 PM
Telephone: 263-2059

Plinio

About a half mile south of Quepos on the left side of the Manuel Antonio road is a favorite hotel and restaurant of locals, tourists and people like me who live too far away from the area to visit comfortably as a day trip. Plinio Hotel has that warm home-away-from-home feel, rustic natural beauty, very reasonable room rates and an excitingly diverse restaurant.

Hans and Sabine are originally German émigrés who have become long time Costa Ricans. They live nearby in Villa Nueva, with their enchanting 12 year old twin daughters, on an organic herb and vegetable farm that supplies the kitchen with green and black pepper corns, lemongrass, cinnamon, chili peppers and many of the ten ingredients that make up Sabine's fabulous house salad dressing. She is the amazing self taught head of the kitchen and teacher to the supporting staff. Over the last few years, she has orchestrated the change of focus from Tico, German and Italian to Thai, Indian and Indonesian cuisines. Now you can choose from all six. They are all remarkably decent due, in part, to the fact that she makes every sauce, curry paste and dressing in house from scratch and without MSG.

Our motley mess of a group descended on Plinio for three nights with a carnivore, vegetarian, Atkins dieter, spice lover and picky eater. After our initial dinner in house, we chose to take all our meals there. We were all delighted with our fare.

From the German part of the menu, you can choose *weisswurst, bratwurst, bockwurst* or smoked porkchops with potato, sauerkraut, pickles, mustard and horseradish.* All dishes come with bread and butter, a salad and great salad dressing. The sausages were $9.50 and the pork chops a dollar more.

The vegetarian loved spinach lasagna ($9), pasta pomodoro ($7.50) and margherita pizza ($7). Picky eater announced that she was going to stick to chicken and, miraculously, devoured, without complaint, whiskey chicken on a bed of fettuccini, Indian cardamom chicken with basmati rice, chutney and *nan* and chicken satay (all were $11). Our Atkins dieter found an appetizer he loved, smoked trout with horseradish cream and sorrel relish ($8). He also enjoyed surf and turf of beef tenderloin and shrimp ($17), tenderloin topped with melted gorgonzola ($15) and broiled fresh catch of the day ($11).

The fire eater ordered all of the following "extra hot": Thai chicken coconut soup ($6), Chiang Mai curry ($11.50), spaghetti arrabiata ($7.50) and red fish curry ($11).

I had and thoroughly enjoyed German style pork chops, Caesar salad, Indonesian *gado gado* salad, sesame crusted tuna steak ($12), Indian *saag panir* ($4), bratwurst and homemade chocolate cake with a scoop of ice cream ($5). Portions are large.

The restaurant is about three flights up from the parking lot. It looks out over tropical vegetation, wires that cross the canopy high above the road for families of capuchin monkeys to cross and flowers galore. The clientele is an eclectic assortment of savvy travelers and talkathon fishermen. Higher still up the hillside jungle is a nature walk and pretty good bird watching. A flight below the restaurant is hot tub, pool, bar and lunchroom. Breakfast is in the main diningroom.

Our sleeping quarters were two story suites with adequate amenities.

The bar and restaurant are open every day from 5 PM to 10.

Telephone: 777-0055

* Bockwurst - smoked and scalded, usually made from finely ground veal; spiced with chives and parsley; resembles a large frankfurter

* Bratwurst - a pale, smoked sausage made of finely minced veal, pork, ginger, nutmeg and other spices;

* Weisswurst - German for "white sausage" is very pale and delicately flavored; made of veal, sometimes beef and pork, cream and eggs; a specialty of Munich and traditionally served at Oktoberfest with rye bread, sweet mustard and, of course, beer.

Restaurant Sofia

In 2004, a reader e-mailed me raves about newly opened Restaurant Sofia on the road the links Santa Elena and Monteverde. She particularly loved "juicy tenderloin in a sauce of cashew nuts..... and my husband had banana (it turned out to be plantain) covered fish (*corvina*) which he loved."

In 2005, we spent four days in Monteverde, and I spread myself too thin, trying to sample the offerings of "a fabulous new chef at the Monteverde Inn", highly acclaimed El Sapo Dorado, and three very popular others, Morphos, Johnny's Pizzeria and Stella's Bakery. They all had their finer points. The star was Restaurant Sofia. El Sapo Dorado also had my attention. I had planned a leisurely nature visit in the spring of 2007 and more in depth looks at both restaurants. Unfortunately, a prolonged drought reduced Monteverde to a dusty shadow of its usual self, with a relative paucity of flora and birdlife. The rough unpaved road through Cerro Plano, on which Restaurant Sophia sits, was described by a friend as bone-jarring with the visibility, at times, of a Sahara sandstorm. Therefore, my feelings about the restaurant are based on a single visit, woefully below my usual standard. Word from others who have been there recently attests to its continuing excellence.

I had a marvelous steak in chipotle chili sauce and my wife had chicken in a sauce of not too sweet reduced guava. We shared a luxurious salad first and had only coffee after – hardly a tour de force of the Nuevo Latino sumptuous sounding menu replete with Thai spices and tropical ingredients.

Had we returned a second time, I suspect that Restaurant Sofia might find itself in the Four Star category today. Did I mention that, unlike the other Nuevo Latino restaurants around the country, its prices are quite reasonable?

We sat in the dining room that overlooks a lovely garden backed by cloud forest. Our between-bites entertainment was watching the comings and goings of more than a dozen bird species.

Open daily from 11:30 AM to 9:30 PM

Telephone: 645-7017

Saga

Great chefs all seem to share the same reverence and passion for the best ingredients perfectly prepared and beautifully presented. On rare occasions, a non-chef shares those same emotions. Simón Mekler, the owner of Saga, sparkles adoringly when he talks about and presents Saga's food. When he teases compliments out of diners, a very easy task considering the fine cuisine, he smiles with his eyes and mouth like a grandfather at the little princess's first dance recital.

Let's start by setting the stage. An enclosed lush garden serves as a warm backdrop for patio and diningroom. The interior is playfully cast in red, black and ivory with imaginative complimentary art and décor. The total concept is very attractive, yet comfortable and unpretentious.

The menu is full of international promise with elements from Argentina, Catalunya, Colombia, France, Greece, Hawaii, India, Italy, Japan, Sicily, Southern U.S., Spain, Thailand and, of course, great local produce and beverages. The fusions work well, components are expertly matched e.g. medallions of tenderloin in teriyaki sauce, jumbo shrimp on individual beds of golden passion fruit purée, salmon tartar with a *shoyu* dressing and corn tortilla chips, grilled chicken breast napped in peanut sauce with fried rice and pineapple chutney, pork tenderloin seasoned with Indian herbs and spices and served with orange flavored sweet potatoes or sesame seed crusted salmon steak sauced with a nice reduction of quality balsamic vinegar.

Presentations are artistically eye popping from humblest breadsticks, appetizers, soups, salads, main courses and desserts. In other restaurants, when the kitchen tries to get artsy, the food arrives cold or poorly prepared. Not here. The Saga kitchen and waitstaff deliver hot food on warm plates with artistic presentations worthy of the Food Network.

Well, what about the taste? So nicely balanced that I never thought to ask for salt, pepper or other flavor enhancers. The vegetables are also worthy of praise. Recently, I ordered pepper steak, a perfectly done (in Costa Rica I order steak *medio,* medium, and it comes medium rare) juicy very tender tenderloin. It came as the top layer of three layers surrounded by a classical pepper sauce. The bottom layer consisted of thick slices of grilled portobellos, crisp thin asparagus spears – heated through but nearly raw to the bite and julienned carrots, a little less crisp but not soft, fanned out across the plate. All three preparations were pleasing to my California Cuisine bent. The second layer was a mound of lumpy yellow mashed potatoes. The steak sat on top, for a while. The plate was stark naked when I finished. Simón and I both smiled.

Salad mavens think Saga is among the best salad places in Costa Rica. The sandwich menu is popular for lunch, but they come on jam packed baguettes, anything but dainty tea types. The ingredients include steak, roast beef, smoked turkey, baby mozzarella cheeses, Portobello mushrooms, sun dried tomatoes, guacamole etc.

The hardest choice is decide between a fine appetizer first or spectacular dessert last. Another reason Simón smiles is that his wife is the pastry chef. All the bread, pastry and ice cream are homemade. Two of the desserts are blue ribbon great. I haven't tried the others. First, good *cannoli* are hard to find in Meso-America. The reason is that ricotta cheese doesn't have the right consistency here. (Neither does cottage cheese, so I have trouble making blintzes.) Saga uses slightly sweetened and kiwi scented cream cheese instead, and pipes it into a tubular lace pecan pastry, crunchy and delicious. Add to it kiwi ice cream and a pale green sauce speckled with kiwi seeds.

Sounds good, but no chocolate? The second exemplary dessert is less rare, but no other version is better. Chocolate Volcano is chocolate ganache or cake baked to order with a molten chocolate center. The cake is typically wider on the bottom than the top. Saga's version is a fluted chocolate ganache filled with dark bittersweet chocolate sauce, hot out of the oven (allow 12 minutes from the time of your order until it arrives). Along side is a scoop of vanilla ice cream topped by a sugar cookie banner striped in chocolate and brown and white sauce.

Prices are not bad for Escazú but are not for people on a tight budget. Appetizers run $5-9, main courses $8-17, salads $6-9, soups $4-6 and sandwiches $8-9.

From the three way corner in front of Paco Center, go north, away from the Escazú – Santa Ana road, for 400 meters. Saga is on the right (east) adjacent to the Dutch ambassador's house.

Open Monday tro Saturday 11AM to 11PM. Sunday 11 to 6
Telephone 289-6615

Saisaki

Guilty as charged – I am an addict of Asian food. There certainly are enough decent Chinese and Japanese restaurants to feed my habit. Taj Mahal meets most of my Indian cravings. Tin Jo's elegance and variety are wonderful. Their Thai dishes are quite nice. Add a few samples of the cuisines of Indonesia, Viet Nam, India, Japan and the Philippines to their Chinese cornucopia, and I hardly find myself wanting. Chili Rojo, El Jardin and Plinio, among others, add more Thai and a little Vietnamese variety. Perhaps, all that I crave to complete my Asian yearnings are variety and quality from Korea, Vietnam and the Philippines.

Two out of three aren't bad. Saisaki is more than just another good Japanese restaurant. The owner/chef is from Manila and learned to cook Korean and Japanese food in Japan. His fifteen page menu has three Filipino pages and a Korean page along with his grand assortment of Japanese goodies.

My favorite two Korean/Japanese restaurants closed in the past two years. Saisaki has emerged as my new favorite for *kim chee, bulkogi, bibimbap, chabchebap* and green onion pancakes. Korean cuisine is loaded with salt, garlic and hot chili peppers – not an ideal trio for Tico palates. Fortunately, Saisaki has a large enough following for its Japanese cuisine to be able to maintain the integrity of its Korean dishes. The *kim chee* (fermented red-hot Napa cabbage) is a little light on the garlic and a little less fiery than typical, but satisfying. Marinated strips of sirloin in the *bulkogi* are flavored expertly. In Korea, *bibimbop* or *bebimbop* is a popular rice bowl mixed with seaweed, spinach, sesame seeds, onions, bean sprouts and barbequed beef strips, topped with a fried egg. The bowl itself is oven-proof ceramic. The dish is baked in a hot oven so that the interface where rice meets bowl browns an outer crust on the rice. Outside of Korea, consider yourself lucky if the bowl is heated ceramic, even without a crust. At Saisaki, the bowl is hot ceramic. The ingredients are fine. A little Japanese chili powder on the side is the perfect condiment. *Chabchebop* is the common noodle dish in Korea.

Among my favorite Filipino dishes are Shanghai-style *lumpia* - crispy little egg rolls, *pancit* – the country's standard collection of noodle dishes, *adobo* – stew of chicken and/or pork in red oil and *pata* – crispy roasted pig's foot. Saisaki has them all. The *pata* is a huge well seasoned *chicharrone* with bones and toes, served with a dark, salty dipping sauce.

How about the eleven pages of Japanese food? They are filled with more variety than most restaurants in Japan: *sushi, sashimi, teriyaki, tempura, donburi*, three kinds of noodles, *teppan-yaki*, skewers, *gyoza* - dumplings ($3), soups, seafood salad ($3.50) and more. A thirteen piece set of *nigiri (*seafood) sushi is $10.50. Seven piece orders of sashimi average $4-5. Among a large number of exotic sushi rolls, an eight piece caterpillar roll is $5. *Nabeyaki udon* $8, miso soup $1.75 and *edamame* soy beans for $3 are similarly priced fairly.

I even had a dessert on one occasion of peach ice cream wrapped in batter, covered with hedge hog-appearing tempura spicules, drizzled with guava sauce ($3).

The décor is modest Japanese. The clientele is yuppie. The star of the show - the tasty, virtually authentic, reasonably priced food.

To get there, head north off Paseo Colón for half a block at Kentucky Fried Chicken on 36th street.

Open for lunch (11-3) and dinner (6-10) everyday.

Telephone 223-7097

Sakura and Fuji

What are more symbolic of Japan than *sakura,* or cherry blossom, and Fuji, the perfectly conical sacred mountain of pilgrimages? No surprise, therefore, that there are dozens of fine restaurants world over named Sakura and Fuji, from South Africa, Switzerland, England, New Zealand, Australia, Hong Kong, Bangkok, New York, Chicago, Little Rock and San Francisco to Costa Rica.

My Japanese food eating desires have been blessed by four situations. Before Costa Rica I lived in San Francisco and New York for most of my life, got to visit Japan three times for several weeks each time, took my cardiology fellowship for two years a few hundred yards away from Japan Town in San

Francisco, where I took more than half my lunches. I was invited to celebrations and feasts by Japanese-American patients in my practice for thirty years.

Like one of Pavlov's dogs, my yen for Japanese food is easily stimulated by certain triggers: sushi and green tea for serenity before a poker competition; warming food on a windy cool day like *nabeyaki udon,* an earthenware pot or a metal kettle, steaming hot, filled with *dashi shiru (*broth made from bonita flakes with a little sweet sake and soy), thick white *udon* noodles, slices of fish cakes (*kamboko)* and/or wheat gluten cakes *(fu),* two tempura fried prawns, occasionally pieces of chicken, spinach or kale, leek, scallion and an egg on top, served with Japanese chili powder on the side; and nostalgia from student days for a plate of *gyoza* – ginger and garlic flavored meat dumplings or *katsu donburri,* a rice bowl with sweet omelette, onions and fried breaded pork loin on top, served with its own special dark brown sauce, *tonkatsu* sauce.

It seems that only authentic fare quenches my hunger. Although there are about two dozen very nice Japanese restaurants here in Costa Rica, few of them satisfy my need for the real thing. Maybe the "real thing" no longer exists. Philadelphia sushi hand rolls with cream cheese and smoked salmon now seem to grace every menu from Vancouver to Patagonia. Sacrilege!

Worldly Costa Rican friends suggested that I try either Sakura or Fuji for authentic Japanese food.

Sakura is a relatively expensive Japanese restaurant with a traditional heritage. The adjacent hotel once had Japanese owners and catered to Japanese tourists. Those days are long gone. The former Hotel Herradura is now the Ramada and the kitchen staff is all Filipino. Still, some of the trappings persist. As you enter the gate, there is a koi pond, but red swordtails have replaced the koi. Azaleas and clump grass augment local shrubbery for an Asian feel. There is even a tiny stand of heavenly bamboo.

Inside, an elegant long sushi bar and lots of wood offset the lack of traditional table settings, porcelains, shoji panels, masks and geisha prints. I was saddened, however when my green tea came in a plastic tea pot and coffee mug. The esthetics of serving tea are paramount to the culture. My *miso shiru* soup was weak. The *gyoza* were prepared traditionally, browned on the bottom and steamed on top, but the flavors that set them apart from Chinese pot stickers, ginger and garlic, were absent. The fault is not theirs alone. Thus far, nearly all the *gyoza* I have eaten in Costa Rica are wanting in flavor. I wonder if many or most Japanese restaurants are using the same frozen Chinese product.

Nabeyaki udon did come in an earthenware bowl with a cover. I asked for and got the right kind of imported chili powder. It came with the requisite soft cooked egg on top, a single medium size tempura-cooked prawn and a few small pieces of chicken, sliced leek and three slices of fish cake. The broth was tasty with enough shaved bonito for flavor and proper sweetness from sweet sake, *mirin*. Too many Japanese restaurants ruin good dishes by overwhelming broths and sauces with soy sauce, that I feel like a hypocrite for complaining that the otherwise lovely broth needed a little *shoyu* to balance the other flavors. The *udon* was perfect, fat pure white and not overcooked. Overall, not a bad dish. On another occasion, the sushi was respectable, pieces a little small and prices on the high side.

11-3 & 6-11 Monday-Saturday, 12:30-10 on Sunday.
Adjacent to the Cariari Ramada Inn.
Telephone: 239-0033

Fuji is closer to my ideal than any of the other options. Enter the lovely lobby of Hotel Tryp Corobici, just past the origin of the Pan American Highway at Sabana Park.

Ascend the stairs at the far end and notice three red lava rocks on a bed of straw colored pebbles that would look at home in Kyoto, traditional lantern and paintings. At the top of the landing, bamboo poles and a heavy wooden door mark the entrance. Inside, the tables are set with fan shaped place mats and carefully folded upright white cloth napkins. Shoji panels backdrop the far wall and geisha prints and a symbolic representation of Mount Fuji draw your attention to the polished wooden sushi bar. Potted palms add greenery around the large room. Most of the other diners and the chef appear to be Japanese.

My green tea comes in a hand painted ceramic pot with bamboo handle and a tastefully chosen ceramic cup. Both sit on worn wooden coasters. The circle of tranquility, the *wah,* surrounds the table.

Homemade *gyoza,* perfectly browned on the bottom and steamed soft on top, emit aromas of Japanese braising. Bits of green fleck the chopped meat juicy filling. Alas there is no discernable ginger or garlic flavor, but the taste is more savory than any other *gyoza* I have had in Costa Rica. For a dipping sauce, I mix rice vinegar and a little soy sauce from the table.

A steaming black kettle of *nabeyaki udon* comes next. Under the wooden lid float all the classic ingredients, a pair of very large tempura battered prawns, fish cake slices (*kamboko),* a coddled egg, pieces of sweet wheat gluten cakes (*fu),* greens and a fragrant broth. My only disappointment is that the *udon* is a less common variety of noodle, not as thick or white as my favorite. Texture and taste are quite good, however.

Second visit is perfection. Two of us enjoy a crisp and light tempura appetizer of shrimp and vegetables ($13) and rare tuna in a citrus-soy *ponzu* sauce ($8) followed by two noodle dishes, cold buckwheat noodles with a dipping sauce($11) and hot thin egg noodles in a *miso* soup ($10)

Three's a charm and so is *kaiseki bento (*$21), an elaborate classic in a lacquer box.

Fine traditional Japanese food in a lovely harmonious environment is even more expensive in Japan as it is at Fuji. Is it worth one and a half to twice the price of the mid range competition? For the Nipponophile aficionado, I would thick so.

Open daily from noon to three and 6:30 to eleven.
Telephone: 232-8122

Sale e Pepe

Hidden behind Pops on Escazú's main drag is "Old Faithful", not the geyser, but the restaurant, Sale e Pepe. Whenever I question friends about their favorite places to eat, they offer up a few four or five star elegant diningrooms and then add, as if rehearsed in unison, "and of course I (we) really like Sale e Pepe." As basic and reliable as are salt and pepper, so too are pasta and pizza at Sale e Pepe. They all agree that the food is consistent, hearty, well seasoned, reasonably priced and served hot and promptly.

The menu offers ample choices. Under the antipasti heading are 17, including the likes of octopus cocktail, *caprese* salad, eggplant *parmagiana*, smoked salmon, and three each *carpaccios, foccacias* and cream soups. They are nearly all $5-6.

Pasta comes as *penne*, spaghetti or *fettuccini* - unstuffed ($5-8) and as ravioli, *tortellini, tortelli* or *cannelloni* - stuffed ($6-12). All told, there are over thirty different varieties including a pair of lasagnas. If you can't decide, the pasta Sale e Pepe is a safe choice. It appears to be no more than a simple tomato sauce, but is actually a mixture of tomato sauce, cream sauce and pesto. The fresh basil undertone and smooth texture are the giveaways.

From the pizza side of the menu there are more choices than the pasta panoply, particularly if you consider two dozen items that you can add to any of the two dozen combinations spelled out. Yes, they are thin crusted and topped most generously.

The sizes, too, seem larger than most pizzeria standards. Smalls average $6, mediums $7.50 and larges $10.

There are daily special meals that go beyond pasta or pizza, desserts and beverage options that include beer and wine.

The back of Pops and a parking lot constitute the minimal view out large windows. Pale yellow walls sport painted grape vines, leaves and fruit. Arches are painted to look like old brick oven doors. First and second floor diningrooms are small, clean and quaint, but hardly romantic. Table-ware is cafeteria simple. Tablecloth colors are solid red, green and yellow, the material synthetic. Service is friendly and efficient. Water glasses and *focaccia* slices appear without asking.

For consistency, quality and value, Sale e Pepe earns its popularity.

Open for lunch and dinner everyday but Tuesday, it closes from 3-6PM Monday, Wednesday, Thursday and Friday. It opens at noon every day and closes at 10PM on Sunday, at midnight on Saturday and at 11PM other nights.

Telephone: 289-5750

Sushi Nippon, Sensu, Samarai, Ichiban, Matsuri

Muro-ji, Kabuki

Costa Rican sushi is generally quite good. If you learn the local fish, you can expand your options to include marlin and snapper. The other fish, including tilapia and tuna, which can be caught here, are generally imported. A few rules of thumb are universal. Go to a busy place where the turnover is most likely to be rapid. In general, don't look for bargains. If the place smells like a fish market, leave. Choose salt water species over fresh. If you are a beginner, start with only a little *wasabi*, the green paste, well-diluted with soy sauce, or risk pain all the way up into your sinuses. Eat the pieces whole in one bite. The fish should be moist and shiny, not dull and dry.

The accompanying pickled ginger is a palate cleanser to freshen your taste buds between different types.

It is impossible to compare all the different sushi bars to each other. I have to rely on opinions of frequent sushi eaters and then visit at least once, myself. We are blessed with five Japanese restaurants that have multiple locations - Ichiban, Matsuri, Moru-ji, Samarai and Sensu. Each has its own devotees. For sushi, Ichiban, Matsuri and Samurai are the most popular, but only their busier locations are considered. I like the sashimi combo at Muro-ji at Plaza Florencia in San Rafael de Escazú. The only real bargain with exceptional quality that I would endorse is Nippon Sushi Restaurant, in the mall just down the hill from McDonalds next to Heredia's University of Costa Rica campus. Another solo operation that appears quite promising in its first few months of operation is Kabuki in Escazú.

Sensu is not bad. It doesn't quite equal the others for sushi, but its other Japanese dishes are OK and priced reasonably. For décor, I prefer Samurai in Santa Ana, Ichiban in La Ribera and Kabuki, which has five elaborate bento boxes for $8-9.50. Ichiban probably has the edge as well for overall cuisine in this price range. More costly venues such as Fuji and Sakura may be better, particularly Fuji.

Japanese Food Comparative Prices May, 2007

	California Roll *	Katsu Don*	Shrimp Tempura*	Gyoza
Fuji	$7	$11	$16	$4.50
Ichiban	$3.50	$8.25	$11	$3.90
Kabuki	$ 4.25	$7.85	$11	$3.85
Matsuri	$6	$8.50	$13	$4.50
Muro-ji	$4.25	$7.95	$10	$3,75
Sakura	$6.50	$9	$17	$4
Sushi Nippon	$3.25	$4.50	$6	$2.50

Samurai doesn't offer katsu-donburi on its menu. When I ordered it at the Santa Ana branch without looking at the menu, the perplexed waitress turned to the sushi chef for help. He spoke to the kitchen and I received a perfect rendition for $10.

Shogun, my favorite little place, changed chefs, lost its menu edge and clientele and closed in 2006.

See index for phone numbers.

Terruño

When I first went to Terruño in early 2007, it was with three men friends. We had large well prepared steaks with too much robust red wine. I had a hard time remembering any subtle nuances after I got home, except that it seemed like a night at a posh men's club in New York, with fake inside windows and old photos. The color scheme went from somber terra cotta to black by way of several shades of brown – strong, male, but not gloomy. The backdrop was a handsome well stocked bar. Wood, wrought iron, dark ceramic tile and leather placemats completed the essence of urban sophisticated gaucho. Genteel watchful service added to the clubby feel and the waiters wore black.

Weeks later, gourmet gab dubbed Terruño as the newest hot spot in town, about the same time people began to notice that the former La Sabana location had closed. The town in this case is Plaza Itskatzú and its wall-to- wall restaurant row. It sits in the back on the right side, next to the Cuban restaurant, Gua Gua and across from the lovely new café, Fitzgerald. Too macho for romantic couples? I put it to the acid test on Valentine's Day and took my most deliciously feminine side there, my lovely wife. Several couples and a few entire families were dining comfortably, with no pall of a testosterone cloud.

Shamelessly I admit to liking cornmeal *empanadas*, deep-fried Costa Rican style, greasy fingers and all, but well prepared Argentinean *empanadas* are clearly in a class above. They are made with wheat flour, filled with juicier and more savory beef or chicken in a little gravy and baked to golden brown perfection. Terruño's *empanada* appetizer is a pair each of meat and chicken filled pastries ($3.75). None better.

Among other starter choices are *ceviche*, flavored cheese, carpaccios of beef, salmon or marlin and an assortment of tempting salads.

Steaks are the name of the game, same as all the other Argentinean restaurants in Costa Rica. They are aged to tenderness, juicy, tasty, large and prepared as ordered ($10-20). Brochettes ($ 9.50-15.50) include a fine seafood choice of salmon, large prawn and tuna. Cherry tomatoes guard the ends. Onion and green pepper fill the gaps. An order consisted of two large skewers, *pico gallo* in extra virgin olive oil and a salad with oil and balsamic vinegar.

Among the chef's suggested specials are small chicken bites *al verdeo* ($9), Beef Milanese ($9.50), small steaks in a smoky Sicilian Marsala sauce ($11), pork cutlets *a la riojana* ($9.50) and pork steak in sweet and sour sauce ($9.50). Add to the options an assortment of fish and chicken dishes ($9-11) and pastas ($3.75-15). The only remaining choices are beverages and dessert.

Costa Rican cheesecake suffers from a penchant to make it very light by adding gelatin to the batter, and, at times, coating the top with a layer of red Jell-O. I don't miss the leaden density of New York's typical version, but, to me perfection is New York's flavor with more density than Tico style. The best cheesecake either of us have ever had in Meso-America is Terruño's, served on a raspberry *coulis* ($5).

Why is Terruño the current rage? For starters, it is a new well run place that offers generous portions of tasty food. However, the baton seems to pass from place-to-place rather quickly. First among the Argentinean "hot spots" was La Esquina de Buenos Aires, then Donde Carlos, then Ni-Fu Ni-Fa despite its name, followed by El Novillo Alegre. Which of these are good? In my opinion, they are all very nice and each has a little difference in their presentation and emphasis. I liked San Telmo, which closed in 2006 and has been replaced by another good one, Bariloche. Surely there are subtle differences more obvious to Argentina cognoscenti than to me. The serious steak eaters seem to prefer Ni-Fu Ni-Fa's cuts of beef to the others. Loyalties are otherwise divided with perhaps a slight edge going to El Novillo Alegre. Only time will tell where in the pecking order Terruño re-emerges after the flame of newness subsides.

Open for lunch and dinner seven days a week
Telephone: 588-2227

Tutti Li

Yet another good restaurant buried in the plethora of Italian competitors, Tutti Li in plaza Itskatzú serves very fine home-made *fettuccini*, thin crusted pizzas, a nice array of appetizers and pastas, standard meat, chicken and fish main courses, *gnocchi*, ravioli, *risotto*, *cannelloni* and *focaccia*. The décor is attractive. The service is professional and attentive. (I haven't been to their original location in Curridabat.)

The prices are typical of the upscale Plaza Itskatzú location (back, left corner). Appetizers range from $6 to $10, the least expensive is a dish of eggplant rolls filled with cheese and accompanied by tomato basil sauce. Most expensive is the multi ingredient antipasto including *prosciutto* imported cheeses and quality olives. Salads run from $5 to $9. *Risotto marinara* and *risotto tres hongos* are $10 and $13. Dry pastas are $7 to $10. Homemade *fettuccinis* are $12 to $20

Main courses come with mixed fresh vegetables and rosemary roasted potatoes. They average $8 for chicken dishes, $10 for fish and $14 for steaks. Pizzas cost $6 to $10 for small ones, about one and a half the price for mediums and twice the price for large.

My only disappointment was the *scaloppini ala Marsala* ($8). What I assumed would be veal turned out to be thinly sliced and pounded beef over-floured in a sauce that was heavily seasoned with vinegar. A nice serving of *cannoli* for dessert more than made up for it.

All in all, the Chinese chef/owner, Mr. Li, does a nice job in a pleasant professional venue that is neither spectacular nor a bargain compared to the stiff competition, but pleases all comers.

It opens every day at noon and closes at 10:30 Monday thru Thursday, 11 on Friday and Saturday and at 9 on Sunday.

Telephone: 588-2405

Chapter 15
Unique Eateries

Restaurant Loveat

Worldwide vegetarian cuisine with a gluten-free option on 500 beautiful acres, that are home to twenty-three Israeli expatriates, meets the criteria for *unique* in my mind.

Between San Ramon and La Fortuna, the two lane road, Route 272, winds through farms, nurseries, quaint towns and a cloud forest. Several roadside stands sell local *palmito* cheese, tightly rolled balls of tart white cooked cheese that peel off in fettuccini sized ribbons. There are a few nice craft shops along the way. As the road descends from the mountains and the dracaena nurseries, billboards announce adventure tours and an Israeli restaurant. Sure enough, 32 kilometers from San Ramon, a large sign marks the entrance of Lands in Love Hotel and Resort and its restaurant, Loveat.

Inside the gate, the road passes through gardens, natural foliage, flowers, a frog pond, past a pet hotel and in sight of lovely sculptures of plants and animals. Twenty-three Israelis came here for peace, tranquility, a healthy lifestyle and a safe haven for them and their myriad pets. They are a sophisticated, eclectic group of adults from age 25 to 55 who eat a vegetarian and gluten-free diet.

Na'ama is the chef. She is charming, charismatic and a culinary wizard. Her repertoire includes dishes from all over the world, seasoned deftly with, among other accents, *za'atar, sumac, tahini, wasabi,* fennel seed, coriander, chilies, cumin, turmeric and spices from Thailand, India and Mexico. You can choose from cheese blintzes, egg rolls, Indian rice, falafel, sushi, lasagna, Mexican tacos, pad Thai, hummus, quiche Lorraine, pasta, soy-based burgers and hot dogs, gluten-free dishes, salads, *gallo pinto,* snacks, omelets, sandwiches and glorious desserts. Her hummus, falafel, lasagna, chocolate fudge cake, pad Thai, and mixed fruit cheesecake are all as good as any in Costa Rica.

The restaurant is open for all three meals, everyday. All meals cost about $10 - $12 before tip and tax. Desserts are$2.

The restaurant is airy, cooled by multiple ceiling fans, pristine and lovely. Art deco panels line the ceiling, pastels and prints adorn the walls. Don't miss the Chagall at the far end.

If you are only passing by on your way to or from La Fortuna, stop for a refreshing *batido* or a cup of rich coffee and slice of cheesecake. If you are interested in adventurous activities, the hotel offers suspended cable rides, rafting, horseback riding in a cloud forest, hiking trails in 500 acres of valley and a large pool.

475-1081

Tilapia Park

If you have young kids or grandkids in tow, consider fishing and eating the catch. Turrucares is a pretty town south of La Garita guarded by a four-way stop sign. A few minutes east of the stop, in the direction of Ciruelas, a sign for **Tilapia Park** points south down a well maintained gravel road. Trucks from the quarry below chug up and down the road from Monday through Friday, but on weekends and holidays, it becomes the gateway to the Land of Oz for tykes who would catch fish.

Snuggled in the crook of a wooded ravine below the quarry, a manmade fish pond beckons. Munchkins rent hand lines for 20 cents and a bag of bait ample to serve six of them for another 20 cents. The rule is simple: you pay market prices for the fish you catch (about $2.50 a pound). There are even pond-side benches and canopies for shade and buckets for the fish. Best of all, the cool open air restaurant serves whole fried tilapia and good tilapia *ceviche* – just like the fish in the buckets, cold beer for the elders and hot dogs, burgers, fries, ice cream, yuca and *refrescos* for the munchkins who love the place. Parents and grandparents kick back and eat and drink.

A plate of two fried fillets, fries and a salad costs about $4.75. For an extra 85 cents, you can have a whole fish fried, one of the ones the kids caught, or one taken from the holding tank. They don't come any fresher. Even though tilapia is a fairly bland fish, when junior catches one and has it served to him or her on a plate with two colored cabbage slaw, seasoned with a squirt of lime, it is ambrosia. Pura vida.

Persa Mex

Yes, indeed, Persa Mex is half Persian and half Mexican. Martha is Bolivian and her husband Iman is Persian. They lived in Mexico for years.

So they opened a restaurant, bar and fusion grill with a menu that includes an eclectic mixture of plates from the Middle East and south of the U.S. Border.

From the Persian menu, care to start with a tasty eggplant and yogurt *Kashko Bademjoon ($3.75)?* For the main course, all four choices are kabobs served with Persian rice and roasted tomatoes. They are cubes of marinated steak, *Barb Kabad de Res* ($9.50), similarly prepared chicken, *Barg Kabad de Pollo* ($7.50), ground beef mixed with puréed onion, *Koobideh Kabad de Res* ($8.50) and a plate that includes all three *Soltani de Carnes* ($11.50).

From the Mexican offerings, you can choose from four kinds of *burritos* ($4.75 - 6.75), two *fajitas (*$ 6-7), *nachos, quesadillas* and *guacamole.*

The other options are an executive lunch of the day ($5.50), fresh fish of the day ($8.50) and house salad, Cesar salad and cream soup of the week all for about $5.

Persa Mex is located just to the right of the entrance to Real Cariari that faces the Pan American Highway in the strip known as Plaza Gourmet.

Open

Telephone: 293-4237.

Xandari Resort and Spa

In the hills above Alajuela sits a veritable Eden, a forty acre coffee plantation turned into a sumptuous resort and spa. The gardens are lush and fragrant, the panoramic view of Costa Rica's Central Valley awesome and the architecture perfect for the setting - sybaritic, lavish, spiritual yet simplistically wholesome in mood and appearance.

The restaurant serves diners, indoors and out, with a view over a balcony and a bed of heliconias that never stops. Inside, the furniture is custom designed and comfortable, the furnishings and art outstanding. Add the creative fusion cuisine of Flor Rojas that she has evolved toward perfection over the past eleven years and Xandari should be listed with the three or four star elites.

The reason it ended up in the "unique" category, is because for half or more of each year, dinner is nearly impossible for the public. Xandari is first and foremost a resort hotel and spa with primary allegiance to its registered guests. Few leave the property for dinner. Many do go out and about on day trips, leaving seats more available during lunch. If you are determined to try for dinner, call the lovely English speaking manager of the restaurant, Marcella Arias, for assistance. She can't reserve a table for you, but she can put your name on a list for available seating. You are more likely to be successful in the off- season. Don't try to come for dinner without calling first. Your best bet is to go there for lunch or book a room.

From the greenhouse and gardens come the lettuce, fresh herbs, cherry tomatoes, sweet red peppers, oranges and bananas. They purchase the finest available fresh fish, chicken and prawns, and good cuts of meat. For the vegetarian, the menu offers tremendous variety, including additions of soy protein prepared to simulate beef, chicken and fish.

Beginning with breakfast, guests (complimentary) and visitors ($8) choose from fruits, granola, yogurt, homemade bread and muffins, bagels, corn pudding, egg and vegetable loaf, cheeses, coffee, tea, fruit juices and a handful of a la carte specialties that include sumptuous Xandari pancakes made with rum, bananas and granola, ($4.50), *choreadas* (corn pancakes $4) and fried plantains ($2).

The lunch menu offers corn chowder, black bean soup and cold gazpacho($4 each); seven salads, including the very popular pura vida chicken salad ($6), a blue cheese, cashew, almond mix on a bed of green dressed in walnut oil and an interesting medley of hummus, babaganoush , guacamole, beet/potato salad and Tico salad ($6). The five sandwich choices come with a small side salad. Served on whole grain rolls, they are crab salad; curry chicken salad with mango or pineapple; guacamole, tomato and cucumber with black olives and hummus; grilled chicken breast with either chipotle or herbed mayonnaise, lettuce and avocado; and fabulous grilled eggplant, roasted red peppers, blue cheese, red onions and pesto mayonnaise. Specialties include very tasty fish tacos, veggie wraps, fruit platters and corn pancakes. If you ask, you may also be able to get the breakfast Xandari pancakes. Of nine desserts, flourless chocolate cake sounds the most unusual. Not to be outdone for creativity, the kids' menu has peanut butter and jelly empanadas along with about another dozen more standard options. Oops, I left out the pizza and snack lists.

For dinner, after about a dozen appetizing sounding starters, you to get to choose from about two dozen main courses - about a third each international, Tico and vegetarian. Without taking you through an exhaustive description of so many creative platters, let me show you just the four sea bass and shrimp items to demonstrate Flor's range of elegant simplicity.

Greek Island sea bass – Sautéed and basted in olive oil that has been infused in oregano, the sea bass is topped with chopped tomatoes, black olives and blue cheese ($12).

Japanese sea bass – Marinated in a sauce of citrus, garlic and soy sauce, the sea bass is pan seared and served with wasabi ($12).

Japanese grilled shrimp – The shrimp are brushed with olive oil and garlic, grilled and served with amari sauce (the same as the marinade for Japanese sea bass) and wasabi ($16).

Grilled shrimp Provençal - Brushed in olive oil and grilled, the shrimp are served with a brandy, tomato, garlic and basil sauce ($16).

To get there: From the Alajuela court house, go north 3.2 kilometers towards Poas, turn left after a small bridge, go for 1.3 kilometers, then right for another 0.9 kilometers.

Open for breakfast, lunch and dinner everyday.

Telephone: 443-2020

Magic's Motown

His parents named him Benjamin. Physically limited by polio as a child, his activities were limited to show and tell entertaining. He earned his second name when he performed slight of hand tricks for his peers. They called him Magic. Some family and friends call him Fraga, the name his Portuguese father called him. Who knows what his preschool-size eight month old son will call him when he talks. We could make a case for calling him Lazarus or Phoenix, but let's go back to teenager Magic and his home in San Francisco's Excelsior District.

Only a few inches shy of seven feet tall, young Magic sold hot dogs at Giant games in Candlestick Park. He rose to become a concessionaire and ultimately had his own fast food emporium on the second floor of the hotel, New York, New York in Las Vegas at the other end of the hall from Nathan's Famous Hot Dogs. He served only chicken wings and burgers, but with more than a hundred different sauces. His idea and a lot of hard work proved quite successful. He sold the business, moved to New York and ultimately ended up here with a lovely wife and child. He brought his formula for success and an enduring love of Motown music and an awesome collection of recordings of its stars, Lionel Ritchie, Stevie Wonder, Smokey Robinson, Diana Ross and the Supremes, to name a few.

He rented the defunct cavernous El Toro Negro restaurant, installed an impressive music system, had murals painted in the likenesses of his favorite performers on the white walls and began serving his chicken wings, burgers and 106 sauces each with a large platter of never-frozen fries. He added 106 *chicharrone* choices and received glowing reviews. Alas, he was duped. The party who rented the place to him, was himself a renter while the property was in probate. The inheritors came by months after his business had taken off and evicted him.

Only a few months later, Lazarus or Phoenix opened Magic's Motown anew in La Garita, diagonally across the main road from Fiesta del Maiz, directly opposite the church. Smaller, family friendly with pool tables, video games, and internet, the new digs have a large parking lot in the back. The neon-blue and white motif is bright and fresh. A few of the Motown murals have been resurrected. Behind the counter are three large flat-screen TV's. After the dish is installed, he will have NFL, NHL, NBA and baseball.

The new menu preserves the big three – wings, burgers and *chicharrones* with a huge side of fries and your choice of 106 sauces. The six piece wings order is $4.95, 12 pieces $7.85 and 24 for $14.50. The quarter-pound burger and fries is $4.95, $7.35 for the half-pounder. Both come with lettuce, tomato, onion and your choice of sauce on the side.

My personal favorites are the medium hot Buffalo wings and half-pound burger with barbecue/garlic sauce. The atomic sauce is hot enough to inflict pain on most mere mortals. The medium Buffalo sauce imparts plenty of lingering warmth on lips and tongue.

In addition, he serves grand American breakfasts from 6AM – 11AM. Omelets, pancakes, eggs, bacon and homemade sausage patties come with a bottomless coffee cup and juice for $4.95 to $6. The pancakes are very nice, the syrup truly maple, the hash browns better than most and the sausage patties loaded with flavor reminiscent of quality American breakfast sausage. Wednesday through Sunday, Beverly, the popular caterer from Savoir Faire in Escazú, prepares a more formal dinner special Wednesday through Sunday evenings.

Hours are 6AM to 11PM everyday.

Telephone 487-5374

Chapter 16
North Pacific Coast Dining

Apologies to the restaurants and readers, but the heat and dust of Guanacaste and the Nicoya Peninsula take their toll on my wife and me. As a result, we can't visit several worthwhile venues often enough to really learn their menus and appreciate the nuances of their kitchens. Too good to be ignored, they are at least entitled to partial reviews gleaned from a combination of one or two visits and information from locals, most of whom are in the restaurant business themselves.

Three are more expensive than the others and one is nearly inaccessible.

La Laguna del Cocodrilo, the northern end restaurant on the beach side of the road, when you enter Tamarindo, is the most expensive in town. It boasts quality creative food, beautifully presented, and a romantic setting by candlelight under the trees in the garden. A friend in the wine business, who spends his life visiting restaurants, considers La Laguna del Cocodrilo to be one of the finest restaurants anywhere with the most appealing plating presentations, but, they are his clients and he may be less than objective.

Papagayo is the name of one of the restaurants at the exclusive Four Seasons Resort. In the true tradition of "Nuevo Latino Cuisine," the essence is in the *mojos,* marinades and sauces that include tropical fruits or their juices. Continental cuisine, including lamb, veal and duck, is nicely enhanced by *mojos* and local ingredients, including fresh lobster. I have not seen the breakfast buffet, but guests rave about it.

Without reservations, you can't even get through the main gate, a thirty minute car ride away. Along with **Di Mare**, the resort's more formal and more modern Italian restaurant, hotel guests can enjoy attentive service, excellent ingredients, lovely presentations and good taste. Both Papagayo and Di Mare are just a cut below the nation's very best, which are less costly. The very attractive wine list also suffers from excessive pricing. Poolside and at the golf course are two other restaurants, featuring less formal American food.

Questions to my friends and acquaintances in the coastal Guanacaste area were -

What and who are your favorite restaurant and chef?

Et Cetera and its chef, **Derek Furlani.** Worthy of honorable mention are **Dragonfly** and **Taboo**.

Where is the best seafood?

With abundant fresh seafood all over, the favorites were **El Coconut** in Tamarindo, **The Happy Snapper** in Playa Brasilito and **Lola's** on the beach in Playa Avellanas.

Where do you go for a romantic quality meal?

El Jardin del Eden in Tamarindo, **Mar y Sol** in Playa Flamingo, **Playa de los Artistas** from Montezuma on the road to Cabuya and **Nectar** in the elegant and romantic Flor Blanca Resort that attracts honeymooners of means.

Who serves the most creative cuisine?

Ginger in Playa Hermosa, **Et Cetera** in Tamarindo, **Nectar** in Santa Teresa, **Lazy Wave** in Tamarindo**.**

What is the best value?

Los Malinches in Palm Beach Estates south of Playa Grande, **Restaurant Lucy** in Montezuma

Where is the most authentic, unspoiled place to eat?

The **Tortilla Cooperative** three blocks west of town in Santa Cruz

Good Costa Rican food?

Restaurant Zully Mar in Tamarindo on the beach, **Lola's, Los Malinches** and **Kike's Place** in Playa Grande

Favorite French restaurant?

Mar y Sol, **Jardin del Eden, Café de Paris** in Playa Nosara

Spicy food?

Louisiana Bar and Grill in Playas del Coco

Unusual cuisine?

Restaurant Chepito's Portuguese in Playa Islita, **Israeli Café** in the Buena Luna Tourist Center in Playa Santa Teresa.

What has changed or is changing?

Lazy Wave Food Company, once considered among the best restaurants in all of Costa Rica, seems to have fallen a notch because of a personality change. It is now more of a singles lounge than ever before, but it remains creative and popular.

Katharine no longer offers lunch at **El Coconut** and Derek has discontinued breakfast at **Et Cetera,** both, to survive the rigors of very long work days. Rumors abound that Derrick has lost his love of the business and may sell or close Et Cetera in the future. These are only unsubstantiated rumors, but they come from many sources.

When John moved **Gecko** from Tamarindo to Playa Brasilito, the restaurant fared better than the owner. Having overcome adversity, John is now reunited with family in Germany – a happy ending except to the fans of the now defunct restaurant.

In the other direction, **Ginger** is now open for lunch and **Louisiana Bar and Grill** is open from 8AM to 10 for breakfast.

In the past few years, the government has dealt with the pothole problem, by grinding up the roads, transforming them into gravel and dust. The dust is often so thick in the dry season that cars drive with headlights on at noon. A bevy of roadside dirt cheap sodas and stands have been forced to close. Late in 2007, paving finally commenced.

Mini-Reviews:

El Coconut

Five years ago, Katharine took over El Coconut and restructured the building on Tamarindo's main street, the menu, the service and the reputation. She is a charismatic, willowy Norwegian who exudes a love for people-pleasing. Watching her comfort a frightened little boy, who overdosed on sun all day, or delight a family by pouring flaming sauce over their banana dessert, you see why her staff is so accommodating. It is contagious.

Under her tutelage, the kitchen has perfected the menu, including imaginative appetizers such as Norwegian smoked salmon with *eggerøre* (herbed fluffy scrambled eggs traditionally served on Scandinavian bread with graavlox), mussels on the half shell in brandy cream sauce, eggplant Provençal filled with imported French *chèvre* and yellow-fin tuna *carpaccio,* all for $9.

While on the subject of yellow-fin tuna, I ordered it as the fresh catch of the day with a choice of four sauces (basil cream, garlic butter, caper and mild creamy curry) and loved the enormous fillet, seared on the outside and rare in the center. Norwegian lime-butter, *sandefjords smør,* is yet another sauce for fish. It came with rice and vegetables ($13.50). They serve large lobsters grilled in the kitchen and flamed with cognac at the table ($39) or plated with pineapple, raisins and ginger ($ 42). The "jumbo" shrimp are as large as they get. Other menu items include surf and turf (filet mignon wrapped in bacon with mushroom sauce on the side and lobster with garlic butter on the side $42), steaks, chicken, pasta and pizza.

The only remaining vestiges of Katharine's days as a major cosmetic strategist in Paris are her high heels. Since she closed for lunch, she gets to take them off and play at the beach.

Telephone: 653-0086

El Jardin del Eden

About five years ago, we stayed at this charming hilltop boutique hotel above the noise and dust of Tamarindo's main street. The restaurant was romantic and food attractively plated, but it wasn't great.

Now it is. The French owners brought in a Peruvian chef two years ago, trained at Cordon Bleu in Paris. Omar is soft spoken, very pleasant and young looking. His food is a lovely meld of classic French and imaginative tropical. We ate in flickering candlelight with soft music in the background and fresh flowers on the table along with gold chargers on woven reed placemats.

Joan had *meru,* a very large bottom feeding grouper that tastes like sweet *mahi mahi.* It was served on a bed of small roasted potatoes, in tarragon cream sauce that she wiped off the plate with a dinner roll ($15). I had lobster martini, five grilled halves atop perfect mashed potatoes dotted with fresh basil. The creamy martini sauce was seasoned with Provençal spices and contained four different kinds of mushroom, Portobello, crimini, button and oyster. Both plates came with crisp fresh asparagus and broccoli. Lobster is offered six different ways (all for $33), grilled and unsauced, grilled separately then bathed in martini sauce, served with tropical fruits, with seafood sauce, Caribbean style and with mango curry.

Our revisit of the hotel and restaurant was prompted by raves for both from three sophisticated friends who were there three weeks before us and brought back a copy of the menu. Among the interesting creations were frozen Andalusian gazpacho garnished with *escargot a la Provençal* and *escargot flambé* in Pernod, both for $8; steamed fish either in a folded banana leaf with pesto or in a timbale with smoked salmon ($14); and scaloppini either in a spicy jalapeño sauce or flambé in Marsala with mushrooms ($15). Rounding out the menu were steaks, jumbo shrimp, ten pastas ($10-17), six desserts ($5) and kids options.

The only caveat for the hotel is that the parking lot, reception, rooms, swimming pools and restaurant are all on different levels with neither ramps for wheelchairs nor elevators.

Telephone: 653-0137

Et Cetera

When Derek Furlani was owner and chef of Lazy Wave Food Company, every reviewer listed it as one of the best restaurants in Costa Rica, some, number one. He started cooking without formal training in Canada twenty years ago, and rose rapidly to run kitchens in Toronto, Vancouver and Los Angeles before coming to Costa Rica 10 years ago. Et Cetera is his third very successful venture here as chef/owner. In time, it will reappear in "best of" lists for five important reasons: location, imagination, quality local ingredients, good service and "scratch cooking" unless Derek changes course again. Everything is made daily, fresh, from scratch – sauces, breads, marinades and he even grinds his own salt.

Derek continues to promise me a copy of his ever-changing new menu, but has yet to deliver. I suggest you resort to daily specials and recommendations of staff or other diners.

Ginger

As you follow the only road to Playa Hermosa, south, parallel to the beaches, a sign points left to the water. Ignore it and continue a few more meters, past the turnoff, to the handsome modern building up the hill on the right. It looks like a Northern Italian hi-tech trattoria, clean lines and simple elegance.

A fellow diner noticed that one of the cocktails on the elaborate list contained *crème de cassis*. She asked if she could have some with white wine, an *aperitif* called a *kir*. As the waiter was responding in the affirmative, she asked about the cocktail - frozen blackberry purée, vodka, lime and the *crème de cassis* and changed her order to a "frozen blackberry blaster." She loved it. Page one of the dinner menu lists five martinis and eleven cocktails, all creative ($5). Next came 24 artistic fusion plates, international "tapas," if you will ($5 on average).

Mongolian ribs in a sauce that tastes of fermented black bean and garlic and hoisin sauce, two of my favorites; Balinese chicken *satay,* skewers of thigh meat rubbed with ground macadamia nuts and spices; pepper crusted seared tuna served sashimi style atop a toasted taco and pickled ginger slaw; hoisin, lime and chili powder marinated jumbo shrimp, grilled in their shells; smoked salmon wrapped around basil, tomato and mozzarella; classic Mexican Aztec soup topped with a dollop of sour cream, crispy strips of fried tortilla and avocado cubes; and zucchini *tzatziki,* hot vegetable chips in a cooling mix of yogurt, grated cucumber, garlic, lime and dill are some of the dishes, all of which are well matched for appearance and complimentary flavors and textures.

The one page lunchtime menu (new since December 2006) features larger dishes. Among others are warm spinach salad topped with crisp pancetta ($6.75), classic Cuban pulled pork sandwich on a crusty roll with cheese and onions ($8) and pizza margarita ($5).

Coffee, dessert, or both in one? Try Grand Marnier moccachino, a tall goblet with espresso, Grand Marnier, chocolate sauce, vanilla ice cream and chantilly cream.

Open Tuesday through Sunday 12-3 and 5-10.

Telephone: 672-0041

Los Malinches

If you follow the signs to Playa Grande and turn left when you reach the beach (south), you reach Palm Beach Estates. Next door to the market is the unassuming small restaurant, Los Malinches, named after the trees with feathery green leaves and glorious yellow and orange flowers. The cuisine is Tico with authentic regional Guanacaste overtones. What sets it apart are the grand jumbo shrimp cocktails in half coconuts or pineapples for $4 and the cheap pinkie shrimp, mayo and avocado salads in avocado shells. Worth a look? The locals say so. Sorry, I don't have a phone number.

Louisiana Bar and Grill

As you approach the town of Playas del Coco, the tranquility of Guanacaste turns into chaos. People, cars, sidewalk venders and buildings compete for cramped space.

Louisiana Bar and Grill is on the second floor of the yellow and red building across the street from the casino and wedged between the Sea Sport Inn with sports fishing and a marlin on its sign and a sports bar called Coconutz.

There are three or four other restaurants that offer a dish or two of blackened or spicy fish dishes, but only Louisiana Bar and Grill really features Cajun and Creole cooking. If you fear spice, relax. The huge menu has something for everyone. If you crave it, you have found a culinary home, and the menu is in Spanish and English.

For New Orleans style fun, you can start with a bowl of gumbo ($ 7.50) or fried shrimp in remoulade sauce ($7) and then go to shrimp creole ($13-20 depending on the size of shrimp you select), jambalaya with rice, shrimp and sausage ($13) or a whole lobster stuffed with Creole sauce ($27.50). If you have a hearty appetite and want a five or six part combo feast, try one of the five ($20-22). As an example, #1, the "big Cajun", includes fish nuggets, shrimp remoulade salad, a bowl of gumbo soup, blackened fish fillet, fried shrimp and seafood and chorizo Cajun jambalaya. You can even order bananas Foster with a scoop of ice cream ($3.50).

The gamut of choices include chicken, steak, smoked porkchops, pasta and a kids menu. The breakfast menu includes six egg combos, six omelets, five kinds of pancakes, three French toasts and a fruit platter.

Open from 8 AM to 10 PM every day

Telephone: 670-0882

Nectar

Begin with 70 acres of private virgin beach in the southern end of the Nicoya Peninsula, add ten villas with privacy and ocean views, sweet smelling breezes from the white blossoms of frangipani trees, air-conditioned bedrooms fit for honeymooners, outdoor sunken tubs and indoor/ outdoor showers and you might think you were in Bali (where my wife and I honeymooned in a similar setting). Spa, massage, gym and one of Costa Rica's best restaurants complete this paradise. The single bedroom villas are about $450 per night.

The restaurant is open to guests and to the public. Soft lights, subdued conversation, soft spoken staff and beachfront al fresco dining combine to make for romantic dining. And the food – very well prepared and presented Asian fusion with excellent sushi and sahimi, a small but ever-changing creative menu, great seafood always, ample vegetarian choices and occasional duck, lobster and lamb specials.

On the simpler side of the kitchen, you can get *gallo pinto* and eggs for breakfast and a hamburger for lunch.

For an appetizer, main course, coffee and dessert without wine, plan on spending about $50 each. Since many of the main courses are in the $15-20 range, Nectar escapes the ultra expensive group by a little.

Telephone: 640-0232

Restaurant at the Rip Jack Inn

When Derek Furlani sold Lazy Wave and bought Et Cetera, his apprentice, Brett, moved north to Playa Grande and the Rip Jack Inn. There he created a Lazy Wave facsimile called Pan. Alas, he had to return to the States. Next came Jim, a new menu and a new name. The restaurant became and remains Restaurant at the Rip Jack Inn. Jim went from onsite chef to overseer. He returned to the States but visits the restaurant about once every three months. Craig Dowling is the new onsite, everyday chef and executor of Jim's menu. Confused? No need. Just remember that the food is creative and nicely prepared, the surroundings homey and the people friendly in the second story restaurant with the long name.

The only chatter comes from a pair of enormous magpie jays in the almond tree off the deck. To the west you can see the ocean, to your feet, a pair of friendly house dogs.

Breakfast is fun. Choose from toasted bagel with cream cheese and fruit or granola with yogurt and fruit for $3; tasty banana flapjacks with maple syrup or the bacon cheese variety

$4; eggs, potatoes and fruit $4; or chorizo and cheddar scramble with fruit $6, all with a bottomless cup of hot coffee.

Jim's menu is not very long, but the selections are well chosen. For a light meal or as a starter for a feast, choose from eight small plates that include crispy seaweed wrapped tuna tempura with *wasabi* cream and *ponzu* dipping sauce ($7); hot garlic shrimp with *hummus* and warm bread ($7.75); and a new twist on a Caprese salad, baked brie with tomatoes and basil pesto($6.50). Or select *ajiaco,* traditional Colombian enriched chicken soup or Mexican *sopa de ajo,* cream of garlic soup with cilantro purée on top ($5).

The interesting main courses include white marlin steamed in banana leaf packets with green onions and ginger, served aside fried brown rice and pineapple and a tangy tamarind sauce ($13); individually baked lasagna with layers of two cheeses, vegetables, hot garlic shrimp and tomato sauce ($13); sesame crusted tuna with *wasabi aioli*, reduced soy sauce, vegetable tempura and white rice ($13); and tamarind glazed pork loin served with chorizo hash and cooked green plantains.

Telephone: 653-0408

The Happy Snapper

Playa Brasilito is one of the few places along the North Coast that, as of the spring of 2007, had not yet succumbed to excess construction, dust and crowds. The charming little bay and beach back right up onto the road and just across the street sits The Happy Snapper, full of boastful local fishermen and diners from Tamarindo to Flamingo. What 's the attraction? How about great seafood, live music, dancing, no dust and better value than its more urban neighbors.

Telephone: 654-4413

Tortilla Cooperative

The north-south main road that runs from Tamarindo to Nicoya passes just east of the Santa Cruz city center. Turn west at the light in front of Banco Nacional and drive through the center. About three blocks past it, on the right, you will see a multi-story metal barn that looks older than the hills. Park close to the road and enter the roadside door. That way you can walk slowly past the series of clay open-topped ovens heated from wood fire below, at which local women make tortillas by hand, without presses. Part two has a few women tending large pots of bean soups, pork and potatoes, *olla de carne (*traditional beef stew with root vegetables), chicken and rice and vegetable *picadillos* at a large stove. They seem to love to talk about their food with proud smiles.

The third and final part of the building consists of two very long tables, plastic table clothes, wooden benches and settings of utensils, condiments and napkins after you are seated. At the counter between parts two and three, order some of what you saw in the pots and enjoy robust authentic Tico food with the best corn tortillas anywhere, for the lowest prices on the Nicoya Peninsula. It is a wonderful cultural throwback experience, one of the few to survive the tourism invasion. The food is good, as well.

Chapter 17
Sodas

In 2006, nearly all the bestselling North American cookbooks were written by home-style cooks or caterers rather than grand master chefs. The revised and simplified *Joy of Cooking* exploded on the market. Comfort food reemerged as a star after a twenty or thirty year hiatus. Ingredients were nearly always ordinary residents of home pantries and refrigerators.

Home-style authentic cooking in Costa Rica lives in every little hamlet in eateries called "*sodas*." Don't be confused by the American slang for carbonated drinks. Club soda is also called *soda* in Spanish, but this chapter is about the luncheonette-greasy spoon- coffee and sandwich shop-diner-café that serves breakfast, lunch, and occasionally early dinner. The basic portion of each menu is identical – combination plates (*casados),* rice and beans *(gallo pinto),* rice dishes (e.g. *arroz con pollo)*, sandwiches, hamburgers, sandwiches made with *tortillas (gallos*), fruit juices, coffee, soft drinks, smoothies *(batidos*), fried and/or roasted chicken, beef slices in gravy, fried or grilled fish, pork cutlets and a few desserts.

The prices are rock bottom. Blue plate specials average about $2.50 and give you your choice of beef, pork, chicken or fish along with rice, beans, salad, fried plantain and tortillas. The décor tends to be Spartan and well worn. All have at least one and as many as three sides open to the outdoors. Some have only hard wooden unpadded benches or metal folding chairs. An architectural euphemism is "rustic." The food is usually fresh and well prepared or the *soda* dies a lonely death. When Costa Rican laborers miss breakfast or lunch at home, they eat similar style food at *sodas*. They also have mid morning and midafternoon snacks before returning home, often eleven or twelve hours after they left in the morning. Many of them frequent *sodas* for those snacks. Except on Sundays, the evening meal is typically a family affair at home.

Food poisoning is rare. Fruits, vegetables, greens, water and ice cubes are all safe as or safer than they are in North America.

For visitors on a budget or for a taste of basic homestyle food, trips to *sodas* are an essential experience. There are enough of them to fill a small phone book. The list below is by no means more than a smattering, based on local popularity, unusual features or advantageous location. They are listed alphabetically by name, not by ranking.

Sodas:

Doña Olga's, Playa Pelada no phone

This open air beachfront no frills soda is unique for its seaside, surfer haven location and for the addition of fresh caught fish to the classic *soda* menu. *Gallo pinto, casados*, whole fresh fried fish and ocean breezes along the Guanacaste Pacific shoreline – wow.

El Jardin, La Fortuna 479-9360

A long time cheap belly filling stop for youth on a budget in the pricey Lake Arenal town of La Fortuna, El Jardin has gone beyond *gallo pinto, gallos, casados, hamburguesas* and *batidos*. The menu now includes steak tenderloin and sirloin and tilapia fish platters.

In the under $2 category are hot dog with fries, taco with fries and plain hamburger. Under $3 are meat, chicken, burger and ham and cheese sandwiches with fries. Soups, salads, *casados* and breakfasts run $3-5.

Open from early breakfast to late dinner, it never appears empty.

It is across from the gas station and looks like a giant bird cage painted white.

Fiesta de Las Pupusas Salvadoreña, Atenas 446-6987

The eastern part of Atenas is called Atenas de Los Angeles. In its mid section is a famous blue statue of cart, oxen and driver carrying coffee beans down the mountain to market.

Twenty meters west on the left side of the road, sits a large *soda* with all the requisite menu parts and hours. In addition, it offers classic *pupusas* from El Salvador and a traditional Salvadoran dessert. *Pupusas* are flat round pancake or crêpe facsimiles stuffed with any combination of your choice of ground pork, cheese or puréed beans, served with vinegared cabbage slaw. *Quesadillas* are a pair of grilled tortillas sandwiching melted cheese. Not so in El Salvador or in this *soda* . Here a *quesadilla* is a sweet dense rectangular golden brown cake only about an inch tall, but covering most of a plate. It is made from corn flour, sugar, butter, cheese and sour cream and is sprinkled with white sesame seeds. A single portion easily can feed two or three.

It is served hot and moist.

La Radial, San Ramón 447-3155

Neither the outside nor the interior looks terribly inviting, yet this narrow little place is always packed with happy chow hounds. Where the San Ramón exit heads north off the Pan American Highway towards town, go a mere hundred fifty meters to the "SODA" sign across the street from the car wash and auto mechanic. The eatery is unadorned except for a wall of inviting menu descriptions. All the usuals are there plus *burritos, pupusas, empanadas, enyucados (empanadas* made with yuca flour instead of corn flour) and a choice of four hot condiments from large jars on the counter.

Las Delicias De La Esquina, San Mateo 428-8365

Most motorists take the La Garita – Atenas – Orotina road when heading for the Central or Southern Pacific Coast beaches. For those travelers who bypass a *pupusa* in Atenas, the next recommended *soda* is forty minutes away, over the winding mountain road on the other side of the mountain rim, in San Mateo. Past the town square and church, you can find *Las Delicias de la Esquina* on the left hand corner of the main road a block or two past the church and just past Super San Mateo (market). Warm smiles from the charismatic sister greet you and tout the imaginative and well prepared offerings of the more serious sister and cook, Sylvia. From a wide selection, even sandwiches are a good bet. My favorite is Sylvia's own variation on a Nicaraguan standard, *vigoron*. The classic is a cabbage salad covered with pieces of fried pork skin, served with generous pieces of boiled yuca. Her version substitutes smoked pork cutlets for the skin, making the dish tastier and much leaner. Despite very simple décor, this eatery has the feel of a spotless family dwelling and makes you feel like a guest.

La Fiesta del Maiz, La Garita 487-5757

I may be stretching definitions a bit in calling this huge weekend madhouse a *soda,* but it is too much fun to miss on a technicality. Open only Fridays, Saturdays, Sundays and holidays from 7AM to 9PM, the place probably seats 150, albeit on unpadded hard seats. Particularly on Sunday afternoons, the ingress and egress of cars into spots in front and across from La Fiesta causes a traffic jam on the two lane road that runs from Alajuela to Atenas. There are half a dozen other typical "corn" restaurants serving hefty portions of inexpensive Tico food along the same road. Some of the others are open every day and serve comparable food with less tumult, less noise, efficient table service and attractive artifacts of rural Costa Rica. La Fiesta is the most westerly of the group, closest to the Turrúcares turnoff. It houses three separate counters to order and pick up your food cafeteria style. It's fun to see the parade of heaping platters being carried off by the hoard. *Chorreadas* (sweet corn pancakes), *chuletas* (smoked pork cutlets), *chicharrones* (cubes of fried pork and pork skin), *tamales* and *maduros* (fried ripe plantains topped with sour cream) seem to be the most popular dishes. All the other *soda* standbys are available.

Soda El Recreo, Turrúcares 487-4098

Unless you live or are staying in the western end of the Central Valley, you are not likely to see the charming little town of Turrúcares. If, however, you are heading to the central Pacific coast through Belén and San Rafael, head north from the center of La Guácima, across bridges and railroad tracks to the next town, Ciruelas. After Pali (a large market), turn west on a beautiful scenic road that crosses a plateau and ends at a four way stop in Turrúcares. Go left one block. On the corner past the supermarket and before the church is *Soda El Recreo.* From the corner, a line of small fixed pedestal bar stools face the counter and galley kitchen. To the left is a small diningroom. *El Recreo* offers much more than the usual stuff. Consider salads, fruit plates, barbecued ribs, *chicharrones,* rice plates, fish, chicken, meats and my departed father's favorite – sliced beef tongue in a tangy sauce. He also adored the friendly people and was moved by the rock bottom prices to tell Depression stories. He lived into his 93rd year.

Soda Isabel, La Guácima, Alajuela 438-0169

A few days after Christmas, 2006, Soda Isabel came tumbling down. Gone were the roof, walls, counters, kitchen and tree that grew up through the dining room floor and out the ceiling. By St. Patrick's Day 2007, it reopened, shiny new with vaulted ceiling, bright yellow, red and blue colors and a modern kitchen. The only unchanged parts were the same old stew pots, wonderful aromas from the kitchen and Isabel's smiling face. Clearly the favorite spot for breakfast, snack and lunch in and around La Guácima, Soda Isabel reemerged like a phoenix. A year earlier, I wrote a column listing readers' favorite dishes and a long time ex-pat included Isabel's *gallo pinto* as the country's best. My favorites include her *batidos, picadillo* and, on Monday, *olla de carne.*

Soda Miss Isma, Puerto Viejo no telephone

When I was last there, the small house and front porch needed paint. The inside was more like a modest home than a restaurant. We were made to feel like houseguests by Miss Isma and a woman I presumed to be a daughter. The food was homestyle Caribbean, delicious and quite inexpensive for a resort town.

Soda Janet, Puntarenas 661-0285

When I think of Puntarenas, I think of Chinese food. With a large Asian population, there is a Chinese restaurant on nearly every street in the downtown area, from the fancy Chong San to the popular more modest Tang Tu. Most of the sodas are cookie cutter similar. One, however, stands alone. Soda Janet is on the street that begins near the beach at the far end of the bus station and crosses the narrow peninsula. It is half a block to the right of the main street that goes toward land's end.

The immaculate little place may be the only *soda* I have seen that doesn't deep fry anything and uses no lard. Pots of chicken in sauce, *picadillo* and pork simmer on the burners. The aromas are intoxicating. The two cooks and waitress are all smiles and charm. The owners, Kenny and Yaneth (Janet is their daughter) buy only the best and freshest comestibles available, unlike most sodas that are inclined to opt for the cheapest. Add shiny black marble-like tiles and spotless counter tops and you have a nice place to stop for an icy watermelon or pineapple drink or tasty meal.

Soda Kathia, Playa Herradura 637-7137

Just a few dozen meters past the entrance to the massive elegant resort, Los Sueños, sits one of the most popular *sodas* along the central Pacific coast. Local working people and visitors to the public beach often fill all the tables. The reasons are obvious. Nearly all the other eateries from Herradura to Jacó are priced for tourists. At Soda Kathia, the prices are reasonable and the portions are generous and well prepared. In addition to the usual, the menu offers a few seafood choices including jumbo shrimp. An engineer friend, who, with his architect wife and son, builds houses in Los Sueños, is addicted to Kathia's pork cutlets.

Soda Margarita, San Rafael de Alajuela 839-1289

San Rafael has many more roast and fried chicken joints and bars than *sodas*. The most popular *soda* is on the road to the airport, across the tracks, next to the auto-body shop, Taller Sura and opposite Pali. Soda Margarita doesn't even sport a sign. If you aren't looking for it, you can easily miss it. It looks like just another gated house front. There is only street parking, not a problem for many of the diners who walk or ride bikes there. The attraction? Simple, well prepared, large portions of inexpensive food.

Soda Piedra Mar, Malpais 640-0069

If the description of Doña Olga's (first listing in this chapter) caught your eye, there is another northern Pacific beachfront *soda* with view of sand and surf and fresh fish on the menu. Add to that a telephone and periodic jumbo shrimp and lobster on the menu, and you have Soda Piedra Mar. You might want to call first to be sure, because it was closed on December 31st and open on New Year's Day, 2006.

Soda Tapia, San Jose & Santa Ana

The original place sits on the congested road along the eastern edge of the *Sabana,* San Jose's huge public park. There is always a traffic snarl out front as cars try to squeeze into or out of the eight or ten parking spots. Seating, just past the single row of parked cars, is only about five meters from the horns, squealing brakes, diesel groans and belched black smoke of buses and trucks. Nonetheless, the driver who actually squeezes in, considers himself most fortunate to reach the city's most popular *soda*. The menu is a checklist and comes with a pencil. Breakfast foods include usual *soda* fare plus omelets, pancakes and French toast (deep fried). The lunch and snack options also include popular large fruit salads, multiple pastry choices and ice cream alone or in combination with other desserts.

In Santa Ana, access is much easier. It shares a parking lot with Taco Bell, Pops and a number of other venues. Farther back from the road (the Santa Ana – San Antonio de Belén road) diners are spared the smell of diesel smoke. The menu is the same. The décor is fresh diner red and white with colorful deco food art on the walls. Service is efficient, albeit slow when the place is packed or they have a huge outgoing-order business. Both locations are open from early morning until after midnight.

Chapter 18
Recipes

Without a governor on my motor, I could turn this chapter into a book.

1) *Agua de sapo* is a refreshing and unique cold drink that I have only had in Costa Rica, but the ingredients can be found anywhere. A *sapo* is a large toad. I don't know the connection. The drink is basically ginger flavored lemonade. The ingredients are brown sugar, lemon or lime juice, ginger and water. The proportions vary depending on the acidity of the lemon or lime and individual taste.

In Costa Rica, we use limes, and the three common types vary greatly. If you use milder Meyer lemons, I suggest the following:

The juice of four lemons, about two inches of fresh ginger – peeled and finely diced, a cup of brown sugar and enough water and ice to fill a pitcher. Let it sit in the fridge for at least an hour, then stir and strain before serving. If you use limes, juice six of them. Not quite the same, but a great quickie variation, is to add a teaspoon of the juice from a jar of Japanese pickled pink ginger slices to your favorite lemonade.

2) Well known in Thai cuisine are salads made with unripe green papayas. Ticos do the same with green mangos. ***Ceviche de mango cele*** is such a salad, simple, crunchy and very tasty. Peeled and sliced green mangos are sold in plastic bags along the roads in December, January and February in most parts of the country. The contents of a bag are about three cups worth.

The salad is simply those slices marinated in lime juice, with the addition of finely diced sweet red pepper and white onion. Approximate ratios are these: 3 cups of raw peeled slices of mango or papaya, the juice of four lemons or six limes, the dice of one large onion and one red pepper, a quarter cup of fresh cilantro leaves and salt to taste. It is best if left to marinate for a few hours before serving in its liquid in a small bowl or drained and set on a bed of lettuce.

Ticos usually add mayonnaise or ketchup to the final salad. Personally I like the flavor as is. In fact, Ticos add the same to condiments to fish and seafood *ceviches* as well, masking, in my humble opinion, the delicate essence of the fish, black clams, octopus or shrimp.

3) How about an egg dish? Ticos aren't accustomed to making or eating fluffy or moist America style breakfast eggs. They prepare a few very simple omelets of thinly sliced deli ham and/or processed yellow cheese. Otherwise eggs are fried in oil until the edges are brown or scrambled bone dry.

Sometimes, you can find ***huevos rancheros*** on the menu. They are easy to prepare at home. All you need are eggs, *tortillas* and a tasty tomato relish or sauce. To make a simple sauce, sweat a finely diced onion and a few cloves of garlic in a little olive oil, add chopped fresh or canned tomatoes to boil off the excess water and salt and pepper to taste. Optional additions are oregano, basil, red pepper flakes, *habanero* or *jalapeño* chili peppers, left over ratatouille or any cooked vegetable blended into the sauce. Toast the bottoms of corn *tortillas,* in a skillet in a bit of butter or oil, two per person. Poach or pan fry two eggs each, sunny side up. Plate two *tortillas* side by side with a little central overlap. Set an egg in the middle of each, nap with the sauce around or over the eggs and garnish with any combination of cilantro leaves, orange sections, cantaloupe cubes or avocado slices.

4) Baked stuffed *chayote* can be a side dish or a main vegetarian course. Chayotes are orange size green squash with a ragged groove along one edge. They should be boiled whole until fork tender in the groove. Slice them carefully in half along the groove to the central pit. Twist the halves apart. Remove the pit. Scoop out the pale flesh without tearing the skin. Mix the flesh, with half as much of a mixture of breadcrumb, salt and pepper to taste, a dash of Salsa Lizano or Worcestershire Sauce, a few pinches of oregano, a few tablespoons of cilantro leaves and a beaten egg. It never hurts to add a little onion and garlic, cooked only to translucency in a bit of butter, to the mixture. Combine well and restuff the squash shells. Top with enough grated cheese to lightly cover and bake until brown on top and heated through.

If you care to make this a dish with meat, mix bacon bits, diced cooked ham or browned ground beef with the filling.

Chayotes are available in the United States in Latin American markets.

5) **Pork in sour orange sauce** is neither common nor rare in Costa Rica. Granted that Costa Rica's most common preparation of pork cubes are fried in their own fat and salted - the ubiquitous weekend dish of *chicharrones*. The second most common preparation for pork is roast tenderloin with enough sauce to counter the meat's inherent dryness. Farther down the list is this rendition that takes advantage of the rich tangy flavor of sour (Seville) oranges. For those unfortunates in North America who can't get the real sour oranges, try half and half mixtures of Valencia orange and Meyer lemon juice. No, it's not the same, but it is not bad.

For this recipe, begin with a cup of apple cider vinegar and continue with a host of two's. Add to the vinegar two teaspoons each of powdered cumin, orange annatto seed powder (*achiote*) and minced garlic. Then, add two grinds of black pepper, two pinches of salt and two pounds of lean pork cubes about two inches in each dimension. Marinate at least two hours. Overnight is preferable. In a large frying pan, heat two tablespoons of oil until it just begins to smoke. Add to the pan the pork cubes after you lift them out of the marinade and pat them dry. When all sides of the cubes have bronzed, take the pan off the heat and pour off the oil, leaving the caramelized bits and pieces behind. Carefully add the marinade to the pan, avoiding hot splatter. Return the heat to high and scrape the tasty bits into the deglazing liquid. Cover the pan and lower the heat to a slow simmer for an hour. Then add the juice of two large sour oranges and two cups of water. Stir the sauce and boil it down a little if it is too thin.

Serve the dish with white rice or potatoes. For entertaining, I like to boil about two pounds of the local pale skinned small yellow potatoes until barely fork tender, and then toss them in butter, salt and flat leaf parsley for a quick browning under the broiler.

6) Red cabbage and pineapple is an occasional side dish featuring two very common year round items here. I like to cut a medium size red cabbage without its white core a little coarser than for slaw. Sweat a large onion in about a tablespoon each of butter and oil, add the cabbage, a cup of fresh pineapple chunks, half a teaspoon of ground caraway, juice from a lime, a few grinds of black pepper, a tablespoon of sugar and salt to taste. Cover and simmer for fifteen minutes. You end up with a Tico combo doctored with a little German influence. If you like, you may add apple slices and raisins as well.

Henry Mora, the chef at Casa Bavaria, makes traditional *rot kohl*. He replaces lime juice with vinegar, caraway seeds with cumin seeds, pineapple with apple and raisins, white sugar with brown sugar, and seasons with clove and bay leaves.

7) Rice pudding is a very common Tico dessert. It is made here to be sweet and creamy. Start by simmering a cup of long grain rice in two cups of water with a whole cinnamon stick in a covered pot. When the rice has absorbed all the water, remove the cinnamon stick, add a pinch of clove, a handful of raisons and a cup of evaporated milk. Some people thicken the mixture even more by adding a tempered egg yolk, but the evaporated milk thickens it enough for me. Return it to the covered simmer until it is velvety smooth. Add a little water and stir if it becomes too thick. Taste in for sweetness and add sugar if you desire more than the sweet evaporated milk has imparted. Spoon into individual serving cups and sprinkle the top with ground cinnamon.

If you like it less sweet and less thick, use regular milk instead of evaporated and add sugar to taste.

8) Chunks of fresh fruit make a wonderful dessert, light meal or side dish. Particularly, when a stand of fifty bananas or a tree full of ripe mangoes, papayas or guava are begging for an alternative presentation, consider **hot fruit in banana**

leaves. Nearly any combination works except perhaps watermelon, passion fruit or pomegranate. Sprinkle chunks of fruit with a little brown sugar and cinnamon, top with a small pat of butter, wrap in washed and trimmed rectangle of banana leaf, fold closed like a *tamale*, place seam side down on a cookie sheet and heat through in a 400 oven for about fifteen minutes. Invert with a spatula onto plates and let the diners open their packets. For fancy entertaining, you can add ice cream, charlottes, chocolate or caramel sauce (on the ice cream) or an edible nasturtium flower to the plate.

9) Hearts of palm salad can also be plain or fancy. Fresh hearts of palm are the best, peeled, boiled in salt water but still crunchy, cut into half inch logs and tossed with your favorite vinaigrette. Costa Ricans use much more mayonnaise than most people. They would toss the pieces in mayo, lime juice and cilantro. Canned hearts of palm are not a bad second choice. Rinse them well or they will be too salty.

For a festive rapid salad that offers wonderful contrasting textures and flavors, consider adding a can each of well rinsed hearts of palm and garbanzos, a small thinly sliced purple onion, half a pint of cherry tomatoes, a handful of cilantro leaves, oil and vinegar and salt and pepper to taste.

Another favorite salad, smart enough for entertaining, mixes the textures of hearts of palm and julienned fennel bulbs with cubes of mango. It balances the sweet and tart with vinegar and sugar marinated finely sliced red onions and dresses the salad with a mild orange juice vinaigrette.

10) Olla de carne literally means a pot of meat. It is really a stew of bone-in cheap cuts of beef and pork like tail, neck, ribs or shin with a grand assortment of root vegetables. Typically, beef pots are weekend fare and seem to coincide with farmers' markets. The cook loads up with whatever combination of the following that are available: pumpkin, hard squash, carrot, beet, yuca, yam, sweet potato, green plantain and a couple of locals, *ñampi* and *tiquisque* that are pink and purple skinned. If I were making this dish in North America, I would substitute turnip and parsnip for the last two. You can probably find yuca and plantains at Latino markets. In addition, most Ticas add one or more each of an onion, a sweet red pepper, corn on the cob, a few cloves of garlic, a couple of diced tomatoes and the leaves from a small bunch of cilantro. The trick is use large chunks of peeled roots, to add them sequentially so that none fall apart and to simmer gently until the meat and vegetables are soft.

Phase one is to simmer the meat in water to cover, seasoned with salt, black pepper, garlic, tomatoes, onion, red pepper and leaves from a branch or two of thyme. Oregano or cumin is sometimes added. After about three quarters of an hour, remove the meat, add the root vegetables in large chunks and enough water to cover, return to simmer until they are soft, usually about another twenty minutes and put the meat back in the pot for another five or ten minutes to reheat. *Olla de carne* is served in soup bowls with white rice on the side, or on a plate alongside the rice, with a separate bowl of broth.

11) *Arroz con Pollo*, chicken with rice, is the main course at nearly every festive event from birthday to wedding. It can also be made from cubed or torn pieces of leftover chicken added to rice made with chicken broth, colored golden with turmeric, saffron or annatto oil to which diced sweated decorative bits of red bell pepper, onion, carrots, scallions and cilantro leaves have been added.

The more authentic version begins with seasoned chicken serving pieces, either marinated in spiced citrus or rubbed in *achiote* powder, salt and pepper, then browned in three tablespoons of oil in a large heavy casserole or Dutch oven. The powder turns the oil yellow orange. Remove the chicken to another pot and simmer the chicken in five cups of chicken broth, white wine or beer until cooked through (twenty to thirty minutes). Add scallions, cooked carrot cubes, diced tomatoes (seeded and peeled) and a pinch of ground cumin to the colored oil in the casserole and sweat for two minutes, add two cups of long grain rice and continue to cook and stir to coat every grain without browning it. Add the liquid from the chicken pot to the rice mixture, simmer covered for about twenty minutes until the rice absorbs the liquid. In the meanwhile, tear the chicken from the bones into small pieces, reunite with the cooked rice and garnish with any combination of peas, corn kernels, capers, olives, hard cooked eggs, chopped chives, roasted red pepper bits and more cilantro leaves.

12) "Waste not, want not" is imprinted on my post depression brain. Here are four recipes to save excess bananas and strawberries. At times it is laughable and I must assure you that I laugh along with you when I spend much more time and money preventing waste than the fruits are worth. We all have our idiosyncrasies.

Banana custard pie and **banana cheesecake** are shortcut recipes born out of such behavior. Our banana trees produce fifty fruit at a time and the freezer still is loaded with banana bread from the last bunch. For nearly instant banana cream or cream cheese pie, begin with a premade graham cracker crust, paint it with a thin layer of egg white, bake for only five minutes in a 350 F (70 C) oven and cool to room temperature. Line the bottom with an inch of overlapping banana slices that have been tossed for only two minutes in a skillet with a bubbling tablespoon each of dark rum, butter and brown sugar. When cool, top with instant vanilla pudding from the refrigerator and serve. To make the pudding almost like cheesecake, for every box or packet of mix, use only half the recommended volume of milk and add, instead, the same volume of equal parts softened cream cheese and sweetened condensed milk. Mix well and refrigerate. To make fancy, sprinkle the top with bits of brittle or crumbled ginger snaps.

A last banana tip is to roast bananas in their skins until they are black and juices start to exude for all dishes in which you mash or purée them. The flavor is miraculously enhanced.

Finally, who can pass up the glorious and cheap large bags of strawberries for sale on the sides of country roads? Even after the strawberries and cream and fruit smoothies, there is a bunch or a bag in danger of perishing. That is the time to make **glazed strawberries on lime curd and meringue.**

Meringue shells appear intermittently at upper end markets. Filled with lime curd and topped with balsamic flavored strawberries, dessert is taken to a new level with little work.

When the round shells are not on the shelves, resort to goblets with broken meringue cookies on the bottom, curd in the center and strawberries on top. Traditional English lemon curd is not very hard to make. We need only substitute our local limes and zest. A shortcut is to make instant vanilla pudding with part of the milk replaced by whipping cream and add lime juice and a little zest to taste. Two options for the strawberries: first slice then toss them either in melted apricot jelly or in syrup made of two parts sugar to one part balsamic vinegar, heated or left to cool a bit. Decorate the top of the faux curd with the dressed berries after they have cooled to room temperature.If you are a purist, here is a recipe for Costa Rican lime curd: Beat three eggs, add strained juice of three limes and ¾ cup of granulated sugar over a stainless steel bowl atop a pot of simmering water. Stir nonstop until it looks like hollandaise sauce (usually about ten minutes), stir in four tablespoons of diced butter pieces until they melt. Pour into meringue shells or goblets, top with a little lime zest and refrigerate or use in this recipe instead of the vanilla pudding.If you don't care for pudding or curd, simply **roast an assortment of fruit** that might well include bananas and strawberries along with chunks of pineapple and papaya (or any combination of fruit at hand) in an ovenproof chafing dish at 375 for 6-8 minutes to soften a little. Serve with syrup made by reducing equal amounts of brown sugar and balsamic vinegar. Toss in a few raisins while heating. Put fruit in serving cups while still warm and drizzle with syrup.

A final treatment for excess fruit turns them into **Tico crumble.** Using the same fruit pieces as above, layer them to completely cover the bottom of a shallow baking dish. Combine a half cup of brown cane sugar (or regular brown sugar), half cup of butter, a cup and three quarters of corn flour and pulse them all together in a food processor until you have crumbs. Top the fruit with the crumbs and bake for 30 minutes in a 400 oven. Options include mixing a little dark rum with the crumbs and putting whipped cream or ice cream atop the warm crumble.

13) Frugal Tico pesto makes two major substitutions from the classic recipe. Most Costa Ricans don't care much for basil and pine nuts are expensive imports. Therefore, I watched a neighbor substitute cilantro and peanuts. She browned half a cup of unsalted peanuts under the broiler and ground them into tiny pieces. Separately, she ground a small clove of raw garlic in the same processor and added a large bunch of washed cilantro stems and leaves (1 & 1/2 cups) and pulsed until fine. She tossed the cilantro-garlic- peanut components in a mixing bowl with half a cup of grated parmesan cheese and tossed. Then she added extra virgin olive oil two Tablespoons at a time and mixed until the consistency suited her. She seasoned with salt and pepper to taste, squeezed in the juice of half a lime, placed it a sterile jar, covered the top with a little more olive oil to act as an air barrier, screwed the top on tightly and put in the fridge for use that evening. She insists that it tastes much better when used the same day, but it can easily keep for a week.

14) Red roasted pumpkin boats are made from roasting wedges of, Costa Rican pumpkin, after they have been coated with an herb, garlic and oil paste.

The pumpkin is similar to butternut squash and you can make the substitution if your aren't in the tropics. Cut it in half and then into slices along the vertical axis. Cut each top to bottom slice across the middle to make two boats. The dry ingredients are a teaspoon each of salt, freshly ground black pepper, red *achiote* powder (substitute sweet paprika if necessary) and a Tablespoon each of dried oregano, cumin and optional thyme or marjoram. Finely chop a clove of garlic, add the dry ingredients and mix well with enough olive oil to make a paste. Rub each boat well with the paste. Roast them skin side down in a 400 oven until fork tender, about 40 minutes. Serve hot as a side dish or vegetarian main course.

15) Corvina *shioyaki* is local delicious sea bass broiled Japanese style. In Japan, fatty fish are coated with coarse sea salt and seared over hot hibachis until the skin becomes crispy and dark. Heat and salt act magically on fat under the skin, enhancing the flavor of the fish and turning ordinary mackerel into a regal delight. Sea bass is much too lean and delicate for the same treatment, but leaving the skin on one side of fillets, using an oily marinade and broiling with the skin next to the heat can achieve a gloriously similar result.

Score the skin on six fillets every inch or so, but not too deeply. For the marinade, sweat a clove of minced garlic in three Tablespoons of olive oil. Remove from the heat. Add juice of a small lime, the leaves of enough fresh cilantro, fresh oregano and fresh tarragon in any combination to equal a half cup loosely packed. Blend them all together and rub the mixture over both surfaces of the fish. After thirty minutes, place the fillets skin side UP, facing the broiler, on a non-stick or lightly buttered baking pan. Sprinkle the skin with a Tablespoon of Kosher salt or sea salt and a grind or two of black pepper. Preheat the broiler to 475. Place the pan on the top rack. When the skin is dark and crisp (usually about 7-8 minutes), remove and serve.

16) Which came first? Like so many people living away from a big city here in Costa Rica, we have a small flock of hens. We made the mistake of naming them and they responded by following us around and squatting in front of me to be petted. So, alas, when their laying days are over, we won't eat them. They will become *pensionadas*. At times, we have many more eggs than we can eat at breakfast, so we boil them and serve **alien hard boiled eggs** to guests.

Let me share a strange fact or two with you about eggs. Try the water test before you boil them. The freshest ones sink to the bottom of a bowl of water because there is little or no air under the shell subsequent to internal evaporation. The older ones float and are easier to peel when hard boiled. Choose the floaters. Second, for reasons that I don't understand, slow simmering of eggs for many hours produces a creamier rather than a drier consistency to the yolk. Red dyed creamy centered eggs are the symbolic focus of first birthday celebrations for boys in China. Probably, a little liquid enters with time. Third and last, because the shells are a little porous, you can flavor and color the eggs by additions to the water. A nice ploy is to boil the eggs first, crack the shells gently with the back of a spoon without removing them and then return them to the flavored colored water. When peeled you have a spider web raku design on a tasty egg with a creamy yolk.

A Sephardic Passover tradition is to simmer eggs for about six hours in water laden with the outer skin of yellow and red onions, coffee grounds and olive oil. I substitute sesame oil for a little more smokiness and add spices (e.g. star anise, pepper corns, coriander seeds) for more flavor.

Place a dozen eggs (floaters), two cups of onion skins, a third cup of coffee grounds, a third of a cup of sesame oil, a tablespoon of kosher salt or sea salt, juice from half a lime or lemon, half a dozen peppercorns, a few cloves and anise stars. Bring to a boil and barely simmer covered for at least six hours, adding enough water to keep the eggs submerged. The eggs store well in liquid covered and refrigerated for a week in their shells. Peel to serve. The color will be pale golden orange, cream colored "whites" and creamy dark yolks. Serve them whole or halved, dusted with paprika.

For a variation and short cut, boil eggs, peel them and marinate them in the refrigerator submerged in flavored liquid that is preferably acidic, for up to a week. Citrus juices provide the proper pH. Use juice from the pickle jar or garlic flavored tomato juice, bloody Mary mix, a mixture of sweet saki and soy, grapefruit-pineapple juice, lemonade spiked with hot sauce or anything else you can imagine.

Chapter 19
Markets

a) Farmers' Markets: Alajuela Friday PM and Saturday AM
San Jose outdoor daily market (has additional flea market on weekends)
San Ramón weekend market
Santa Ana Sunday market

b) Buy in bulk markets: Price Smart in Escazú
Belca in San Antonio de Belén
Italicnam in San Antonio de Belén – cheese and Italian imports

c) Ethnic markets: Tom Tom in Escazú - German
Han in San Jose - Asian
Sorreto's in Escazú - Italian
Little Israel in Rohrmoser and Escazú – Jewish
Kosher Center in Pavas - Jewish

d) Supermarket chains:
Auto Mercado
Hypermas (Walmart)
Jumbo
Mas x Menos
Pali
Perimercado
Super Mercado

Chapter 20
Ethnic Restaurants

My **personal favorites,** based on quality and value, appear in **bold type.** A star indicates * some dishes in the named category.

a) **Argentinean**: Bariloche, Donde Carlos, **El Novillo Alegre**, La Esquina de Buenos Aires, La Gauchada, Terruño

b) **Brazilian: A Churrascaria Brasileira**, Fogo de Brasilero, La Fogueira

c) **Caribbean**: Casa Creole, Casa Creole Bistro & Cafeteria, Claro Que Si, **Delicias Caribeñas de Mami**, La Casona Restaurant, **Miss Edith**, Restaurant Cha Cha Cha*, Soda Miss Isma, Soda Tamara, The Great Waltini's, W'hapin

d) **Chinese**: **Chef Oriental**, **Chinese Cultural Center-Casa China#**, Don Wang# , Flor de Loto, Fulusu, King's Garden, Lotus, Palacio Real, Restaurante Fuente de Fortuna, **Restaurante Villa Bonita#**, **Tin Jo**, Villa Rey
(# = Hong Kong style Dim Sum)

e) **Cuban**: La Gua Gua, **Club Cubano**

f) **French**: Cha Cha Cha*, Chez Jacques, **Colbert, El Jardin Del Eden,** La Bastille, **La Brasserie, Le Chandelier**, **L'Ile De France**, Le Monastère, Le Petit Paris, Restaurant Exótica

g) **German**: Café Europa & German Bakery, Casa Bavaria*, German Bakery, Hamburgo, Los Héroes Restaurant (Swiss)*, Plinio*, Willy's Caballo Negro *

h) **Indian**: **Taj Mahal**, Coconut Spice*, Plinio*, Saga*, Tin Jo *

i) **International**: Ambrosia, Azucar, **Bakea**, Balcón Uvita, **Bistro Rouge**, Boemios, **Café Mundo**, Casa Creole, Chile Rojo, Crokante, Curime, Dragonfly Bar & Grill, El Cerdo Dorado, El Loco Natural, El Patio Bistro Latino, **Essencia**, **Et Cetera**, Gecko's, **Ginger**, Hotel Casa Turire, Hotel Finisterra, Fish and Meat Restaurant, **Jürgen's**, **La Laguna del Cocodrilo Bistro (E)**, La Luz, Lazy Wave Food Company, **Loveat Restaurant,** Mar y Sol, **Nectar**, Paragon, **Park Café**, Persa Mex, **Plinio**, Restaurante Cha Cha Cha, Restaurant Exótica, Restaurante Oasis, **Saga**, **Saisaki**, Sebastian, **Sunspot Grill, Tin Jo**, Trocadero, Wall Street, Xandari

j) **Israeli: Loveat Restaurant,** Israeli Café in the Buena Luna Tourist Center in Playa Santa Teresa.

k) **Italian**: Alfredo, Amimodo, Andiamo'la, Antonio's, **Bacchus, Café Mediterráneo, Cerutti, DaMarco, Di Bartolo,** Di Mare, El Balcon de Europa, **Il Ritorno,** La Focaccia, La Fonte, La Pizza, La Piazzetta, L'Olivo, Lo Spago, **Mangiamo**, Pan e Vino, Peperoni, **Pizza Gino**, Ristorante Cugini, Sabor a Leña, Sale e Pepe, Tre Fratelli, Tutti Li

l) **Japanese**: Benihana, **Fuji**, **Ichi Ban**, Kabuki, Little Seoul*, Matsuri, Muro-ji, **Saisaki***, Sakura, Samurai, Sensu, Shil La*, Soda Tempestad Azul, **Sushi Nippon Restaurant**, Tin Jo*, Tropical Sushi

m) **Korean**: Benihana*, Little Seoul*, **Saisaki*,** Shil La*

n) **Kosher:** Kosher Center

o) **Lebanese, Middle Eastern, Moroccan**: Al Muluk, **Lubnan**, Beirut, Café Moro*, La Mamounia, Omar Khayyam, Persa Mex*, Sash Restarante

p) **Mexican:** Chipotle, El Fogoncito, Huaraches, Jacó Taco, Jalapeños, Jalapeños Central, La Fonda Azteca, Las Mananitas, Los Antojitos, Mochados, Pancho's, Persa Mex*, San Clemente

Bar and Grill, Santa Ana's Tex Mex, Tacontento, Tequila Bar & Grill

q) **Nuevo Latino**: El Patio Bistro Latino, Papagayo, **Sofia**

r) **Peruvian**: **Bohemia**, Ceviche del Rey, Chalito's*, Chancay, Inka Grill, Inta Raymi, **Machu Picchu**, Sebastian*, Señor de Sipan

s) **Philippine**: Tin Jo*, **Saisaki***

t) **Salvadorian:** Fiesta de Las Pupusas Salvadoreña, Pupusas El Barrio San Jose de Alajuela, Pupuseria Marya, **Pupuseria Quirigua**

u) **Sandwiches: Bagelman,** Il Panino**, Il Torino,** Kosher Center, Quiznos, Subway, Wall Street

v) **Seafood**: Anthony, Barba Roja, Ceviche del Rey, El Ancia Restaurant, **El Banco de los Mariscos**, **El Coconut**, **El Dorado,** Elegant Restaurant Camaron Dorado, El Gran Escape, El Pelicano, Fish Shack, **La Leda,** La Fuente de los Mariscos, La Princessa Marina, Lola's, **Louisiana Bar & Gril**l, Mariscos #1, Mar Luna, Paso Real, Restaurante Zully Mar, Restaurant Juberths, Steve n Lisa's, **The Happy Snapper**

w) **Spanish**: Casa de España, **Casa Luisa**, Club Cubano*, El Gaitero, Ginger*, La Isabela, La Luna de Valencia, La Masia, **Las Tapas de Manuel**, La Tasca del Novillo, Marbella, Mundo *, Rancho Grande, Sancho Panza (E)

x) **Steaks**: A Churrascaria Brasileira, Azucar, Cima Hospital, **Donde Carlos**, **El Chicote, El Establo**, **El Novillo Alegre**, El Rodeo, Factory, Hacienda El Estribo, JR's House of Ribs, La Cascada, La Esquina de Buenos Aires, La Fonda, Los Anonos, Outback, Parrillada El Churrasco, Restaurante Patagonia, Tony Roma's

y) **Sunday Brunch/ Lunch: Casa Bavaria, Hotel Intercontinental**, **Hotel Marriot**, **Restaurante Villa Bonita**, Restaurant La Casona del Cafetal

z) **Tapas:** Casa de España, El Gaitero, **Ginger, La Isabela, Park Café, Tapas de Manuel**

aa) **Thai**: Bangkok, Chile Rojo*, **Coconut Spice**, El Jardin*, Los Amigos, Plinio*, **Tin Jo***

bb) **Traditional Costa Rican**: **Casa Vieja**, **Chalito's**, **Cooperativo de Tortillas**, **Don Próspero**, **El Chicote,** El Stablo, Fogón Casero, Hacienda El Estribo, La Casona de Cerdo, **La Cocina de Leña**, La Fiesta del Maiz, La Fonda, Las Delicias del Maiz, Las Delicias de Mi Terra, Las Malinches, Los Adobes, Los Anonos, Los Mangos, Manolo's, Pollos del Monte, Restaurant la Cocina de Jose, **Restaurante Oasis**, Restaurante Zully Mar, **Soda J&M**, Soda La Puerta del Sol.

cc) **United States**: Big Dog's, **Café De Los Artistas**, **Chi Chi's**, Denny's, JR's House of Ribs, Mac's, **Magic's Motown**, Mighty Rivers Café, Pub, **Rock 'n Roll Pollo**, TGIF, The Lighthouse, Tony Roma's and all the burger, chicken and pizza chains.

dd) **Vegetarian:** GreenDLights*, **Loveat Restaurant,** Shakti, Vishnu, Tin Jo*, Xandari*

ee) **Australian, British, Burmese, Canadian, Chilean, Colombian, Czeck, Danish, Dutch, Egyptian, Greek, Guatamalen, Hawaiian , Hungarian, Indonesian, Polish, Puerto Rican, Russian, Salvadorean, Singaporean, Sweedish, Turkish, Vietnamese, :** none currently worth mentioning.

ff) **Coffee, pastries and café food:** Cafeteria Azúcar Canela, Delicias, Eiffel, Fitzgerald's, Giacomín, Grand Café, Spoon, Trigo Miel gg) **Buffets:** International – **Hotel Intercontinental,** Sunday**; Hotel Marriott,** Sunday**.** Chinese **- Restaurante Villa Bonita,** Sunday**.** Spanish – **Cubano Club**, Thursday and Friday**.** Tico **– Don Próspero,** daily**; Rosti Pollo**, daily. Barbecue – **Casa Bavaria** Saturday, 11 AM to 10 PM, German and Tico – **Casa Bavaria** Sunday, 11AM to 5PM

Chapter 21
Best Bites

Favorites: (very subjective, relying on small number of opinions from friends and people who have e-mailed or phoned me. Some choices are based, at least in part, on value.)

American Breakfasts Azucar in Santa Ana, Denny's chain, Café de los Artistas in Escazú, Louisiana Bar & Grill in Playas del Coco, Magic's Motown in La Garita, Rock & Roll Pollo in Santa Ana

Antipasto Pan y Vino chain, Café Mediterráneo and Il Torino in Escazú

Asian Restaurant Tin Jo in San Jose, Saisaki in San Jose

Bagels Bagelman's chain

Banana Split Soda la Parada west of La Fortuna, Café Grande in San Antonio de Belén, Pops

Bar Food Chi Chi's in Escazú, Henry's Beach Café and Grill in Escazú, Rock & Roll Pollo in Santa Ana, San Clemente Bar & Grill in Dominical

Bargain – most decent food for least cost Las Malinches south of Playa Grande, Restaurante Fuente de Fortuna in Alajuela, Sabores in La Guácima, Soda Mana Y Pizza in Ciruelas, Tortilla Cooperative in Santa Cruz on the Nicoya Peninsula

Bi Bim Bop Saisaki in San Jose

Buffalo Wings Jalapeños Central in Alajuela, Magic's Motown in La Garita

Cafés that serve pastries Cafeteria Azucar y Canella in La Guácima, Eiffel in Santa Ana, Giacomin chain, Spoon chain and Trigo Miel chain

Cajun Louisiana Bar & Grill in Playas del Coco, Los Amigos in Jacó, Henry's Beach Café & Grill, Paragon* (Cajun chicken) in San Jose.

Casino Food Casino El Colonial in San Jose, Pirates Sports Bar & Grill in La Fiesta Casino in Alajuela near the airport

Ceviche Paso Real in Liberia, Mariscos #1 inside Alajuela's Central Market, Machu Picchu chain, El Dorado in San Antonio de Belén

Cheesecake Terruño in Plaza Itskatzú, Loveat along the San Ramón-La Fortuna road

Chocolate Cake Loveat Restaurant's chocolate fudge cake along the San Ramón-La Fortuna road, Chocolate volcano at Saga in Escazú

Chocolate Sauce Jo Stuart's home-made sauce. Reach her through AMCostaRica.com

Crêpes Cocorico Verde in San Pedro, Couleur Café in Ocotal, Eiffél in Santa Ana, Oui Oui La Crêpe in both Multiplazas, Viva La Crepa in Escazú, Il Ritorno (orange, cointreau crêpe) in San Jose, and the cheese blintzes at Loveat Restaurant

Deli's Il Torino in Escazú, Tom Tom in Escazú, Wall Street in Escazú and Little Israel in Escazú and Rohrmoser

Desserts Bacchus in Santa Ana, Jürgen's in Los Yoses, Giacomin's and Spoon's multiple sites, three chocolates Bavaria at Café Mundo, kiwi cannoli and chocolate volcano at

Saga in Escazú, cheesecake at Terruño in Plaza Itskatzú and at Loveat Restaurant on the San Ramon – La Fortuna road.

Dim Sum Casa China in San Jose, Restaurante Villa Bonita in Pavas, Don Wang in San Jose

Doughnuts Doña Dona chain, Samuelito's in San Jose

Eggs Benedict Café de los Artistas in Escazú

Falafel Al Muluk in San Pedro, Café Red Stripe in Puerto Viejo, Loveat Restaurant on the road from San Ramon to La Fortuna (fabulous)

Fish Tacos Nogui's Sunrise Café in Tamarindo, San Clemente Bar & Grill in Dominical, Taco Bar in Jacó, Tequila Bar & Grill in Playas del Coco and Xandari

Focaccia Bacchus in Santa Ana, La Focaccia in La Garita. Pan e Vino

French bread Colbert in Vara Blanca

French Restaurant Le Chandelier (4) in San Pedro, L'Ile de France (3) in Los Yoses and Colbert (3) in Vara Blanca, La Bastille in San Jose (2), La Brasserie in San Antonio de Belén (2) and El Jardín del Eden in Tamarindo (2)

French toast Café de Los Artistas in Escazú

German sausage German Bakery in Nuevo Arenal, Plinio in Quepos, and Tom Tom German Deli in Escazú (supplier of the other two).

Hamburger Azucar in Santa Ana, Chi Chi's in Escazú, Henry's in Escazú, Magic's Motown in La Garita, Outback in Plaza Itskatzú, Morpho's in Santa Elena, Tony Roma's in Escazú, Wall Street – chain.

Hot Dogs Grand Café in San Antonio de Belén and chili dog at Jalapeños Central in Alajuela, Price Smart snack bar, Il Torino sells Hebrew National and Nathan's hot dogs to take home.

Huevos Rancheros La Fonda Azteca in Sabana Sur, Jalapeños Central in Alajuela.

Ice Cream Pop's chain and Häagen Dazs in Escazú

Indian food Taj Mahal in Escazú (6), Tin Jo (2) and Coconut Spice(2) in Dominical, Plinio in Quepos (2)

Irish stew O'Conner's Irish Pub in Santa Ana

Italian market Soretto's in Escazú, Italicmam in Santa Ana

Italian restaurant Multiple votes each for Andiamo'la, Bacchus, Café Mediterráneo, Cerutti, Da Marco, Di Bartolo, Gino's and Il Ritorno.

Jalapeño pepper dish Jalapeño & Chicken crêpe at Viva La Crepa

Japanese authenticity Fuji

Korean food Saisaki in San Jose, Shil La in San Jose

Lobster El Jardin del Eden in Tamarindo, Factory in Escazú, La Cascada in Escazú (call first to see if they have them), La Fonte in Jacó, Papagayo at the Four Seasons Resort (E), Sabores in La guacima, Taboo in Playa Langosta

Lumpia, pancit and crispy pata Saisaki in San Jose

Milk shakes Pops

Mole Papagayo at the Four Seasons Resort (E), TacoNtento in Plaza Itzkasú, Huaraches (*mole rojo*) in La Garita

Old Clothes *(ropa vieja)* Cubano Club in Guachipelin

Orange sauce La Brasserie in Belen, Colbert in Vara Blanca, Il Ritorno in San Jose

Paella La Lluna de Valencia in San Pedro de Barva, Maribella in San Pedro, El Dorado in San Antonio de Belén

Pancakes Restaurant at the Skip Jack Inn in Playa Grande, El Grano de Oro, Xandari, Magic's Mortown

Pasta Tie among Andiamo'la, Ciao in Quepos, Lo Spago in Santa Ana, Pan y Vino chain, Pizza Gino in Pozos de Santa Ana and Sale e Pepe in Escazú

Pecan pie C afé de los Artistas in Escazú, Café Mediterráneo in Rohrmoser, Kay's Gringo Postres in Atenas, Oporto in Heredia, Desserts and More in Escazú

Persian kabobs Persa Mex in Real Cariari

Peruvian restaurant Bohemia in Barrio Escalante, Macchu Pichu – all three, Bariloche, El Novillo Alegre chain, Chancay and Inka Grill

Philippine food Saisaki in San Jose

Pickled herring Little Israel in Rohrmoser and Escazú, Tom Tom in Escazú

Pinchos Casa de España in San Jose's Sabana Norte

Pizza Too many different favorites including multiple votes for Pizza Gino in Pozos de Santa Ana (3), Pan y Vino chain (3), Sale e Pepe in Escazú (3), La Pizza in Santa Ana(2),

Tutti Li in Plaza Itskatzú(2), Lo Spago in Santa Ana(2), Ciao in Quepos(2) and Andiamo'la in Curridabat(2).

Presentations Bakea in Barrio Amón, Essencia in Brasil de Moro, Ginger in Playa Hermosa, Jürgens, La Laguna del Cocodrilo Bistro in Tamarindo, La Luz in Santa Ana, Park Café in San Jose, Saga in Escazú

Pupusas In Santa Ana's Sunday farmers' market (the stand run by the Salvadoran man and his Russian wife and their Ukrainian friend) and their family pupuseria in Santa Ana, Pupuseria Quirigua

Ribs La Casa del Viñedo in La Garita, Soda J&M in San Rafael de Alajuela, Tony Roma's in Escazú, Los Años Locos on the pista in Santa Ana, Rock & Roll Pollo's Saint Louis ribs on Thursdays

Roast chicken Costipollo in San Rafael de Alajuela, Pollos del Monte in both locations

Romantic Bacchus, Cerutti, El Grano De Oro, Essencia, La Luz, Le Chandelier, Nectar, Sunspot Grill, Xandari

Salads Azafrán in Rohrmoser and Escazú, GreenDLights in Santa Ana, Outback in Plaza Itskatzú, Restaurant Cha Cha Cha in Cahuita, Saga in Escazú, Tin Jo in San Jose, Xandari and Matsuri's seafood salad.

Salmon Il Ritorno in San Jose, La Brasserie in La Ribera, Paragon in San Jose, Saga in Escazú.

Sausage Sharon Wallace's homemade Italian in Ciudad Colon, Carnes Melissa's homemade chorizo in SanRafael Alajuela, Johnson's frozen brats and Italian in Auto Mercado, La Pizza's spaghetti with meatballs and Italian sausage (chorizo) in Santa Ana and the homemade breakfast sausage patties at Magic's Motown in La Garita.

Seafood There were virtually as many favorites as there were opinions. The numerical favorite was De L'Ola Del Mar which closed more than a year ago. Second favorite was the popular, but unheralded, El Banco de los Mariscos in Santa Barbara de Heredia, a long way from either coast. More votes were cast for ocean side local fish shacks and sodas than for multistar restaurants. El Coconut in Tamarindo, The Happy Snapper in Playa Braselito, La Leda Mata de Limón in Caldera Puntarenas and Mar y Sol in Playa Flamingo were the favorites of Guanacaste/Puntarenas natives, along with an inland Liberia location for very good ceviche – Paso Real. Los Malinches, a Tico place with Guanacaste style food, in the southern end of Playa Grande, was touted as the best buy for shrimp cocktail and shrimp salad. Luna Azul near Playa Ostional was the most remote. Juberths was the favorite of locals in Quepos. Sebastian in Escazú is earning a reputation for its fish and shrimp dishes. El Dorado in San Antoio de Belén is my favorite unknown spot for dorado fillets in Catalan sauce and ceviche.

Steaks Too many different favorites. None received more than three votes. Best two steaks I have had were at Le Chandelier in San Pedro and Ni-Fu Ni-Fa along the pista between Santa Ana and Escazú. Ni-Fu Ni-Fa would clearly have been number one, had I done the ranking, but it closed suddenly in August, 2007. Most unusual multiple vote getter (2) was the cafeteria at Cima Hospital. El Novillo Alegre in Santa Ana is the only surviving venue with three votes, now that Ni Fu- Ni Fa has closed. Two votes each also went to La Cascada, Donde Carlos and El Chicote.

Steak Sandwich Pirates Sports Bar & Grill in La Fiesta Casino near the airport, Don Fernando chain

Sushi Ichiban in Pavas and San Antonio de Belén, Matsuri Sushi in Curridabat and Santa Ana, Sushi Nippon Restaurant in Heredia and Samurai chain

Tandoori Taj Mahal on the Santa Ana – Escazú old road, Plinio is Quepos

Tapas El Gaitero, Las Tapas de Manuel in Itskatzú, Ginger in Playa Hermosa, Olio in Barrio Escalante, Park Café in San Jose

Veal Dishes Di Bartolo in Guachipelin

Vegetarian **Loveat Restaurant** on San Ramón – La Fortuna road

Waffles Café de los Artistas, Eiffel, Viva La Crepa

Not Recommended

Some restaurants that have spent lots of money on décor, advertising and/or presentations but, in my humble opinion, don't match the effort on the freshness, flavor or preparation of the food, or have problems with service, hygiene, dirty bathrooms or oppressive cigar smoke. Many of you may disagree with justification. Some restaurants may correct their problems in time. It is only my opinion based on two or more visits but I don't recommend the following: **Antonio's, Bar Marlin, Big Dog's, Chef Jacques, El Patio del Balmoral, Fulusu, Gua Gua, Héroes Restaurant, Hong Fu Lou, Hooters, Joanna, Li Qun, Mil Sabores, Miriam 2, Okinawa, Parioli Tavern Restaurant, Pasta Café, Sabor a Leña, Sen Fa, Tre Fratelli.**

Best Day Trips from or in the Central Valley

A. Climb out of the valley through coffee plantations and fern nurseries to Poas Volcano, back down a little way to the Vara Blanca turnoff to La Paz Waterfall Park to see butterflies, hummingbirds, snakes, frogs, bromeliads, three large waterfalls, oxen and painted cart and aviary. For a perfect ending to a great day, go back Vara Blanca, turn left at the gas station intersection for a very short ride to Colbert, a marvelous French country restaurant for a leisurely elegant but very affordable meal.

B. Drive through Braulio Carrillo National Park and its pristine verdant splendor, head north to the Sarapiqui River and take a two hour boat ride among monkeys, sloths, caimans and all sorts of waterbirds.

C. Drive to Carrara National Park and hire a guide to take you bird-watching along the trail that leads to the lagoon, the earlier in the morning the better. It is a great place to see scarlet macaws and monkeys. Then head south to Jacó for lunch, a gelato and a walk along the main street to peek into the galleries and souvenir shops. Return along the main road north with stops at the Tárcoles River bridge to see the large crocks in the water below, at Los Sueños to see the architecture, gardens and marina of this elegant resort and a final stop in Orotina to buy fresh fruit to sustain you on the slow curvy roads back up to the Central Valley.

D. The rountrip train ride to the Pacific Coast includesTico entertainment. A cab ride to Puntarenas offers beachside market and snacks.

E. The Café Britt coffee tour followed by a tasty and healthy buffet lunch at Don Próspero on site.

Chapter 22
Chains (Favorite in bold type)

Occasionally travelers, most often children, crave comfort food from home. When the occasion arises the following American chains have Costa Rican franchises: Burger King, China Express, Church's Fried Chicken, **Denny's**, Domino's Pizza, **Häagen Dazs**, KFC, McDonald's, Papa John's, Pasta Express, Pizza Hut, Quiznos, Starbucks, Subway, Taco Bell, TCBY, TGI Fridays, Tony Roma's, Wendy's and assuredly a few more.

Among the non-American chains are **Bagelman's** (New York style bagels, lox and cream cheese and more); Big Dogs (sports bars); Campero (fried chicken); Ceviche Del Rey (Peruvian seafood houses); Comida Mi Tierra (Tico); El Fogoncito, Huarache's and Los Antojitos (Mexican food); Hamburger Factory (hamburgers plus); Il Panino, Il Pomodoro, Pizzeria Tramonti and 2 X 1 Pizza (Italian); **La Casa de Doña Lela** (Tico dinners, snacks, kid's menu, weekend breakfasts and rustic décor); La casona de Cerdo (*chicharrones,* ribs, Tico); La Princessa Marina (seafood); **Matsuri**, Samurai and Sensu (sushi, sashimi, bento boxes and Japanese dinners); **Macchu Pichu** (Peruvian dinner houses); **Pan Y Vino** (good pizzas, antipasto, focaccia and sea food pasta at reasonable prices); Pollo Frito de Papi, **Pollos del Monte** and Pollos Raymi (chicken emporia); Pop's (quality and variety ice cream parlors); Spoon's, **Giacomin** (coffee and desserts); Rostipollo (spit roasted chicken, a luncheon buffet and much more); Rustic (Tico dinners); Vishnu (vegetarian).

Chapter 23

The Food Calendar
Seasonal crops, festivals and holidays

Year-round fruits and vegetables

Watermelon, papaya, pineapple, coconut, banana, oranges, limes, tangerines, grapefruit, tomatos, peppers, cabbage and onions are available all year round, though there are seasonal peak harvests, indicated by roadside vendors selling at very low prices. Virtually all vegetables are available in all seasons, due, in part, to micro-climates that complement each other.

Chicken and rice, *arroz con pollo,* is a very common dish for weddings, birthdays, anniversary parties, Christenings and holidays. For family gatherings, the menu is frequently *chicharrones, frijoles molida, guacamole, ensalada de repollo* and corn chips for the bean and avocado purées.

January

New Year's Day is a national holiday.

Also in January is the Patron Saint local festival in Alajuela, with parade and pilgrimage. Virtually every community of a few thousand people or more has a patron saint (*patronale)* celebratory weekend, ushered in at 5 PM on Friday by booming canon-like fire crackers and closed at midnight Sunday by the same blasts. It seems that most of them occur between November and February. The food stalls offer everything from cotton candy and shaved ice with syrup and dried milk powder (*granizadas)* to cauldrons of pig parts (*frito)* and chicken with rice (*arroz con pollo).* At the larger gatherings, you might find *empanadas, chicharrones,* kabobs, *pupusas,* chow mein, fried rice and eggrolls. Elaborate firework displays are common.

Palmares has a rodeo with music, dancing, a gentler version of bullfights (I'll call it "bull teasing" hereafter), carnival rides, bingo and food booths attended by thousands.

Santa Cruz offers similar activities to Palmares, on a smaller scale, with marimba music as well, honoring its patron saint, the Black Christ of Esquipulas, the week of January 15th.

Alajuelita celebrates the same patron saint, the same week - the Black Christ of Esquipulas, with an oxcart parade and procession up the mountainside to a large lighted cross.

The Costa Rican Country Club hosts the *Copa del Café,* an international under 18 tennis tournament.

Guanacaste String Festival is held in Tamarindo. It includes some unusual music.

February

Guavas start to ripen and continue through May.

Green mango slices (*mango cele)* appear in bags with a lime wedge and salt along the roads and in street stands in San Jose.

Carnival celebration in Puntarenas is not on Rio's scale, but does include a parade of dancers, marchers and floats. It usually occurs the third or fourth week of the month.

Ciudad Colón hosts the Orange Expofair with citrus displays and sales, traditional food, music, entertainment, dances and crafts.

In San Isidro del General, early February is the time for its harvest festivals, cattle exhibits, industrial and livestock shows and bull teasing. It is the center of Valle del General, a large agricultural area.

Re Curré is a Boruca Indian town south of San Isidro del Géneral that celebrates the Day of the Devils with a stylized reenactment, with masks and costumes, of their battle with the Spaniards. They portray themselves as little devils and the Spaniards as a bull. The festivities include fireworks, tribal dances and sale of local crafts.

The last week of February coincides with the Mayan New Year (the 25th). An annual Sun Festival celebrates progress in solar energy with a Mayan fire ceremony, exhibits of solar-powered devices and food cooked in solar ovens in Santa Cruz, Guanacaste.

Expoferia Orosi Colonial is a fair of crafts and food in front of the Colonial Church in Orosi.

Expo-Alfaro Ruiz, the last week of the month, consists of a livestock show, music, dance, concerts, rides and food in Zarcero.

La Fortuna also has a livestock show and more, in the first half of the month.

March

Cherry-like *nances* and plum-like purple mombins reach sweet ripeness in the Central valley.

The second Sunday in March, San Antonio de Escazú relives the tradition of pairs of oxen pulling painted carts down from the highlands , loaded with coffee beans. Sans beans, a long line of oxen and carts parade, accompanied by games, music and dancing. Local priests bless the animals and harvest.

Orotina has a fruit harvest festival at the fairgrounds with melons galore - cantaloupe three or four for a dollar, canary melons and honeydew. A food court caters to the hungry and thirsty with a variety of local eats.

Mangoes ripen earlier at sea level and appear there with red and yellow skins and succulent flesh.

March may be the best month for San Jose with its annual Arts Fair (puppets, dance troupe performances, classical music and jazz with internationally acclaimed performers); Book Fair; its horse and cattle show, horse races, rodeo and bull teasing; and orchid show of more than 1500 varieties from here and abroad.

The Central American Grand Prix is held at the race track in La Guácima.

Farmers' Day, with colorful folk costumes and dance, comes to Tierra Blanca on the fifteenth.

The Association of Residents of Costa Rica puts on a fair in San Jose to match up volunteers with organizations (First "annual" event in 2007).

On the Ides of March (15th), a religious processional marches from Cartago to the ruins of the country's first church in Ujarrás.

On the 19th, local communities celebrate San Jose Day with religious services, and many people observe the tradition of visiting Poas Volcano.

Coronado is the site of the Annual International Food Fair. Proceeds help the poor.

In the middle of the month, Zarcero hosts the Chiverre Fair, which celebrates the huge squash described in the April section, with music, cultural events, singing and competitions.

April

Holy Week, the week that leads up to Easter Sunday, includes national holidays on Thursday and Friday. As a result, many businesses, factories and government agencies close for the entire week, leading to a mass exodus to the beaches. Processions of Jesus on the cross are common.

Ripe mangoes hang from Central Valley trees by the hundreds. *Jocotes* are everywhere but most are green. Guavas fall from overloaded trees.

Roadside stands sell *chiverre* for the holidays. They look like pale oblong large squash. They are oven or grill roasted until the entire outsides are charred. Then they are cracked open. The shell is so hard it requires a mallet or cleaver to crack it. Inside is what appears to be pure white spaghetti squash, which is removed, thrown into a pillow case and dried in the clothes drier. Although the squash appears to be dry, when added to a pot with either two pounds of brown sugar or two cakes of cane sugar, it exudes enough liquid to make thin syrup, when simmered covered. It is seasoned with cinnamon and clove and allowed to cook for up to two hours. If it is not stirred frequently, it will burn. The jelly-like *miel (*honey) *de chiverre* is a favorite holiday treat, particularly as the filling for pastry turnovers.

Another Easter traditional food is *flor de itabo,* a cluster of white flowers. Usually they are coated with beaten egg, rolled in bread crumbs and fried. They are also boiled, mixed with diced hard-boiled eggs, sautéed onions and tomato, topped with grated cheese and browned under the broiler.

An Easter Log, *Tronco de Pascua,* is made from stale ladyfinger crumbs, coffee and eggs, glazed in chocolate, sprinkled with nuts.

Alajuela celebrates its favorite son, a barefoot farm boy named Juan Santamaria, who won the day and lost his life, defending the country against an American named William Walker and his mercenary army who were in the process of trying to capture all of Central America in 1856. If you go to see the parade of marching bands on April 11, notice the mango trees in the central park, thought to be among the tallest in the world. The day is a national holiday. A visit to the Juan Santamaria Museum is historically interesting and contains a nice orchid display.

University Week happens in San Jose with concerts, exhibits and a parade.

May

In Limon, May Day looks strangely British with cricket matches as well as music, dominoes, picnics and dancing.

May first is also Costa Rica's national Labor Day holiday and the day of the President's State of the Nation address.

San Isidro del Géneral has an oxcart parade on May 15th, similar to the one in San Antonio de Escazú. San Isidro is the patron saint of farmers and livestock, so every town in the country that is called San Isidro de *something*, celebrates the day with parades, fairs and blessings for animals and crops.

The *Carrera de San Juan*, a large national marathon, is run on the 19th.

Mangos, red peppers, tomatoes, papayas, *nancis*, water apples and pineapples line the roadsides in stands and on the back of pickup trucks. Cantaloupe disappear abruptly near the end of the month.

June

With the rainy season in full swing, many fruits ripen- *jocotes*, mangos, *nancis*, dragon fruit, oranges, mandarins and the last of the guavas. Fresh corn reappears. Few outdoor activities are scheduled because of the afternoon tempests. There are no major holidays except, of course, if you are a father. Father's Day happens on the third Sunday with only a fraction of the Mother's Day fanfare that happens in August.

July

In Puntarenas on the Saturday closest to the 16th, a gala celebration of the patron saint, the Virgin of Mount Carmel, includes a regatta of colorfully decorated yachts and fishing boats, religious services, fireworks, sporting events, concerts and dances. The festival is called "Virgin of the Sea." Craft and food booths line the seaside.

Alajuela has its Mango Festival - parade, crafts fair and music.

A series of classical and jazz concerts constitute an International Music Festival that holds performances in several different locations in July and August.

Roadside stands sell corn, *jocotes,* sweet limes, mandarins and papayas. Citrus time begins in the Central Valley.

Guanacaste Day, July 25th, is celebrated in Santa Cruz with a folklore festival.

In Liberia Guanacaste Day is huge, with bull teasing, rodeos, livestock exhibitions, music concerts, folk dancing and traditional regional food and costumes. It is the anniversary of annexation of Guanacaste from Nicaragua in 1812.

August

More citrus. With pale yellow green skims, nearly the size of oranges, sweet limes abound. They lose their flavor rapidly after picking. If you harvest them yourself and juice them soon after, they have a light sweet flavor as is. Mandarins and grapefruit ripen in the Central Valley by the end of the month. *Jocotes*, water apples and corn (8-10 / dollar) sell at roadside stands.

Religious processions mark the Day of the Virgin of the Angels in Cartago. The nation's patron saint, *La Negrita,* is an eight inch black stone statue that looks like Mary holding the Christ Child. The basilica is built on the spot where the statue was found in 1635. Pilgrims come from all over Central America on August 2nd, on foot, horseback or crawling on hands and knees.

Mother's Day is a major national holiday on the 15th. Restaurants are packed. Flower vendors reign.

On the last day of the month, the streets of San Ramón come alive. The obvious patron saint, San Ramón, is honored as neighboring towns carry depictions of thirty saints to the church in San Ramón amid street dancing and parades.

September

Limon hosts a celebration of its African/Caribbean roots with its Black Culture Festival. The week of Costa Rican–African Culture includes seminars, exhibits and displays of historic and cultural significance.

September 15th is Costa Rican Independence Day. At 6 PM, the Freedom Torch is supposed to arrive in the original capital, Cartago, as every schoolchild in the country sings the national anthem. The torch is carried from Guatemala by relay runners all the way to Cartago. Every school in every hamlet sends its marching band (often only drums) into the streets on parade the following day. Food, music and dance accompany the kids in most communities.

October

More music and marching bands mark the Corn Festival in Upala on the 12th, with the crowning of a Corn Queen in an October pageant. Corn pancakes or pudding, anyone? Costumes are made from corn husks, kernels and silk.

Grapes and apples are frequently imported from temperate climates. The smaller versions of both fruit hit the markets from Costa Rican highlands in October and November. They are not bad.

Carnival comes four months early to Limón, Mardi Gras Caribbean style.

The city of San Jose and the ministry of Culture sponsor an annual crafts fair.

Sarapiqui hosts an annual hearts of palm, *palmito,* fair with a variety of dishes on sale.

In Cartago, a similar event demonstrates and sell dishes made from the palm fruit *pejibaye* at the Expo-Feria del Pejibaye, the last weekend in October and first in November.

Halloween is celebrated a little, but is generally thought of in ominous terms as an event related to pagan devil worship.

November

The month begins with religious processions all over the country on All Soul's Day, also called "Day of the Dead." Families visit cemeteries and adorn crypts with flowers.

The Central Highlands host a coffee festival with bean picking contests.

The National Baroque Festival is held at the old stone church in Santa Ana.

The International Theater Festival comes to San Jose's streets and theaters.

Oxen and their painted carts parade down San Jose's Paseo Colón, the last Sunday of the month. The party begins the night before in La Sabana, the large city park, with singing and fireworks adjacent to the camped oxen.

As the rainy season ends, fruit trees sprout blossoms galore.

Frozen turkeys, canned cranberry sauce and packaged stuffing mixes hit the shelves of up-scale markets that cater, in part, to ex-pats.

December

Christmas decorations begin to appear in stores, on streets and around homes as early as late September, but by early December, they are everywhere. Employees get an extra month's salary to offset the cost of Christmas. Tricycle and bicycles sales displays multiply like fruit flies.

The very same *miel de chiverre* that appeared in sweet profusion during Easter Week, returns in pastries and turnovers for Christmas. Apples, grapes, eggnog and cookies are also part of the holiday food tradition.

San Jose's National Theater hosts recitals of Christmas choirs from all over the country, early in the month.

The Festival of Lights Parade in San Jose includes elaborately lighted floats and fireworks.

From Christmas until New Year's Eve, Zapote is the site for the enormous carnival, Festejos Populares, with rides, music, food and fireworks.

Every December the aroma and squeals from rural Alajuela pig farms desist. Christmas and edible pork products are wed in Latin America.

The winds of Christmas arrive as if to freshen the air, and a local flock of guinea fowl vanishes about a week before Christmas. All over South America, but especially in Colombia, a 10- to 15- pound whole roast suckling pig is the centerpiece of the Christmas dinner table. Glazed hams are also becoming more popular south of the Rio Grande.

There is no doubt in my mind that more pork goes for tamale filling in Costa Rica in December than for anything else. In my pueblo, as in the rest of the country, two or even three generations form a family assembly line to mass produce the plantain leaf-wrapped packets of pork filled corn meal cakes. Neighbors give each other boxes of Christmas tamales and add a critique of preparation skills to the usual front gate gossip: "Cecelia's spices are amazing . . . Martha left out the raisins this year . . . Sandra ties the most perfect twine patterns . . . Josefina doesn't use fresh corn, does she?"

What happens to the rest of the pig? The belly goes for bacon. The skin crisps in *chicharrone* cauldrons. The ribs are roasted and barbecued, often along with chickens over coffeewood fires, *a la leña.*

In the 60s, I lived in a Chinese neighborhood in San Francisco and bore witness to the adage that Cantonese people eat every part of the pig except the squeal. Cheeks, snouts, ears, tails, kidneys, livers, hearts, spleens, stomachs, skin, feet and intestines appeared in thick rice soups, clay pot stews, on dim sum platters, at banquet tables, in braised sauces over rice and on buffets of cold hors d'oeuvres. Dozens of puns emerged from that neighborhood playing on the words "offal" and "awful."

What happens to those nether parts here? In Brazil, *feijoada,* the national dish, is a black bean stew containing at least five different pig parts to gain respectability and authenticity. They include combinations of feet, necks, snouts, ears, tails, jowls, blood sausage and, rarely, intestines.

Here in Costa Rica, I haven't seen stomach or intestine used. I assume they make their way into sausage, hot dogs and cold cuts. The tripe used in *mondongo* and *menudo* is from cows. A Brasilera friend bought frozen "cleaned" pig intestines for her *feijoada,* but still boiled and recleaned them before using them in the stew-pot.

In the southern U.S., chitterlings, or chitlins, are made from pig intestines. They were part of the slave culture in which the masters gave their slaves only those pig parts they wouldn't eat. Pig intestines have a vile smell and require hours to clean and prepare. Now, they survive nearly exclusively as nostalgia food.

In Salley, South Carolina, the annual Chitlin' Strut is a festival that attracts about 75,000 people. In Guatemala, I had a bowl of *revolcaldo,* pig offal stew including intestines and brain. It wasn't bad, but one of my sons noted that *caldo* meant soup-pot and *revol* was short for revolting.

In Jamaica, there is a dish of beans and pickled pig tails. Methinks all food preferences are cultural.

Have you ever eaten *frito?* It is the same word as "fried" but is a common and much loved fiesta food served in dozens of pueblo festivals across Costa Rica. It is pig part and organ meat stew without intestines – a dice of heart, lung, liver, spleen, kidneys, ears, nose, cheeks, ribs, rind, neck, head and feet. Kidneys need to be pre-boiled and rinsed a few times before dicing.

The dice is marinated in lemon juice, mashed garlic, oregano, thyme, sliced onion, salt and black pepper, for several hours or overnight. Dry and brown the dice in a skillet, put it in a pot with any unabsorbed leftover marinade, enough water to cover, optional diced aromatic vegetables – carrot, onion, celery stalks with leaves, sweet pepper, tomato, plantain, zucchini and cubed potato.

It is seasoned with salt and salsa Lizano to taste. I thought the last ingredient was a cut up guinea hen. I didn't know why, but I guessed that was where the pre-Christmas flock went. My ear for Spanish led me astray.

The cook who shared her recipe for frito with me said *guineos* – small green bananas, not *guineas* — guinea hens. The stewpot is then simmered for about two hours until everything is tender (an extra half hour if you live at an altitude higher than the Central Valley). All the different meats, despite their disparate origin, become tender and tasty. If you are tempted to make it, when it is finished, refrigerate it overnight, remove the top layer of white fat, reheat, garnish with chopped cilantro and serve with white rice.

If you are offal challenged, you can go to the December *chicharrone* festival in Puriscal, west of Ciudad Colon, for festival food, arts and crafts, music and a horse parade.

More pork? What is a cardiologist doing, writing about pork? What is the skinny about pork? The truth is that pork is not "the other white meat." Neither is it poison for your heart.

Pork is a red meat. Redness is defined by the USDA according to the amount of a muscle substance called myoglobin. The US Pork Board began the "other white meat" ad campaign in 1987. Pork and beef have much more myoglobin than the white meats of chicken or fish. Veal has less than pork when it is very young. That pork lightens when it is cooked, is irrelevant. All meats carry saturated fats, the unhealthy kind. Poly or mono saturated fats are better for you.

Artificially produced trans-fats are worse. Different cuts of pork can be lean or fatty.

Pork tenderloin has similar fat content as skinless chicken breast. Boneless loin roast and extra lean ham are similar to sirloin chops in fat content, but bacon and sausage are much worse. Nice juicy pork chops are juicy because they have lots of fat, as are marble-streaked steaks.

What about pork ribs? When I make them at home, I boil off a lot of the fat before they go into the oven. It also makes them "fall off the bone tender." The largest ribs are Chinese country-style with a generous chunk of meat attached. The red color is due to artificial dye. They are moderately fatty. Next come spareribs from the side of the animal. They are perhaps the tastiest but have more bone and less meat than the others.

Ribs from the back, called baby-backs, have less bone and more meat. The tiniest with only a little piece of bone or cartilage are the Chinese dim sum variety steamed in black bean sauce. I love their flavor but they are about half fat. Fortunately for those with little restraint, the servings are tiny.

Chapter 24
Restaurant Spanish for the neophyte

Greetings Good morning *Buenos dias*
Good afternoon *buenas tardes* Good evening *buenas noches*
Breakfast *desayuno* Lunch *almuerzo*
Dinner *cena* Please *por favor*
Thank you *gracias* You are welcome *con mucho gusto*

Purpose I am hungry *tengo hambre*
Do you have a table? *Hay una mesa*
(non-smoking)? *(sin fumar)* For 2 *para dos*
I am thirsty *tengo sed* Where is ... *donde esta*
Diningroom *El Comedor* Bathroom *el baño*
Kitchen *la cocina* The menu, please *el menu, por favor*
Is there a menu in English? *Hay un menu en inglés*
The check, please *La cuenta, por favor*
The food is delicious *La comida es deliciosa*

On the table: Cutlery *los cubiertos*
Glass *el vaso* Cup *la taza*
Wine glass *la copa* Plate *un plato*
Bowl *la sopera* Napkin *la servieta*
Pitcher *el pichel* Fork *el tenedor*
Knife *el cuchillo* Teaspoon *la cucharita*
Soupspoon *la cuchara* Salt *sal*
Black pepper *pimiento negro* Hot sauce *salsa picante*
Sugar *azúcar* Ketcup *salsa de tomate*
Mustard *mostaza* Mayonnaise *mayonesa*
Vinegar & Oil *vinagre y aceite* Bread *pan*
Butter *mantequilla*

Drinks *bebidas* Water *agua*
Coffee (decaf) *café (descafeinado)*Beer *cerveza*
Wine(white, red) *vino (blanco, tinto)* Club soda *soda*
Fruit smoothie *batido* Soda *gaseosa*
Cold dink *refresco* Tea *té*

Hot chocolate *chocolate caliente*

Menu specials

Blue plate special *casado*

Set menu *menú del dia*

Local specialities *specialidades locales*

House specials *especialidades de la casa*

Menu items

Beef *carne*

Chicken *pollo*

Fish *pescado*

Seafood *mariscos*

Pork *cerdo, lechon*

Soup *sopa*

Vegetables *verdures*

Appetizers *entradas*

Dessert *postre*

Salad *ensalada*

Rice *arroz*

Potato (fried, mashed) *papa (frito, pure)*

Pasta *pasta*

Salt *sal*

Pepper *pimiento*

Sugar *azúcar*

Milk *leche*

Eggs *huevos*

Bacon *tocino*

Ham *jamon*

Sausage *salsiccha*

Shrimp *camarones*

Mushrooms *hongos*

Onions *cebollas*

Avocado *aguacate*

Hamburger *hamburguesa*

Hot dog *perro caliente*

Veal *ternera*

Lamb *cordero*

Beef *carne de res*

Tongue *lengua*

Chop *chuleta*

Rib *Costilla*

Rare *poco hecho, rojo*

Medium *término medio,medio*

Well done *bien hecho*

Hot *caliente*

Cold *frio*

To go *para llevar*

Tasty *que rico*

Delicious *delicioso*

Chapter 25
Adios mis amigos

Tourists have complained frequently that, after a costly taxi ride, they arrive at a restaurant, closed for months or years. There is no way for guide books to stay abreast of change. Delays in printing, distributing and purchasing usually set the information back a year or two. The restaurant business is a crap shoot even in the best of circumstances. Many a fine kitchen closes when the chef retires, when the owner dies and the kids want no part of the business, when adverse publicity (even if bogus) depletes the clientele, when new competition floods the market, when a vital supplier folds or doubles prices, when a reviewer reports on a bad experience, if the project is under-funded and can't sustain itself long enough to become profitable etc.

To minimize the risk of a wild goose chase, look at this incomplete list of closures in 2005, 2006, and 2007, among which are some of my former **favorites** (in bold type). A tip of the cap and a word of thanks for the memories to the following: Abbracci, **Al Molino**, Ambrosia, Ave Fenix, **Bokaös**, Bouzouki, Brendee's, **Café Couleur**, **Cha Cha Cha**, Chango, Chef Jacques, Chile Rojo, Chipotle, Crazy Fish, **De L'Ola Del Mar**, El Balcon de Peruana, El Cañaveral, **El Campeon**, **El Invernadero**, El Toro Negro, El Torreón, Gecko (Brasil de Mora), **Gecko** (Playa Brasilito), Goyi, Gula's, Gustare, Icarus, Indio Hatuey, La Fragata, La Fuente, La Galeria (both in San Pedro and Escazú), La Giradilla, La Jarrra Garibaldi, **Mighyy Rivers Café**, **Mundo**, **Power Chicken**, **Ni Fu- Ni Fa,** Rancho Grande, Restaurante Patagonia, Restaurante Tipico Neolatino, Rock and Ride Café, **San Telmo** in Escazú and Curridabat, **Satto**, **Shogun**, Solera, Sushi Itto,**Tico Mex**, Toad Hall, Toku and Voulez Vous. Azucar closed in San Jose, but reappeared with a splash in Santa Ana.

Chapter 26
Restaurant Index

My personal favorites are in bold type. There are hundreds more that are not listed because I haven't visited them or don't know of anything unique about them. Assuredly I have missed a number of good ones. With feedback from readers, I'll add them to updated editions and remove the names of those which have closed.

Abbreviations: Ala. = Alajuela, B. = Barrio, C.R. = Costa Rican, Inter. = international, Rest. = restaurant, S.A. = San Antonio, S.J. = San Jose, Vegi. = vegetarian, E= expensive, V= view

Name	Location	Cuisine	Phone
A Churrascaria Brasileira	S.A. de Belen	Brazilian	2239-1532
A La Leña	Chain	Pizza	
Alfredo	Escazú	Italian	2208-2138
Amimodo	Puerto Viejo	Italian	2750-0257
Andiamo'la	Curridabat	Italian	2272-1838
Anthony	La Guácima	Seafood Tico	2438- 0143
Antojitos Del Rey	Heredia	Fast food	2293-7953
Antonio's	Cariari	Italian	2293-0622
Azafrán	Chain	Salads, sandwiches	2220-2008
Azucar	Santa Ana	Steak, Int.	2282-9210
Bacchus	Santa Ana	Italian	2282-5441
Bagelmen's	chain	sandwiches, deli	
Baalbeck Bar & Grill	San Rafael de Heredia	Tico, Lebanese	2267-6482
Balcón de Uvita	Uvita	International	2743-8034
Bangkok	Sabana Sur	Thai	2296-6110
Bar Tintos y Blancos Wine	Terramall	Tapas	2278-6900
Barba Roja	Quepos	Seafood	2777-0331
Benihana	Sabana Norte	Japanese	2291-4572
Big Dog's	Santa Ana	Bar food	2282-9935
Boemios	St. Elena	International	2645-5750
Bohemia	B. Escalante	Peruvian	2253-6348
Bugsy's	San Ramón & La Fortuna	Hamburgers	2445-5557
Caballo Blanco	Moravia Brasil,	bar food	2236-8626
Café de los Artistas	Escazú	American	2288-5082

Name	Location	Cuisine	Phone
Café Europa& German Bakery	Liberia	German	26681081
Café Galeria El Aguacate	Brasil	International	2249-0687
Café Kavehaz	Curridabat	Hungarian	2283-1616
Café Mediterráneo	Rohrmoser	Italian	2290-5850
Café Mundo	San Jose	International	2222-6190
Café Ruiseñor	B. Escalante	Bakery plus	2225-2562
Café Teatro Nacional	San Jose	Desserts, snacks	2221-1329
Café Té con Té	Escazú	Desserts, snacks	2288-5028
Cafeteria Azucar Canela	La Guácima	Desserts, café	2438-0029
Cafetería 1830	San Jose	International	2221-4011
Cafetería Gourmet	Atenas	International	2446-0493
Caliente, Caliente	Pavas	Tico	2231-3327
Capital Grill	Escazú	Steak, Inter.	2288-6362 E
Casa Bavaria	Alajuela	German	2483-0716
Casa Creole	Cahuita	Caribbean	2755-0035
Casa Creole Bistro & Cafeteria	SJ	Caribbean	2256-2316
Casa de España	San Jose	Spanish, tapas	2290-8526
Casa Pasta	Tibás	Pasta, pizza	2241-5278
Casino	Cahuita	International	2394-4153
Casino Club Colonial	San Jose	Steaks, Tico	2258-2807
Ceviche del Rey	chain	Peruvian, seafood	
Chalito's	Las Vueltas	Tico, Peruvian	2439-1029
Chancay	Plaza Itskatzú	Peruvian	2588-2318
Chef Oriental	Moravia	Chinese	
Chelles	San Jose	24 hour Tico	2221-1369
Chez Cristophe	Curridabat	Sandwiches, Fr.	2224-1773
Chi Chi's	Escazú	American	2228-1173
Club Cubano	Guachipelin	Cuban, Spanish	2215-2001
Club del Mar	Jacó	Seafood, int.	2643-3194
Coconut Spice	Dominical	Thai, Indian	2829-8397
Cocorico Verde	San Pedro	Crêpes	2224-9744
Comida China	Chain	Chinese	
Comida para Sentir	San Pedro	Vegetarian	2224-1163
Costipollo	San Rafael, Ala.	Chicken, Ribs	2438-6835
Couleur Café	Ocotal	French	2670-1696
Crokante	B. Otoya	International	2258-1017
Curime	Cariari	Steak, Fusion	2239-0022 E
Da Marco	Piedades	Italian	2282-4103
Delicias	Grecia, San Ramón	Pastries, Café	2444-6301
Delicias Caribeñas de Mami	Heredia	Caribbean	2262-0359
Delicias de Mi Tierra	La Garita	Tico	2433-8536
Del Mar	San Jose	International	2257-7800
Denny's	La Sabana, Alajuela	24 hour American	2231-3500
Di Bartolo	Guacipelin	Italian	2228-2800

Name	Location	Cuisine	Phone
Di Mare	Papagayo	Italian	2696-0006 E
Doña Dona	Chain	Donuts	
Doña Olga	Playa Nosara	Soda, Fish	
Donde Carlos	Los Yoses Peru,	Steak	2225-0819
Don Fernando	chain	Steak	
Don Próspero	Barva	Tico buffet	2277-1500
Don Wang	San Jose	Chinese	2223-5925
Domino's Pizza	chain	Pizza	
Dos Locos	Quepos	Tico	2777-1526
Dragonfly Bar & Grill	Tamarindo	Tico/Asian	2653-1506
Eiffel	Santa Ana	Pastry, Café	2282-0814
El Ancia Restaurant	Playa Samara	Seafood	2656-0716
El Balcon de Europa	San Jose	Italian	2221-4841
El Banco de los Mariscos	Santa Barbara	Seafood	2269-9090
El Caballo Rey	Punta Leona	Tico, steak	2824-3360
El Cerdo Dorado	Tacacori (Ala)	International	2430-7474
El Chicote	San Jose	Steak, Tico	2232-0936
El Coconut	Tamarindo	Seafood	2653-0086
El Dorado	S.A. de Belén	Seafood	2239-7226
Elegant Rest. Camaron Dorado	Playa Brasilito	Seafood	2654-4028
El Fogoncito	chain	Mexican	
El Gaitero	S.A de Escazú	Spanish	2228-1850
El Gran Escape	Quepos	Seafood	2777-0395
El Grana de Oro	San Jose	International	2255-3322
El Hicaco	Jacó	Tico, seafood	2643-3226
El Jardin	La Fortuna	Soda	2479-9360
El Jardin	Playa Brasilito	Italian, Thai	2654-4397
El Jardin De Edén	Tamarindo	French, Seafood	2653-0137
El Novillo Alegre	Curridabat	Argentinean	2524-0353
El Novillo Alegre	Escazú	Argentinean	2288-4995
El Novillo Alegre	Santa Ana	Argentinean	2203-4735
El Patio Bistro Latino	Quepos	International	2777-4982
El Pelícano	Playa Herradura	Seafood, Tico	2637-8910
El Rodeo	S. A. de Belén	Steakhouse	2293-2692
El Sapo Dorado	St. Elena	International	2645-5010
Entrepanes	San Jose	Sandwiches	2257-9303
Essencia	Brasil de Mora	International	2203-7503
Factory	Escazú	Steak, Lobster	2208-2137
Fiesta de Las Pupusas Salvadoreña	Atenas	Salvadorian	2446-6987
Finca Bonanza	Ciudad Colón	Dutch, Tico	2249-1185
Fish Lips	Dominical	Seafood	2787-0091
Flor de Loto	Sabana Norte	Chinese	2232-4652
Fogo Brasil	San Jose	Brazilian	2248-1111
Fogón Casero	SA de Belén	Costa Rican	2589-4646

Name	**Location**	**Cuisine**	**Phone**
Fogón Sano	Playa Hermosa	Health food	2643-7108
Fuji	Sabana Norte	Japanese	2232-8122
Giacomin	S.J. & Santa Ana	Pastries	2234-2551
Ginger	Playa Hermosa	International	2672-0041
Grand Café	S.A. de Belén	coffees, sandwiches	2239-1830
Green D'Lights	Santa Ana, San Pedro	Salads, sandwiches	2234-2617
Green Dragon	Monte de la Cruz	French, Interl	2267-6222
Häagen Dazs	chain	Ice cream	
Hacienda El Estribo	Santa Ana	C.R. & steak	2282-5339
Hamburgrer Factory	chain	Hamburgers	
Hamburger Grill	chain	Fast food	
Henry's Beach Café & Grill	Escazú	Cajun, Bocas	2289-6250
Hooters	Pl. Itsktzú	American	2289-3498
Hotel Casa Turire	Turrialba	International	2531-1111
Hotel Vista de Valle	Naranjo	Costa Rican	2451-1165
Huaraches	chain	Mexican	
Ichiban	chain	Japanese	
Il Padrino	Pavas	Italian	2220-1614
Il Panino	Curridabat, Escazú	Sandwiches	2524-0335
Il Pomodoro	Chain	Pizza	
Il Ritorno	B. California	Italian	2225-0543
Isla Verde	Pavas	Chinese	2296-5068
Il Torino (Café)	Escazú	Italian deli	2288-4476
Inka Grill	chain	Peruvian	
Jacó Taco	Jacó	Mexican 24hr	2643-1313
Jalapeños	Atenas	Mexican	2446-6314
Jalapeños Central	Alajuela	Tex-Mex	2430-4027
Jamon, Jamon	La Garita	Spanish	2433-7944
Jazz Café	San Pedro	Sandwiches	2253-8933
Joanna	Escazú	International	2228-7381
J.R. House of Ribs	Bario Amón	Ribs, steaks	2223-0523
Jürgen's	Los Yoses	European Int.	283-2239
Kay's Gringo Postres	Atenas	American, desserts	2373-3629
King's Garden	Sabana Norte	Chinese	2255-3838
Kosher Center	Pavas	Kosher Deli	2290-1576
La Bastille	San Jose	French	2255-4994
La Brasserie	S.A. de Belén	French	2239-5410
La Casa de Doña Lela	chain	Tico	
La Casa del Viñedo	La Garita	Tico	
La Cascada	Escazú	Steak, Lobster	2228-0906
La Casona de Cerdo	chain	Tico, Pork	
La Casona Restaurante	Tortuguero	Fish & Caribbean	2709-8092
La Cava Grill	Escazú	International	2228-8515 V
La Chosa de Laurel	La Fortuna	Tico	2479-7169

Name	Location	Cuisine	Phone
La Cocina de Leña	El Pueblo (S.J.)	Costa Rican	2255-1360
La Divina Comida	Escazú	Peruvian, Italian	2201-9353
La Esquina de Buenos Aires	San Jose	Argentinean	2223-1909
La Fiesta de Pollo	Alajuela	Tico	2430-8073
La Fonte	Jacó	Italian	2643-3890
La Radial	San Ramón	Tico soda	2447-3155
La Station	Curridabat	Steak, seafood	2283-0681
La Fiesta del Maiz	La Garita	Tico, Corn	2487-5757
La Flor	San Jose	Costa Rican	
La Focaccia	La Garita	Italian	2433-8382
La Fogueira	Plaza Itskatzú	Brazilian Meats	2588-0080
La Fonda	La Guácima	Tico, steaks	2438-2193
La Fonda Azteca	Sabana Sur	Mexican	2296-6048
La Fuente de los Mariscos	La Uruca	Seafood	2296-1256
La Gallera	La Uruca	Mex, Peru Argentinean	2291-6785
La Guachada	Sabana Oeste	Argentine, Empanadas	2232-6916
La Gua Gua	Plaza Itskatzú	Cuban	2288-5112
La Isabela	Alajuela	Spanish, Tappas	2298-0168
La Laguna del Cocodrilo	Tamarindo	Fusion	2653-0225 E
La Leda	Caldera	Seafood	2634-3097
La Lluna de Valencia	San Pedro de Barva	Paella, tapas	2269-6665
La Luz	Santa Ana	International	2282-4160 V
La Masia	Sabana Norte	Spanish	2296-3528
La Piazzetta	San Jose	Italian	2222-7896
La Princesa Marina	chain	Seafood	
Las Delicias de Mi Tierra	La Garita	Costa Rican	2433-8536
Las Delicias de Maiz	La Garita	Tico	2433-7026
Las Tapas de Manuel	Moravia, Itskatzú	Spanish	2288-5700
La Tasca del Novillo	Santa Ana	Spanish	2282-3042
Las Tucas	Playa Negra	Tico, smoked pork	
Le Chandelier	San Pedro	French	2225-3980
Le Monastère	Escazú	French	2228-8515 V
L'Ile de France	Los Yoses	French	2283-5812
Little Seoul	Rohrmoser	Korean, Japanese	2232-5551
Lola's	Playa Avellanas	Luncheonette	2658-8097
L'Olivo	Sabana Norte	Italian	2232-9440
Los Adobes	S.A. Belén	Tico	2239-0957
Los Amigos	Jacó	Wraps, Thai, Cajun	2643-2961
Los Anonos	Escazú	Tico, Steak	2228-0810
Los Años Locos	Santa Ana	Steak	22037663
Los Antojitos	chain	Mexican	
Los Héroes Restaurant	Lake Arenal	Swiss, European	2692-8014
Lo Spago	Santa Ana	Italian	2582-2121
Los Vitrales	Santo Domingo de Heredia	International	2244-1414

Name	Location	Cuisine	Phone
Louisiana Bar & Grill	Playas del Coco	Cajun & Seafood	2670-0882
Lubnan	San Jose	Lebanese	2257-7061
Luna Azul	Ostional	International	2821-0075
Machu Picchu	chain	Peruvian	
Mac's American Bar	Sabana Sur	Tex-Mex	2231-3145
Magic's Motown	La Garita	Wings, burgers	2467-5374
Maiz Tico	Chain	Tico	
Manolo's	San Jose	24 hour Tico	2221-2041
Marbella	San Pedro	Spanish	2224-9452
Mar y Sol	Playa Flamingo	International	2654-5222
Mas Tkila	Pl. Itscatzú	Cantina	2228-1815
Matsuri	Curridabat & Santa Ana	Japanese	2280-5522
McDonalds	chain	American	
Mirador La Trance	Aserri	Costa Rican	2230-3505 V
Mirador Ram Luna	Aserri	Costa Rican	2230-3060 V
Mirador Tiquicia	Escazú	Costa Rican	2289-5839 V
Mirador Valle Azul	Escazú	Italian	2254-6281
Miss Edith	Cahuita	Caribbean	2755-0248
Mi Tierra	Volcán Irazú	Tico	2822-9432
Morphos	Santa Elena	International	2645-5607
Muro-Ji	Escazú	Japanese 228-1992	
Nectar	Mal Pais	International	2640-0232
Nogui's Sunrise Café	Tamarindo	Seafood	2653-0029
Non-Solo Café	Escazú	Pastry, Italian	2289-4909
Nuevo Latino	Los Sueños	Nuevo Latino	2630-9000 E
O'Conner's Irish Pub		Santa Ana Bar Food	2282-0199
Okinawa	Curridabat	Pan-Asian	2283-0709
Olio	B. Escalante (SJ)	Tapas	2281-0541
Oporto	Heredia	International	2263-2058
Oui Oui La Crêpe	Multiplazas	Crêpes	
Outback Steakhouse	Plaza Itskatzú	Australian style	2288-0511
Pacific Bistro	Jacó	International	2643-3771
Pacifico Restaurante	San Jose	Japanese, Korean	2257-9523
Pan e Vino	chain	Italian	
Papa John's	chain	Pizza	
Papagayo	Four Seasons Resort	Nuevo Latino	2696-0006 E
Parioli Tavern Restaurant	Alajuela	Costa Rican	2441-3537
Park Café	Sabana Sur	Inter. tapas	2290-6324
Parrallada El Churasco	B. Escalante	Argentinean Steak	2225-0778
Paso Real	Liberia	Seafood, meats	2666-3455
Peperoni	S. A. de Belén	Italian	2293-2248
Persa Mex	Real Cariari	Persian, Mexican	2293-4237
Pirates Sports Bar	Alajuela	American 380-0573	
Pizza Gino's	Pozos	Pizza , pasta	2282-3859

Name	Location	Cuisine	Phone
Pollos Del Monte	chain	Chicken, Tico	
Port City Java	Santa Ana	Coffee shop	2203-8211
Pupusas El Bario	San Jose de Alajuela	Pupusas	2433-3169
Pupusa Salvadoreñas La Flor de Izote	Escazú	Pupusa	2228-2463
Pupuseria Mayra	Tibás	Salvadorian	2236-0991
Pupuseria Quirigua	Santa Ana	Salvadorian	2203-4128
Quiznos	chain	Sandwiches	
Ranchito Miriam	La Garita	Tico	2433-2312
Restauran Sushi-Ko	Sabana Oeste	Japanese	2291-1285
Restaurant at the Skip Jack Inn	Playa Grande	Inter.	2653-0408
Restaurant Beirut	Sabana Norte	Lebanese	2296-9622
Restaurant Casa de Miguel	Grecia	Costa Rican	2444-6767
Restaurant Don Rufino	La Fortuna	International	2479-9997
Restaurant Exótica	Ojochal	French, International	2786-5050
Restaurant Friday's	San Pedro	American	2224-5934
Restaurant Juberths	Quepos	Seafood	2777-1292
Ristorante Cugini	Alajuela	Italian	2440-6893
Rstaurante Isla Verde	Pavas	Chinese	2296-5068
Rest. Fuente de Fortuna	Alajuela	Chinese	2431-2268
Restaurante Lotus	Escazú	Chinese	2228-8105
Restaurante Magnifico	San Jose	Chinese	
Restaurante Mariel	La garita	Tico	2433-8240
Restaurante Oasis	San Jose	Tico	2255-0448
Restaurante Picachos	Cartago	International	2574-6072
Restaurante Playa de los Artistas	Montezuma	Mediterranean	2642-0920
Restaurante Villa Bonita	Pavas	Chinese	2232-9855
Restaurante Zully Mar	Tamarindo	Tico, Seafood	2653-0023
Restaurant Chepito's	Punta Islita	Portugese	
Restaurant La Casona del Cafetal	Orosi Valley	Inter.	2577-1414
Restaurant La Cocina de José	Liberia	Tico	2666-1202
Restaurant Sofia	Monteverde	Nuevo Latino, fusion	2645-7017
Rock and Roll Pollo	Santa Ana	American, sports bar	2282-9613
Sabor a Leña	Escazú	Italian	2288-2503
Sabores	La Guácima	Tico, seafood	2438-5707
Sabor Nicaraguenses	San Jose	Nicaraguan	2223-1956
Saga	Escazú	International	2289-6615
Sash Restaurante	Rohrmoser	Middle Eastern	2232-1010
Saisaki	San Jose	Japanese, Korean	2223-7097
Sakura	Cariari	Japanese	2239-0033
Sale e Pepe	Escazú	Italian	2289-5750
Samurai	chain	Japanese	2228-4124
Sancho Panza	Cariari	Spanish, tapas	2239-0033
San Clemente Bar & Grill	Dominical	Mexican, Seafood	2787-0055

Name	Location	Cuisine	Phone
Santa Ana's Tex Mex	Santa Ana	Tex Mex	2282-6342
Sebastian	Escazú	Peruvian, fusion	2289-9468
Señor de Sipan	Tres Rios	Peruvian	2278-2978
Sensu	Escazú, Curridabat	Japanese	2228-2443
Shil La	Pavas	Korean, Japanese	2296-1808
Soda El Recreo	Turrúcares	Tico	2487-4098
Soda Gimbel	Heredia	Tico	
Soda Isabel	La Guácima, Ala.	Tico	2438-0169
Soda Janet	Puntarenas	Tico	2661- 0285
Soda Kathia	Playa Herradura	Tico soda	2637-7137
Soda La Puerta del Sol	Sarchí	Tico, Seafood	2454-4620
Soda Margarita	San Rafael Ala.	Tico soda	2839-1289
Soda Miss Isma	Puerto Viejo	Caribean, Tico	
Soda Piedra Mar	Malpais	Seafood, Tico	2640-0069
Soda Tapia	S.J. and Santa Ana	Tico	2222-6374
Soda Tempestad Azul	Tibás	Japanese	2240-4933
Soda y Pizza Mana	Ciruelas	Tico, pizza	2438-3118
Spoon	Chain	Café, pastry	
Stan's Irish Pub	Zapote	Irish Pub	2253-4360
Steve and Lisa's	Tárcoles	Seafood	2637-0494
Subway	chain	Sandwiches	
Sunspot Grill	Quepos	International	2777-0442
Sushi Nippon Restaurant	Heredia	Japanese	2260-1329
Taboo	Playa Langosta	International	2653-1422
Taco Bar	Jacó	Mexican, Inter.	2643-0222
TacoNtento	Pl. Itskatsú	Mexican	2588-8231
Tacotitlan	Coronado	Mexican	
Taj Mahal	Escazú	Indian	2228-0980
Té con Té	Escazú	Café	2288-5027
Terruño	Plaza Itzkatsú	Argentinas	2588-2227
Tequila Bar & Grill	Playas del Coco	Mexican	2670-0741
Tequila Joe's	Santa Ana	Tex-Mex	2282-0199
TGIF	Escazú	American	2228-8443
The Great Waltini	Playa Grande	Caribbean, Inter.	2653-0975
The Happy Snapper	Playa Braselito	Seafood	2654-4413
The Lighthouse	Jacó24 hour	American	2643-3083
The Pub	Escazú	American	2288-3062
Time Out Tavern	Escazú	American, bar	2289-3217
Toad Hall	Nuevo Arenal	Vegi. Inter.	2692-8020
Tony Roma's	Escazú	American	2288-0800
Tre Fratelli	Escazú	Italian	2289-4389
Trocadero	B. California	International	2223-8408
Tropical Sushi	Quepos	Japanese	2777-0395
Tsunami Sushi	Jacó	Japanese	2643-3678

Name	Location	Cuisine	Phone
Tutti Li	Pl. Itzkasú	Italian	2588-2405
Villa Rey	Escazú	Chinese	2289-5028
Villas Río Mar	Dominical	International	2787-0052
Viña Romantica	Las Pilas de San Isidro	Inter.	2430-7621
Viva La Crepa	Escazú	Crepes, Waffles	2588-1805
Vishnu	chain	Vegetarian	
Wall Street	Escazú, Santa Ana	Deli, sandwiches	2289-6493
Whapin'	B. Escalante	Caribbean	2283-1480
Willey's Caballo Negro	Arenal	California, German	2694-4515
Xandari	Alajuela	Inter. spa	2443-2020
Xandari (Pacific)	Esterillos Este	International	2778-7070

Chapter 27
About the Author

Lenny Karpman has written articles, essays, reviews and books on food, travel, human rights, and medicine. His two prior books are *Chana's Legacy* and *Noni, Baloney, Puddin' & Pie*. His shorter pieces have appeared in anthologies *Best Travel Writing 2005*, and *Venturing in Ireland*; in magazines Salon, Troika, PanGaia, the Jewish Magazine, Journal of the American Medical Association, Circulation; and in newspapers Dallas Morning News, San Francisco Examiner, Newark Star Ledger, Pittsburgh Post Gazette, Pacific Sun, A.M. Costa Rica, and many others. He was editor of San Francisco Medicine and Chanticleer.

Dr. Karpman practiced medicine for more than thirty years as a cardiologist for Kaiser Permanente in San Francisco, served on the Marin County Human Rights Commission and on legislative committees of three California non-profits, and received the Benjamin Dreyfus Civil Liberties Lifetime Achievement Award from ACLU.

Lenny and his wife Joan Hall live in Costa Rica on a farm, surrounded by a menagerie of rescued furry and feathered critters. They have three children and five grandchildren.